Rossa's Recollections
1838–1898

DIARMUID O'DONOVAN ROSSA

ROSSA'S RECOLLECTIONS
1838–1898

Introduction by
SEÁN Ó LÚING
and a new index

IRISH UNIVERSITY PRESS
Shannon · Ireland

First edition New York 1898

This IUP reprint is a photolithographic facsimile of the first edition and is unabridged, retaining the original printer's imprint.

© *1972*

Irish University Press Shannon Ireland

All forms of micropublishing

© *Irish University Microforms Shannon Ireland*

ISBN 0 7165 0010 8

Irish University Press Shannon Ireland

T. M. MacGlinchey Publisher

PRINTED IN THE REPUBLIC OF IRELAND AT SHANNON
BY ROBERT HOGG PRINTER TO IRISH UNIVERSITY PRESS

INTRODUCTION

Jeremiah O'Donovan Rossa's *Recollections* first appeared serially between 11 January 1896 and 7 May 1898 in his newspaper the *United Irishman* (New York). The first newspaper chapter is sub-titled '60 years of an Irishman's life' and the fact that Rossa proposed to write a full review on his career is confirmed by the title page of the published volume which indicates that the *Recollections* would cover the period 1838 to 1898. The date 1838 is puzzling, since Rossa was born in 1831 and the book includes ample childhood memories previous to 1838 of his fosterage in his grandfather's Irish-speaking household. An announcement of the book's publication appears in the *United Irishman* of 13 August 1898.

That volume, now reprinted, brings the story of Rossa's life up to the middle of 1863. A continuation of the *Recollections,* in fourteen chapters, ran in the *United Irishman* from 4 June 1898 to 18 November 1899, bringing Rossa's narrative as far as the seizure of the Dublin *Irish People* in September 1865 and linking up with the experiences already related by him in his *Prison Life,* first published in book form in 1874. The *Prison Life* brings the story of his career up to 1871 with his arrival in America and some events of that year, including a brief account of his election contest for state senatorship with the colourful Boss Tweed. The remainder of his life and especially the controversial years of it from 1872 to 1890 must be documented from various Irish American and American newspapers, mainly his *United Irishman* (1881 to 1910 approximately), the John O'Mahony papers in the Catholic University of America, Washington D.C., and other sources. Rossa wrote no memoirs of his American career. He tried to do so several times but had to give up, explaining that he felt unable to write about so painfully controversial a period. The closing years of his life are documented in John Devoy's *Gaelic American* 1913–15 and a notable series about his last illness and funeral, written by his talented wife, appears in the *Gaelic American* between 11 September 1915 and 15 January 1916.

Perhaps the best introduction to the *Recollections* is his own preface, which somehow got mislaid as he explains in the *United Irishman* of 3 December 1898:

Three years ago I sat down to write a book of "Rossa's Recollections". The first thing I wrote was the preface to that book. The book is now written and published, but the preface I wrote three years ago is not in it; it got mislaid; I find it now and print it, that you may have an idea of what the book is, and what I intended it should be.

This is the preface:

I sit down to write this preface before I have written a line of the book. I want to put before you and before myself what the book of "Rossa's Recollections" is to be. This day is Sunday, January 29, 1895. Last night I was at the house of Wicklow Byrne, 150 East 28th street, New York. I talked with him and his sister and mother till 11 o'clock. I told him I was thinking of writing a book that would give an account of all I knew about the Irish movement since I was born, and all the people I had met connected with that movement.

Just as I left Wicklow Byrne's house in 28th street I met at the corner of Third avenue and 27th street John E. Fitzgerald of Boston and P. J. Cody of Galway. Last April in Paris I was the guest of John E. Fitzgerald for an evening. Answering some of their inquiries, I told them I was going to write this book, a book that children could read, and that people who were not children would want to read, that they might learn from it a true account of the habits, manners, customs and actions of the Irish people for the last sixty years, and of their relations with England for many years more. No true or correct history of the movements of my day was yet written, and though my book was to be a historical one, the story of my life-time is, if I can tell it properly, such a story as will tend to set right many things that many writers have set wrong, and will also tend to make the Irish-blooded children of this country and this generation grow up to be men proud and helpful of the land of their fathers.

Cody and Fitzgerald were in glad glee at my going to write such a book, and spoke for it an immense circulation, bespeaking for themselves several copies of it. Fitzgerald spoke of how immensely my wife, "Mary Jane", could help me in the compilation of it. It gave us a subject for conversation; so, on and on we talked, of bookmakers, of writers, of Boyle O'Reilly, Dr Joyce and others till day was breaking. How was I to enlist the aid of my Mary Jane in getting out the book? "Out all night" was a bad way.

When I got home, Sunday morning, I put the whole blame for being out all night on the accident of meeting John E. Fitzgerald and talking about this book, and as she has been urging me these years past to write that book, the black looks went away, she brightened up, and told me how the other night after I had, at the supper table, told some stories about my boyhood days, and had gone to bed, Jerry (13 years old) said: "Mamma, what a pity it is papa wouldn't write a book and tell those stories in it!"

There are around this supper table of mine six of these young children (five girls and one boy), between the ages of eight and nineteen. It is for children such as they, as well as for the fathers and mothers of them, that I intend to make this book of "Rossa's Recollections" a book of interesting reading.

If you notice that I, at any time, or many times, wander away from the main road of my story into byways and bohreens, you will bear in mind that I only do in narrative what has been my lot to do going through life.

O'Donovan Rossa.

Rossa does indeed wander away from the main road of his story, roving back and forth as fancy takes him. Incidents from his London visit of 1895 figure in the chapter on his schooldays. Recital of traditional November and May-day customs shares chapter space with a discourse, subjective enough, on the bad doings of Gladstone. He introduces a sizeable quotation from his *Prison Life* in chapter XIX. In pages 263–66 there are echoes of Irish-American controversies of the 1880s. Rossa feels bound by no conventions of time or order and the book cannot be described as well organized. It is the product of a *seanchaí* or storyteller. The last chapter in the book does not properly belong to the series, being the recollections and family traditions of his New York friend Thomas Crimmins which originally appeared in the *United Irishman* of 25 December 1897.

There is a variety of interesting and valuable material in the *Recollections*. It has something of use in his particular field for the folklorist, the historian, the genealogist and the ballad collector. Reading through it we see the nineteenth century demographic links between the United States and Ireland, forged so heavily out of social tragedy, in the process of being created. Rossa, living in the most modern of cities, could not divest himself of the ancient traditions of his people. He genuinely believed in fairies and has written elsewhere that he heard the *cóiste gan cheann*, the headless hearse, rolling through Brooklyn. He puts down as the most natural thing in the world (p. 217) that a 'fairy puck', or injury, was something better avoided. By contrast we are brought up two pages later against one of the grim realities of American history as he records that his West Cork Fenian relative had charge of the military company present at the execution of Mrs Surratt in Washington. Irish words and phrases are numerous throughout the book. Eviction scenes are witnessed against the sombre canvas of the Famine and the great migration to the United States.

It is interesting to note that Rossa refers to the I.R.B. as the Irish Revolutionary, not Republican, Brotherhood (pp. 199, 243, for example). Replying to a query from a San Francisco correspondent, he writes in the *United Irishman* of 11 April 1896:

> The letters "I.R.B." meant the "Irish Revolutionary Brotherhood". Without showing your letter to some of the Old Guard whom I met in New York this week past—Tom Brennan of Dublin, Tom Ronayne of Midleton, Charley O'Connell of Cork, John W. Keogh of New York, I asked each of them what the letters "I.R.B." meant when he was a young man in Ireland, and each, without hesitation, answered 'Irish Revolutionary Brotherhood'.

This statement of Rossa's opens up an interesting avenue of speculation. Was the Fenian organization less a republican movement than one which sought freedom allied to no exact definition? The Fenian chief James Stephens shows himself to be no doctrinaire in a letter, printed here, introducing John O'Leary, no republican, to John O'Mahony with the advice that principles of government were best not discussed with him 'before some of our extreme friends' (p. 274); though the letter might also be taken as suggesting that responsible Fenian leaders applied a deliberate if tacit policy of subordinating all other issues to the primary one of achieving free political status. The Rossa of 'A Chapter on Genealogy' who appears in this book, although a not unwilling American democrat, is by taste and preference a Gaelic aristocrat, proud of his descent from an old Irish family and carrying with pride his ancestral patronymic. O'Donovan Rossa, the most typical Fenian, is likewise here less a Fenian democrat than a Gaelic clan leader. This sense of aristocracy and nationhood we find him sharing with John O'Mahony (p. 235). There were others like them, but there is no incongruity in finding them involved in a nationalist movement with thousands who had no clan traditions to sustain them.

Politics apart, a study of Rossa's life would give the romantic novelist some absorbing material. He was three times married. His first marriage, to Nanno Eagar of Milltown, County Kerry, a relative of The O'Donoghue, is described in the *Recollections*. His third marriage, in 1864, to Mary Jane Irwin of Clonakilty, County Cork, is related in his *Prison Life*. But although the romantic circumstances of his engagement and marriage to Ellen Buckley of Castlehaven, County Cork, which took place in 1861, might be supposed to fall within the scope of this book, there is not a word about them. Ellen Buckley died in 1863 at the age of twenty and Rossa's almost total silence about her in all his writings suggests that her death must have affected him too deeply for mention.

Rossa was a great student of history and antiquities and became a member of the Kilkenny and South East of Ireland Archaeological Society. He found congenial company in his kinsman, John O'Donovan, LL.D., editor of the *Annals of the Four Masters*, and their friendship, which began through correspondence in 1854 and lasted until John O'Donovan's early death in 1862, is illustrated here by a selection of John O'Donovan's letters. Less than a score are printed, out of a total in his possession of 'twenty or thirty' (p. 240) or 'about thirty or forty' (p. 335)—Rossa is endearingly unspecific at times. The correspondence shows how much Rossa was indebted to John O'Donovan for the historical research which enabled him to claim his hereditary title of O'Donovan Rossa. Some fifteen letters of Rossa's side of the correspondence are preserved amongst the letters and papers of James Graves in the library of the Royal Irish Academy.[1] They confirm his debt to John O'Donovan. In a postscript to an early letter in the Graves papers dated 10 July 1854, signed 'Jer. O'Donovan Rossa', he adds 'I often thought I should not write the latter until I could prove my title to it.' In the course of another letter in the Graves collection dated 24 October 1858 Rossa writes 'I am now delighted to hear that you are in a way perhaps of clearing away the little difficulty that existed in the way of my—I should have said *your*—researches, a few years since'.

Rossa, himself a founder of the Phoenix National and Literary Society, which merged with the Fenian movement, gives a useful account of the rise of Fenianism in the south-west, although his claim that the movement had its origins there is firmly rejected by Thomas Clarke Luby in his manuscript memoirs in the National Library and, following him, by John O'Leary.[2] Some of the most valuable content of the *Recollections* is found in the selection of letters, written by Fenian leaders, which Rossa prints. He explains to a correspondent in the *United Irishman* of 23 December 1899 how they came into his possession:

> I was on the council of the Fenian Brotherhood when John O'Mahony died [1877]. The council decided to give up the tenancy of the Fenian headquarters. The other members of the council asked me to give storage to all the ledgers, letters, books and papers of the Fenian Brotherhood. They were carted to my house. I have them in my house to-day.

These papers were used by William D'Arcy, O.F.M. Conv. when writing *The Fenian Movement in the United States: 1858–1886* (Washington D.C., 1947). At Rossa's death in 1915 they

1. I am indebted to Éamon de hÓir, Ordnance Survey, for indicating this source.
2. John O'Leary: *Recollections of Fenians and Fenianism* I, 84, footnote.

were stored in twenty-two barrels and trunks in Staten Island where they remained until 1944.[3] They are now in the archives of the Catholic University of America, Washington D.C., but the entire collection is available on microfilm in the reference department of Cork County Library, Courthouse, Cork.[4]

Chapter XXI is given wholly to a letter from Stephens to O'Mahony dated 6 April 1859 advising amongst other things the modification or omission of the recruitment test to meet any scruples of prospective members. This advice O'Mahony was already acting on, as may be seen from his letter of 4 April 1859 to William Sullivan of Ohio in which he describes the American Fenians as 'an Irish army, not a secret society' (p. 302). A particularly interesting passage (pp. 302–3) in this letter, but one which must be accepted with caution, states that a member of the Belfast Arms Club had brought news that the Ribbonmen of the North, with an extensive organization, and a 20,000 stand of arms in Belfast (surely an exaggeration) were determined to join the Phoenix (i.e. Fenian) society.

There is plenty of evidence in these pages that Rossa, despite controversies, had a wide circle of friends both in America and Ireland. Many who disagreed with his policies respected him personally. One of these was Tom Somerville, member of a distinguished West Cork family, whose goodwill towards Rossa is represented by a friendly note on page 260.[5] Rossa is in error, as recent research has shown, in saying (p. 315) that James Mountaine was a Protestant.[6] His admiration for Thomas Francis Meagher is patent. There are cherished memories of Michael O'Brien, hanged at Salford Jail in 1867, and of minor Fenian personalities like Captain William O'Shea, begrimed with the mud of Gettysburg, and Brian Dillon, all of Cork, but let it not be supposed that this is a parochial book. Rossa the humanitarian is seen fighting a legal battle with the Skibbereen Board of Guardians which took it ill that he shared out poor relief with a man's heart. The *Recollections* is mellow and retro-

3. William D'Arcy: *The Fenian Movement in the United States*, p. 413.
4. *Evening Echo* (Cork), 19 April 1969. See also Seamus Pender, 'Fenian Papers in the Catholic University of America—A Preliminary Survey' in *Cork Historical and Archaeological Society Journal*, Jul–Dec 1969, pp. 130–40, and subsequent issues.
5. Herber (John T. Collins): 'The Somervilles and O'Donovan Rossa' in *Southern Star*, 25 April 1936.
6. Walter McGrath: 'James Mountaine', *Evening Echo* (Cork), 30 and 31 Dec 1968, 1 Jan 1969.

spective, with tinges of regret and pessimism, lacking the fire and anger of the *Prison Life*, but of real value for a knowledge of the social genesis of Fenianism and the Fenian movement. A friend not mentioned in the *Recollections* is Douglas Hyde, an admirer of Rossa not only for his devotion to the Irish language, but for other reasons, as some very earnest rebel poetry of Hyde's younger years bears witness. The continuation of the *Recollections* includes Rossa's account of his tours on behalf of the Fenian organization throughout Great Britain and Ireland. One detail of interest out of the many he tells is that John O'Donovan's sons were initiated into the Fenian movement by Patrick (Pagan) O'Leary. On his second visit to America in 1865 he carried letters to John O'Mahony from James Stephens, Thomas J. Kelly and Frederick Millen. These letters which are printed in chapter XIII of the second series are of great importance in showing the state of the Fenian organization in Ireland in the summer of 1865. In his letter, of 24 June 1865, Stephens expresses strong criticism of the action of his American colleagues in sending Colonel Kelly to Ireland earlier that year to inspect the strength of the I.R.B. He ends the letter:

And so you will excuse any apparent ungentleness in this letter. I assure you I have done my best to be what I should to men struggling with me in so high and holy a cause, and for all my shortcomings I ask your pardon. This you will freely give me, for you are too well used to free speech to take it amiss in me. In any case we shall square up all on the battle-field.

Yours fraternally
J. Stephens[7]

In the preceding paragraph of the same letter Stephens has this to say of Rossa:

And now a word about the bearer. That he is dear to me and almost all here I need not say. But this is not why he has been chosen to go out on the present occasion. Two considerations have determined our choice. First, he can tell you more than any other man about our work. And second, he is a

7. *United Irishman* (New York), 23 Sept 1899.

well known friend of the H.C. [John O'Mahony, Head Centre]. He has other recommendations to your favor, but these, we trust, you will consider enough to secure it.

The last chapter of the second series, number XIV, is mainly a reprint from the contemporary Dublin *Irish People* (1899) of an interview with James Stephens containing a review of the I.R.B. which Rossa endorses as correct.

Rossa lived in America from 1871 until his death in 1915, except for part of 1906 when he returned to Ireland to take up a clerical post under Cork county council from which he resigned in September of that year. For a brief period in the early 1870s he edited a Republican party paper, the *Era*. From 1881 until about 1910 he edited the weekly *United Irishman*. This paper is important for documenting his American career and giving his views and comment on contemporary affairs, as an extract, from the issue of 3 April 1886, illustrates:

> The Knights of Labor are making a noise in the Land. But we hope they will do something better than make a noise—we hope they will free labor from the combination corporative tyranny of the capitalists that has been grinding the workman and his wife and child into poverty. We know what that combination is; we have been locked up in the Tombs Prison, in New York, by it, because we resisted it and trampled upon its rules and regulations. Yes, and we have been indicted by a New York Grand Jury for an alleged offense, and very likely that indictment stands over our head still, because we were never brought to trial . . . . Success to the Knights of Labor, and to all who labor for the right!

Some characteristic comment from it is reprinted in the supplementary chapter (pp. ix–xiii) to the 1882 and 1899 editions of his *Prison Life*. In the last fifteen years or so of its existence it declined to a monthly and became repetitive, varying little in content from one month to another.[8]

8. For instance, chapter XIII, second series, appears in the issues of 23 and 30 Sept, 7, 14 and 21 Oct 1899.

One of Rossa's books has an interesting bibliographical history. In 1884 S. W. Green & Son, Beekman St., New York, published the 300 page novel *Edward O'Donnell*, sub-titled *A Story of Ireland of our day*, with the facsimile signature 'Jer. O'Donovan Rossa' on the title page and simply 'Rossa' on the cover. D. J. O'Donoghue apparently had doubts about whether Rossa wrote it,[9] and Edmund Downey ascribes the authorship to Edward Moran, elder brother of D. P. Moran, founder-editor of the Dublin *Leader*.[10] Edward Moran was a native of Waterford who practised as a solicitor in Brooklyn, where he died in 1914. A reference by Rossa to the origins of the book supports Downey's ascription.[11]

Seán Ó Lúing.

9. D. J. O'Donoghue: *The Poets of Ireland*, Dublin 1912, p. 351; *Irish Book Lover*, VII no. 1: 15.

10. In a note in the *Irish Book Lover*, VII no. 2: 27 Downey says: '*Edward O'Donnell* was written by the late Edward Moran. He sent me a copy of the book at the time it was published, and on the half-title he wrote "Six weeks work—all my own . . .". See also Stephen J. Brown S.J., *Ireland in Fiction*, I, Dublin 1919, I, 216–17. Reprint, Shannon 1968.

11. 'To make a long story short. a book was written and published under the name of *Edward O'Donnell*, and that book is in the market now. The Waterford gentleman did the writing, and we did the editing.' *United Irishman*, 3 Nov 1884.

Devoy, John. *Recollections of an Irish Rebel*. New York 1929. Reprint, Shannon 1969.

Gibson, Florence E. *The Attitudes of the New York Irish towards State and National Affairs 1848–1892*. New York 1951. Includes details of the Rossa-Tweed contest 1871.

McHugh, Roger. *Rossa*. Tralee n.d. Abbey theatre prize-winning play, first performance 31 March 1945, with W. O'Gorman as Rossa.

O'Brien, William and Ryan, Desmond., eds. *Devoy's Post Bag*. 2 vols. Dublin 1948.

O'Donovan Rossa, Jeremiah. *O'Donovan Rossa's Prison Life*. New York 1874. Reprinted, with a supplementary chapter as *Irish Rebels in English Prisons*. New York [1882] and 1899. Abridged edition, *My Years in English Jails*. Edited by Seán Ua Cearnaigh. Tralee 1967.

O'Donovan Rossa, Margaret. *My Father and Mother were Irish*. New York 1939.

O'Donovan Rossa Funeral Committee. *Diarmuid Ó Donnabháin Rosa 1831–1915*. Souvenir of public funeral. Contributors include Pearse, Griffith and Connolly. Dublin 1915. A 1954 souvenir booklet reprints some articles from 1915 souvenir.

Ó Lúing, Seán. *Ó Donnabháin Rosa*. Baile Átha Cliath 1969.

Report of the Proceedings . . . of the Special Commission . . . for the trial of Thomas Clarke Luby and others for treason-felony. Dublin 1866. Pages 855–1059 consist of Rossa's trial.

Report of the Commissioners on the Treatment of the Treason-Felony Convicts in the English Convict Prisons. London 1867. This is the Knox and Pollock report commented on by Rossa in his *Prison Life* pp. 239–44.

Report of the Commissioners appointed to inquire into the Treatment of Treason-Felony convicts in English Prisons together with Appendix and Minutes of Evidence. Vol. I, *Report and Appendix*: Vol. II, *Minutes of Evidence*. London 1871. The chairman of this commission was Lord Devon. One of the commissioners, Hon. George Charles Brodrick, later warden of Merton, was the writer of the letter to

Rossa printed on p. 419 of *Prison Life*. The holograph of Rossa's reply, printed on p. 420, is amongst the Brodrick papers in the National Library. Rossa used this report extensively in his *Prison Life*.

The last two reports above are included in the volume *Crime and Punishment: Prisons 21* of the British Parliamentary Papers, IUP, Shannon 1970.

ROSSA'S RECOLLECTIONS.

1838 TO 1898.

CHILDHOOD, BOYHOOD, MANHOOD.

Customs, Habits and Manners of the Irish People.

ERINACH AND SASSENACH—CATHOLIC AND PROTESTANT—ENGLISHMAN AND IRISHMAN—ENGLISH RELIGION — IRISH PLUNDER.

SOCIAL LIFE AND PRISON LIFE.

The Fenian Movement. Travels in Ireland, England, Scotland and America.

By O'DONOVAN ROSSA.

O'DONOVAN ROSSA,
MARINER'S HARBOR, N. Y.
1898.

CONTENTS.

3

4   CONTENTS.

ROSSA'S RECOLLECTIONS.

Sixty Years of an Irishman's Life.

CHAPTER I.

THE CRADLE AND THE WEANING.

In the Old Abbey field of Ross Carbery, County of Cork, is the old Abbey Church of St. Fachtna. Some twenty yards south of the church is the tomb of Father John Power, around which tomb the people gather on St. John's eve, "making rounds" and praying for relief from their bodily infirmities.

On the tombstone it is recorded that Father Power died on the 10th of August, 1831. I was at his funeral; I heard my mother say she was "carrying" me that day. It is recorded on the parish registry that I was baptized on the 10th of September, 1831; that my godfather was Jerrie Shanahan, and my godmother Margaret O'Donovan. When I grew up to boyhood I knew her as "Aunty Peg." She was the wife of Patrick O'Donovan "Rua," and was the sister of my mother's father, Cornelius O'Driscoll. Jerrie Shanahan's mother was Julia O'Donovan Rossa—my father's uncle's daughter. She is buried in Flatbush, Brooklyn.

5

Her granddaughter Shanahan is the mother of nine or
ten children of the Cox family, the shoe manufacturers
of Rochester, N. Y., who by "clounas" are connected
with the family of ex-Congressman John Quinn of
New York, as John Quinn's mother was the daughter
of Denis Kane of Ross, whose wife was the sister of
John Shanahan. I don't know if John Quinn knows
that the Coxes of Rochester are cousins of his; I don't
know would he care to know that his mother's first
cousin, Jerrie Shanahan is my second cousin, and my
godfather. There were forty men of my name and
family in my native town when I was a boy; there is
not a man or a boy of my name in it now. One
woman of the name lives as heritor of the old family
tomb in the Old Abbey field.

And that is the story of many another Irishman of
the old stock. Families scattered in death as well as
in life; a father buried in Ireland, a mother buried in
Carolina, America; a brother buried in New York, a
brother buried in Pennsylvania, a sister buried in
Staten Island. The curse that scattered the Jews is
not more destructive than this English curse that scat-
ters the Irish race, living and dead.

This place of my birth, Ross Carbery, is famed in
Irish history as the seat of learning in the early centuries. Shrines of St. Fachtna, holy wells and holy
places are numerous all around it. Distinction of
some kind—special good fortune or special misfortune
—belongs to the life of every one born there. It is
the birthplace of Maurice J. Power, the right-hand
man of ex-President Grover Cleveland, in the city of

New York. It is the birthplace of Richard Croker, the right-hand man of the Government of the Tammany Hall Society, in the city of New York.

Of the Fates that hover over my life I have no reason to complain. They have mixed my fortunes; given me a strong constitution, a light heart, and a light pocket, making my struggle for existence active enough to keep the blood in a healthy state of circulation, fortifying me with strength to stand firm under difficulties, and filling my mind with strong hope in the future if I do all that I deem right in the present.

The Maurice J. Power in New York that I speak of is the same family of Powers as the Father John Power at whose tomb the people pray to God for relief from their infirmities. And the belief is that many have obtained relief through their prayers there. I know that I have gone through that Abbey-field the day after a St. John's eve, and I have seen, propped up by stones, a pair of crutches that were left there by a man who came into the field on those crutches the previous day. The holy words say, " Faith will move mountains," the whole world is the temple of God, and the pilgrim cripple, full of faith, praying to Him in that Abbey-field, became able to walk away without his crutches, and leave them standing there as monuments of the miracle.

Father Jerrie Molony, the priest of the parish, discountenanced the rush of people to Father Power's tomb every St. John's eve : he spoke against it from the altar on Sundays. All to no use ; the people came ; came in thousands. Of course, where people congregated in such numbers, abuses began to grow; the votaries of sin came into his parish as well as the votaries of prayer, and very probably the good priest thought it better to stop the gathering altogether than have it made the occasion of shame and scandal.

I will here leap some years ahead, to record my recollection of one St. John's eve that I was in Ross. It was in the year 1858.

James O'Mahony of Bandon wrote to me that he wished to meet me to have a talk over Irish national affairs. He suggested that St. John's eve in Ross would be a good place, as crowds of people would be there, and we would escape any prying notice. We met there that day. We had our talk, and then we walked toward the Abbey field. The blind and the halt and the lame were there, in every path and passage way, appealing for alms—appealing mostly in the Irish language. We stood behind one man who was sitting down, his bare ulcerated legs stretched out from him. His voice was strong, and his language was beautiful. O'Mahony said he never heard or read anything in the Irish language so beautiful. Taking his notebook and pencil to note down the words of the appeal, some traveling companion of the cripple's told him that a man was taking notes, and the cripple turned round and told us to go way. He wouldn't speak any more until we went away.

This James O'Mahony was a draper in Bandon; he was the brother of Thaddeus O'Mahony who was a professor of the Irish language in Trinity College, Dublin. He went to Australia in the year 1863. I hope he is alive and happy there. With him went another comrade of mine, William O'Carroll, who kept a bakery in North Main Street, Cork. They were among the first men in the South of Ireland that joined the Stephens' movement. It was James O'Mahony that first gave James Stephens the name of Seabhac; shouk; hawk. The Shouk shoolach—the walking hawk—was a name given in olden days to a banned wanderer. Stephens, at the start of this organization, traveled much of Ireland on foot. A night he stopped at my house in Skibbereen, I saw the soles of his feet red with blisters.

This is a long leap I have taken in the chapter of "from the cradle to the weaning"—a leap from 1831—the year I was born—to 1858, the year I first met James Stephens. So I will have to leap back now, and talk on from my childhood.

I must have been very fond of my mother, or my mother must have been very fond of me, for I must have lived on her breast till I was up to three years of age. I know she tried often to wean me from her; she put me to sleep with one of the servant maids, and I remember well the laugh my father and mother had at me next morning, when I heard her telling them how often during the night I tried to get at her bosom. I am more than three years older than my brother Conn, and I suppose it was the advent of his coming that brought about the arrangement to have me taken into the country to my grandfather's place.

CHAPTER II.

AT MY GRANDFATHER'S.

IT may be doubted that I remember things that happened to me when I was at my mother's breast, or when I was three years old; but I have no doubt on that matter. Prominent in my forehead is a scar. I got that scar this way: The girl whose chief duty was to mind me had me on her back one day. I was slipping off; she bounced herself, to raise me up on her shoulders, and she threw me clear over her head, on the street. My forehead came on a stone, and from the cut I got remains the scar. I could to-day point out the spot where I got that toss—between Billy O'Hea's house and Beamish's gate. I got it before I went to my grandfather's. I did not come back to town till I was seven years old—the time I began my schooling.

Those four years I spent in a farmhouse photographed my memory with all the pictures of Irish life, and fashioned my tongue to carry the Irish language without any strain. Some say I have a "brogue." I have. I am proud I have, and I will never endeavor to have any other kind of tongue. I gave a lecture in Detroit one night; coming out the main doorway, there was a crowd, and behind me coming down the steps I heard one lady say to another: "What a terrible brogue he has!"

Every allowance is made by English-speaking society for the man of every other nationality on earth speaking broken English, except for the Irishman. The Dutchman, the German, the Frenchman, the Russian, the Italian, can speak broken English, and it won't be said he speaks it with a brogue, and is, consequently, illiterate; but the Irishman who speaks it—a language as foreign to his nationality as it is to the nationality of any of the others—is met immediately with ridicule and contempt. But—'tis part of the price or penalty of slavery, and until Irishmen have manhood to remove that slavery, the name of their language or their land will not have a respected place among the nations. We may bravely fight all the battles of all the peoples of the earth, but while Ireland's battle for Ireland's freedom remains unsuccessfully fought—while England continues to rule Ireland—all the historical bravery of our race in every land, and in every age will not save us from the slur of the unfriendly chronicler who writes that we fight well as "mercenaries," that we fight bravely the battles of every land on earth, except the battle of our own land.

The Irish language was the language of the house at my grandfather's place. It was the language of the table, the language of the milking baan, the language of the sowing and the reaping, the language of the mowing, the "mihal" and the harvest-home. The English language may be spoken when the landlord or English-speaking people came the way, but the language natural to every one in the house was Irish, and in the Irish language I commenced to grow. The

household of Renascreena consisted of my grandfather Cornelius O'Driscoll, my grandmother Anna-ni-
Laoghaire, my aunts, Nance, Johanna, Bridget, Anna;
my uncles, Denis, Conn and Michael. Michael was
the youngest of the family. He keeps the old home-
stead now (1896). Last year, when I was in Ireland,
he drove into Clonakilty to meet me, looking tall and
straight. I asked him his age. He said seventy-five.
All the others—aunts and uncles—are dead, except
Aunt Bridget, who lives at No. 11 Callowhill, Philadelphia, the wife of Patrick Murray. In the family, had
been four more daughters. Mary, married to John
O'Brien; Margaret, married to Jer. Sheehan, of Sha-
nava; Kate, married to Martin O'Donovan-Ciuin, of
Sawroo, whose son is Martin O'Donovan of San Francisco; and Nellie, the oldest of the children, married,
at the age of fifteen, to Denis O'Donovan Rossa, of
Carrig-a-grianaan, whose son I am.

Yes, married at the age of fifteen my mother was,
and born thirteen years after she was married, was I.
There isn't much of a courtship story, as far as I could
hear. This is how I heard it: My father was riding
his horse home from the fair of Ross one evening.
The girls at the roadside well, there in the valley of
the Renascreena road, stopped his horse and challenged
him for a "faireen." He gave them a guinea; my
mother was the recipient of the gold piece. After that,
came a proposal of marriage. My mother's people visited at the house of my father's people at Carrig-a-
grianaan, one mile to the north, to know if the place
was a suitable one. All seemed right, and the mar-

riage came off. But a story is told about there being some angry words between my two grandfathers after the marriage. My father's father kept a bleachery on his farm, and the day my mother's father visited the place, the storehouse of that bleachery was well packed with the "pieces" of bleached linen, which were looked upon as belonging to the stock of the house. But, when, after the marriage, the people who sent the pieces in to be bleached took them away, Grandfather O'Driscoll charged that everything was not represented fairly to him; he talked angrily, and said he'd drown himself: "Baithfid me fein, baithfid me fein"—"I'll drown myself, I'll drown myself."

"Oh," said the other grandfather, "bidheach ciall agat; ba ghaire do'n fhairge Donal O'Donobhue 'na thusa, as nior bhathaig se e fein"—"Oh, have sense; Daniel O'Donoghue was nearer to the sea than you, and he didn't drown himself."

Daniel O'Donoghue was after giving his daughter in marriage to my uncle, my father's brother Conn, a short time before that.

There were always in my grandfather's house at Renascreena a couple of servant girls and a couple of servant boys; twenty cows had to be milked, and horses and goats, pigs, poultry and sheep had to be attended to. And what a bright picture remains in my memory in connection with the milking time in the baan field back of the house! The cows, munching their bundles of clover and looking as grave as Solomons, the milking maids softly singing while stealing the milk from them into their pails; the sweet smell of the new milk and the new clover; the larks singing in the heavens overhead, as if keeping time with the joyous voices on earth.

That was the time when everything in the world around me had a golden hue. I was the pet of the house. And, how I'd bustle around on a Sunday morning, giving orders to the boys to get the black horse with the white face ready for mass! and when the horse was ready, how I'd run through the bohreen into the main road to look at my granddaddie riding out, the big buckle in the collar of his great coat shining like gold, with my Nannie in her side-saddle behind him!

A small kitchen-garden orchard separated the house and outhouses from the other family homesteads on that hillside slope. They were the homesteads of my grandfather's two brothers, Patrick and Denis. As each of the three homesteads was well populated, the population of the three of them made a little village, and when the neighboring boys came around at night to see the girls, there was sport enough for a village. There were fairies in Ireland then, and I grew up there, thinking that fairy life was something that was inseparable from Irish life. Fairy stories would be told that were to me and to those around me as much realities of Irish life as are the stories that I now read in books called "Realities of Irish Life." I grew up a boy, believing that there were "good people" in this world, and I grew up in manhood, or grow down, believing there are bad people in it, too. When I was in Ireland lately the population wasn't half what it was when I was a boy. I asked if the fairies had been extermi-

nated, too, for there seemed to be none of the life around
that abounded in my time. Yes, English tyranny had
killed out the "good people," as well as the living
people.

The O'Driscolls did not own the town-land of Renascreena themselves, though the three families of them
occupied nearly the whole of it. The O'Driscolls did
own it at one time, and other lands around it, but the
English came over to Ireland in strong numbers; they
coveted the lands of the Irish; they overran the
country with fire and sword; they beat the Irish; they
killed many of them: they banished many of them;
and they allowed more of them to remain in the land,
on the condition that they would pay rent to the English, and acknowledge them as their landlords. That is
how the old Irish, on their own lands, all over Ireland
to-day are called tenants, and how the English in Ireland are called landlords. The landlord of Renascreena
in my day was Thomas Hungerford, of Cahirmore.
The landlord to-day is his son Harry Hungerford, a
quiet kind of a man, I understand. The father was a
quiet kind of a man, too. He was, in a small way, a
tenant to my father. My father had the marsh field on
the seashore. Tom Hungerford rented from him a
corner of it, out of which to make a quay on which the
boatmen would land sand for his tenants. My father
would give me a receipt for a pound every gale-day to
go up with it to Cahirmore. Giving me the pound
one day the big man said:

"If I was so strict with my tenants as to send for
the rent to them the day it fell due, what a cry would

be raised against me." I told him the rent in this case wasn't going to beggar him, and as he was prospering on the estate, it wasn't much matter to him paying it. He smiled. He is gone; God be good to him; he was not, that I know of, one of those evicting landlords that took pleasure in the extermination of the people.

The Irish people learn through oral tradition what many people learn from book history. Before I ever read a book, before I ever went to school, I got into my mind facts of history which appeared incredible to me. I got into my mind from the fireside stories of my youth that the English soldiers in Clonakilty, convenient to where I was born, used to kill the women, and take the young children, born and unborn, on the points of their bayonets, and dash them against the walls, and that the soldiers at Bandon Bridge used to tie men in couples with their hands behind their backs, and fling them into the river.

Those very two atrocious acts are, I find, in Daniel O'Connell's " Memoirs of Ireland," recorded this way:

" 1641. At Bandon Bridge they tied eighty-eight Irishmen of the said town back to back, and threw them off the bridge into the river, where they were all drowned.—Coll. p. 5."

" County Cork, 1642. At Cloghnakilty about 238 men, women and children were murdered, of which number seventeen children were taken by the legs by soldiers, who knocked out their brains against the walls. This was done by Phorbis's men and the garrison of Bandon Bridge."

O'Connell's Memoirs give accounts of similar atrocities in every county of Ireland, and his accounts are taken from Englishmen writers of Irish history. In the fireside history of my childhood home, I learned that the English soldiers in Clonakilty took some of the infants on the points of their bayonets and dashed them against the walls.

At a flax-mihal, or some gathering of the kind at my grandfather's, one night that some of the neighboring girls were in, they and my aunts were showing presents to each other—earrings, brooches, rings and little things that way. One of them showed a brooch which looked like gold, but which probably was brass, and wanted to make much of it. " Nach e an volumus e !" said one of my aunts. " What a molamus it is." That was making little of it. Perhaps the boy who made a present of it was "pulling a string " with the two girls. The word " volumus " is Latin, but the Irish language softens it into "molamus," and uses it as a name for anything that is made much of, but is really worth very little. You will see in Lingard's history of Ireland how the two words came into the Irish language. After the time of the Reformation, when England formulated the policy and practice of expelling from Ireland all the Irish who would not turn Sassenach, and all particularly who had been plundered of their lands and possessions, she passed laws decreeing that it was allowable for landlords and magistrates to give "permits" to people to leave the country, and never come back. But, that the person leaving, should get a pass or permit to travel to the nearest seaport town to take shipping. And if a ship was not leaving port the day of his arrival at the port, he, to give assurance of his desire to leave the country, should wade into the sea up to his knees every day till a ship was ready. There were printed forms of such permits; and the first word in those forms, printed in very large letters, was the Latin word " Volumus," which meant: We wish, or we desire, or it is our pleasure, that the bearer be allowed to leave Ireland forever. A royal permit to exile yourself, to banish yourself from your native land forever! Nach e an volumus e! What a molamus it is!

A political lesson was graven on my mind by the Irish magpies that had their nests in the big skehory tree on the ditch opposite the kitchen door. I had permission to go through the tree to pick the skehories, but I was strictly ordered not to go near the magpies' nest, or to touch a twig or thorn belonging to it.

If the magpies' nest was robbed; if their young ones were taken away from them, they would kill every chicken and gosling that was to be found around the farmyard. That is the way my grandfather's magpies would have their vengeance for having their homes and their families destroyed; and it made every one in my grandfather's house " keep the peace " toward them. I have often thought of my grandfather's magpies in connection with the destruction of the houses and families of the Irish people by the English landlords of Ireland. Those magpies seemed to have more manly Irish spirit than the Irish people themselves. But there is no use of talking this way of my childhood's recollections. I'll stop. If childhood has pleasure in plenty, I had it in this house of my grandfather, from the age of three to the age of seven.

I am publishing a newspaper called The *United Irishman*. In it, I printed the two preceding chapters.

Ex-Congressman John Quinn, whom I have spoken of in them, sends me the following letter:

DEAR ROSSA—I read with delight in the last issue of your truly patriotic journal what to me is the most interesting of all stories; namely, " Rossa's Recollections."

The traveling along with you, as it were, carries me back to the early morning of my life in that dear land beyond the sea, and I feel that I hear over again the tales as told by a fond mother to her listening, her wondering children, of saintly Ross Carbery, and the wild, the grand country from there to Bantry Bay.

Yes, I have heard her tell of the miracles which were performed at the tomb of Father John Power, and, I feel that if ever the afflicted were healed of their infirmities on any part of this earth, they were, at the grave of that saintly priest.

I was not born in that county, for " under the blue sky of Tipperary " my eyes first saw the light of day, but, as you say, my mother was born in Ross Carbery; and where is the son who does not love the spot where his mother was born? I do, with a fondness akin to veneration.

Oh, what memories you will call up in those recollections of yours! How the hearts of the sons and daughters of Ireland will throb as they feel themselves

carried back in spirit to the abbeys, the raths and, alas!
the ruins, around which in infancy their young feet
wandered. For to no people on earth are the loved
scenes of childhood half so dear as they are to the sons
and daughters of our Green Isle.

It is very interesting to me to have brought to my
mind once more the dear old names from whence I've
sprung. And, you ask, "Would John Quinn care to
know that the Kanes, the Shanahans, the Coxes, of
Rochester; the O'Regans, of South Brooklyn, and the
children of the exiles, are cousins of his and mine?"
Why, Rossa; I certainly would be more than delighted
to know of them, and to meet any of them; the more
so, as leaving Ireland with my parents immediately after
the "Rebellion" of '48, I never had much of an opportunity of meeting any of them, or knowing of their
whereabouts. No matter where they are, or what their
lot might be, they would be to me as dear as kindred
could be.

When first I learned that the same blood, through
the Shanahan line, flowed through your veins and mine,
I seemed to draw you the more closely to me.

I had long admired you for your devotion to motherland. I have in other days wept as I read of your sufferings in British dungeons; when, with hands tied behind your back, you were compelled, for days at a time,
to lap up the miserable food given you. I did not know
that we were united by ties of kinship then, but I felt
bound to you by the strongest ties of country and of
home, for I recognized in you a son of the Gael who,
no matter what your sufferings might be, had vowed to

keep the old flag flying; to keep the torch blazing brightly to the world, proclaiming that all the power of perfidious England could not quench the fires of faith and Fatherland in Ireland.

Yes, you proclaimed, not only from the hilltops and the valleys of our native land, but also from the cells of an English jail, that Ireland was not dead, but would yet live to place her heel on the neck of England.

For this, every Irishman should admire, should honor you. Your paper and your "Recollections" should be in the hands of every true Irishman. The reading of such stories will keep alive the faith of our fathers, faith in the sacred cause; yes, and make hearts feel young again as they read of those grand old hills and valleys of holy Ireland.

And those noble, those prominent figures, the sons and daughters of other days, who played their various parts in the great drama of Irish life and patriotism— we shall read of them, and though of many, very many, we must feel that in this world we shall never meet again, yet we know that in leaving, they have but gone a short time before us to enjoy in heaven that reward, which hearts so good and pure as theirs were, shall surely receive.

Wishing you success in your "Recollections," your *United Irishman*, and all your undertakings. I am,

Sincerely yours,
JOHN QUINN.

CHAPTER III.

MY SCHOOLDAYS.

AT the age of seven, I was brought home to my father and mother in Ross, to be sent to school, and prepared for Confirmation and Communion. I had received those sacraments of the Church before I was nine years of age. Confirmation day, the boys were lined along the chapel aisle in couples, the boy who was my comrade going up to the altar was Patrick Regan, and it was a singular coincidence that nine years before that, he and I were baptized the same day in the same chapel. And we went through school in the same class.

That time, when I was only a very little boy, I must have been a very big sinner, for I remember the day of my first confession, when I came out the chapel door, relieved of the weight of my sins, and faced the iron gate that stood between me and the main road, I felt as though I could leap over that gate.

If you at any time notice that I occasionally wander away from the main road of my narrative in these "Recollections," and run into byroads or bohreens, or take a leap of fifty years in advance, from the days of my boyhood to the present days, I have high and holy authority for doing that. Father Brown, of Staten Island reading the Epistle of the day at mass yesterday (Feb. 16, 1896) read these words: "When I was a

22

child, I spoke as a child, I understood as a child, thought as a child; but when I became a man, I put away childish things."

I am speaking as a child, so far, and very likely my words will give less offense than the words I will have to say, when I grow up, and speak as a man.

In preparing for confirmation, the school broke up about noon on Saturdays, and the boys were led by the master to the chapel, which was near by. There, were Father Jerrie Molony, and his nephews, Michael and Jerrie Molony, who were home from college on vacation, and Tead Red, to help our master in instructing us in our catechism. Tead Red was the instructor in the Irish language. He had a class of his own. I saw Father Molony take hold of a boy in my class one day, and take him over to the class of Tead Red, telling him it was in the Irish language he should learn his catechism. How often here in America have I thought of Father Molony, when I met priests from the most Irish-speaking part of Ireland, who could not speak the Irish language. No wonder that our nationality should become diluted and corrupted, no wonder it should become poisoned with—Trust in the English to free Ireland for us.

But, my schoolmaster! How can I speak of him! He is dead. God be good to him. I often wonder how he got his schooling. I often wonder how the people of Ross of my early days got their schooling, for they spoke the English language more correctly than it is spoken by many of the people of this day who are called educated; and, with that, they naturally spoke the Irish language. The priests used to preach in the Irish language.

I say I wonder how the people of Ross in the genera-tion of my father's boyhood got their education, for they were born in a time when education was banned in Ireland. The schools that are called National schools were not established till I was born. The hedge-schools and hedge-schoolmasters were around in the genera-tions that preceded my time. In the summer time, the children assembled in the shade of the hedges and trees, and the masters taught them their lessons. In the winter time the hedge-school was in the shelter of some farmhouse. As it was in the schooling of the Irish people, so it was in their religion. That was un-der a ban too; the priests were boycotted as well as the people. Yes, for two hundred years after the English religion was introduced into Ireland, any priest caught saying mass was subject to a fine; caught a second time, it was fine and imprisonment, and caught a third time it was banishment or death. Any Irishman caught attending mass was heavily fined; caught a second time, was doubly fined, and when the fines increased and were not paid, the lands of the people were confis-cated, and sold out by the English. That is how the tradition is implanted in the minds of many exiled Irish men and women to-day—that their people lost their lands in Ireland on account of sticking to their re-ligion.

There were two of the old-time schoolmasters in Ross when I was a child. Daniel Herlihy was one, and Daniel Hegarty the other. I remember being at the house of each; but it was only for a few days, or a few weeks. They had their schools in their own houses, and they turned out good scholars, too; scholars that knew Latin and Greek.

But 'tis to John Cushan that I give the credit for my schooling. When I went to his National school, I wasn't much beyond my A-B-C, if I was out of it at all; because I recollect one day that I was in my class, and the master teaching us. He had a rod called a pointer, and he was telling a little boy from Maoil what to call the letters. The little boy could not speak any English; he knew nothing but Irish, and the master, putting the tip of the pointer to the letter A on the board, would say to him, " Glao'g A air sin," then he'd move the pointer to B, and say, " Glao'g B air sin," and so on to the end of the lesson.

Another recollection satisfies me I had not much learning when I went to John Cushan's school. I was in my class one day, that one of the monitors had charge of it. All the small classes were up in the hallways around the school, reading their lessons off the boards that hung on the walls. It was a day that the Inspector visited the school, and with the Inspector was the priest, Father Ambrose. Each boy in my class was to read one sentence of the lesson, until the lesson was ended; then the next boy would commence again, at the top of the card. It came to my turn to commence, and after commencing I did not stop at the end of the first sentence. I read on—

" John threw a stone down the street. He did not mean to do any harm. But just as the stone slipped out of his hand, an old man came in the way, and it struck his head and made him bleed."

I read on to the end of that lesson, which is about the last one in the A-B-C book, or "First Book of Lessons of the National Schools." I forgot myself; I was thinking of birds' nests, or marbles, or something else; when I got out of my reverie, there were the boys tittering, and the master and the priest and the Inspector looking at me with a smile-turn on their faces.

My memory would do those times what I cannot get it to do now. It would get into it by heart, and retain it for some time—a pretty long time indeed—every lesson I got to learn. Those lessons hold possession of it to-day, to the exclusion, perhaps, of memories that are more needed. Yet, I find them no load to carry, and I use them occasionally, too, to some effect. A year ago in giving some lectures to my people in Ireland and England, I made audiences laugh heartily, by telling them how much they needed learning some of the lessons I learned at school. They'd understand the application of my words, when I'd repeat for them these lines that were in my second book at John Cushan's school:

"Whatever brawls disturb the street,
   There should be peace at home,
Where sisters dwell and brothers meet
   Quarrels should never come.

"Birds in their little nests agree,
   And 'tis a shameful sight,
When children of one family
   Fall out and chide and fight."

The men who were in those audiences, to whom I spoke, were divided. Thirty years ago, I knew them to be united. Thirty years ago, they had no trust in the English parliament to free Ireland for them. Last year, all their trust for Ireland's Freedom seemed to be in that parliament. This one little story will enable my readers to clearly understand me:

Last May, I was in London. One day, passing by the office of the Land League rooms there, I called in to see the Secretary, James Xavier O'Brien. I .had known O'Brien long ago. I and my wife had slept a night at his house in Cork city in the year 1864. I had traveled with him among his friends in Waterford in the year 1864. He and I were in the prison of Millbank, London, in the year 1867. We tried to write letters to each other; the letters were caught; we were punished; I was transferred to the Chatham Prison.

When in London in 1895, I thought I would like to look at O'Brien and have a little talk with him about those old times. I went into his office. We recognized each other. After the first salutation, the first words he said, and he said them soon enough, were:

"Rossa, I can't do anything for you in regard to your lectures."

"Stop, now," said I, "stop. Never mind the lectures. I called in to see you, just to look at you; to have one word with you, for old times' sake; if I had passed your door, or that you had heard I passed your door without calling in, wouldn't people think that we were mad with each other for something; wouldn't we be giving scandal?"

He smiled, and we talked on. But again, he spoke of not being able to do anything for my lectures, and again I stopped him; and a third time he brought the matter up, and a third time I had to stop him, and tell him it was not to talk of lectures I came in, but to have a look at himself. In traveling through England and Scotland and Wales after that day, I learned that part of the duties of his office in London was, to write to the McCarthy party clubs telling them the lectures of O'Donovan Rossa were not officially recognized by the confederation; but that individual members were not prohibited from attending them, as individuals, if they desired to attend.

I will now take myself back to school again.

I spoke of getting all my lessons by heart in short time. That's true. They are in my head still. One of them tells me not to believe in dreams; that—

"Whang, the miller, was naturally avaricious. Nobody loved money more than he, or more respected those who had it. When any one would talk of a rich man in company, Whang would say, 'I know him very well; he and I are intimate.' "—And so on.

But Whang did not know poor people at all; he hadn't the least acquaintance with them. He believed in dreams, though; he dreamed, three nights running, that there was a crock of gold under the wall of his mill; digging for it, he loosened the foundation stones; the walls of his mill fell down, and that was the last of my Whang, the miller.

Many lessons were in the schoolbooks of my day that are not in the schoolbooks to-day. "The Exile of

Erin " was in the Third book in my day; 'tisn't in any of the books to-day. "The Downfall of Poland," in which "Freedom shrieked as Kosciusko fell," was in one of the books in my day. 'Tisn't in any of the books to-day. England is eliminating from those Irish national schoolbooks every piece of reading that would tend to nurse the Irish youth into a love of country, or a love of freedom, and she is putting into them pieces that make the Irish children pray to God to make them happy *English* children.

But apart from politics, there were some good lessons in those books that have remained living in my mind all through my life. This is a good one—

I would not enter on my list of friends,
Though graced with polished manners and fine sense,
Yet, wanting sensibility—the man
Who needlessly sets foot upon a worm.
An inadvertent step may crush the snail
That crawls at evening in the public path,
But he that hath humanity, forewarned
Will step aside, and let the reptile live.
The creeping vermin, loathsome to the sight,
And charged with venom, that intrudes —
A visitor, unwelcome unto scenes
Sacred to nature and repose :—the bower,
The chamber, or the hall—may die ;
A necessary act incurs no blame.
Not so, when held within their proper bounds,
And guiltless of offense, they range the air,
Or take their pastimes in the spacious field,
There they are privileged.
And he that hurts or harms them there
Is guilty of a wrong ; disturbs the economy
Of nature's realm ; who, when she formed them,
Designed them an abode. The sum is this :

If man's convenience, health or safety interferes,
His rights and claims are paramount, and must extinguish theirs;
Else, they are all, the meanest things that are,
As free to live, and to enjoy that life,
As God was free to form them at first —
Who, in His sovereign wisdom made them all,
Ye, therefore, who love mercy,
Teach your sons to love it too.
The springtime of our years is so dishonored and defiled, in most,
By budding ills that ask a prudent hand to check them.
But, alas! none sooner shoots, if unrestrained,
Into luxuriant growth, than cruelty,
Most devilish of them all.   Mercy to him
Who shows it is the rule, and righteous limitation of its act
By which heaven moves, in pardoning guilty man;
And he who shows none, being ripe in years,
And conscious of the outrage he commits,
Shall seek it, and not find it, in return.

That poem is in my mind, whenever I step aside, lest
I tread upon a worm or a fly in my path.   And here,
from my school-book are —

THE SIGNS OF RAIN.

The hollow winds begin to blow,
The clouds look black, the glass is low,
The soot falls down, the spaniels sleep,
And spiders from their cobwebs creep.
Hark ! how the chairs and tables crack,
Old Betty's joints are on the rack ;
Loud quack the ducks, the peacocks cry,
The distant hills are looking nigh,
How restless are the snorting swine.
The busy fly disturbs the kine,
"Puss," on the hearth with velvet paws,
Sits wiping o'er her whiskered jaws.
Through the clear streams the fishes rise
And nimbly catch the incautious flies.

The frog has changed his yellow vest,
And in a russet coat is drest,
My dog, so altered in his taste,
Quits mutton bones, on grass to feast,
And see yon rooks—how odd their flight,
They imitate the gliding kite.
And headlong, downwards, seem to fall,
As if they felt the piercing ball.
'Twill surely rain; I see, with sorrow
Our jaunt must be put off to-morrow.

Then, there is the little busy bee :—

How doth the little busy bee
Improve each shining hour
And gather honey all the day
From every opening flower.

How skilfully she builds her nest,
How neat she spreads the wax
And labors hard to store it well
With the sweet food she makes.

In works of labor, or of skill,
I must be busy too;
For idle hands, some mischief still
Will ever find to do.

Those poems may not be exactly word for word as
they are printed in the books; but I am not going to
look for the books, to see if they are correct. That
would be a desecration of myself and my story, as I
have told my readers I am taking my writings from the
stores of my memory.

Nor, must I run away from school either—to tell
stories outside of school. I ran ahead in my classes
when I was at school. The master would have a

patch of one of our fields every year, to sow potatoes
in. My father, on some business of his, took me with
him to the master's house one night; the master had
two little girls, daughters; he was telling my father
that I was getting on well at school, and that if I continued to be good 'till I grew up to be a big boy, he'd
give me his Mary Anne for a little wife.

My grandfather and grandmother would come to mass
every Sunday. They'd come to our place first, and let
the horse be put in the stable till mass was over. I was
that time such a prodigy of learning, that my innocent
Nannie feared the learning would rise in my head.

I was put sitting up on the counter one day to read
a lesson for her, and after I had finished reading, I heard
her say to my mother, "Nellie, a laodh! coimead o
scoil tamal e; eireog a leighean 'n a cheann "—"Nellie,
dear! keep him from school a while; the learning will
rise in his head." Oh, yes; I was a prodigy of learning
that time. My learning ran far and away ahead of my
understanding. I was in my class one day, reading
from the little book of "Scripture lessons," and I read
aloud that the mother of Jacob and Esau "bore twines"
—"What's that? What's that?" said the master,
smiling, and I again read that that lady of the olden
time "bore twines." I did not know enough to pro-
nounce the word "twins," and probably did not know
at the time what "twins" meant. If the schoolmaster
was teaching me my natural language—the Irish, and
if I had read from the book—"do bidh cooplee aici," I
would readily understand that she had a couple of
children together at the one lying-in.

My master often slapped me on the hand with his wooden slapper, but he never flogged me; though I must have suffered all the pains and penalties of flogging from him one time, for, before he struck me at all, I screeched as if he had me half-killed.

I was put into the vestry-room one evening, with five or six other boys, to be flogged, after the rest of the scholars had left school.

The master came in and locked the door, and gave the orders to strip. I unbuttoned my trousers from my jacket, and let them fall down. I commenced screeching, and I'd emphasize with a louder screech every lash of the cat-'o-nine tails that every little boy would get. I was left for the last. He caught me by the shoulder. "Now," said he, "will you be late from school any more?" "Oh, sir, oh, sir, I'll never be late any more." "You'll keep your promise—sure?" "Oh, yes, yes, sir; I'll never be late any more." Then, with cat-o'-nine tails lifted in his hand, he let me go without striking me.

This school I was at was called the Old-Chapel school. It was built on the top of the hill field, and on the top of the Rock. Very likely it was built in the days of the persecution of the church, when it was a crime for the priest to say mass, and a crime for the people to attend mass. From the location of it, any one coming toward it from the north, east, south or west, could be seen. The watchman in the belfry house on the tiptop of the rock could see all around him. "The Rock" is a seashore hamlet, inhabited chiefly by fishermen. The hill field was one of my father's fields, and often I went over the wall on a Sunday morning to look at Corly Keohane ringing the bell for mass.   I had to be up early those mornings to keep the Rock hens out of the cornfield; often and often the bedclothes were pulled off me at daybreak.

CHAPTER IV.

IRISH FIRESIDE STORY AND HISTORY.

I MUST have been at John Cushan's school about six years. Paying a visit to the school after his death, I looked at the roll-calls, and I could not find my name on them after December, 1844. So I had been at school from the age of six to the age of thirteen. Bad times came on then. The year 1845 was the first year of the great blight of the potato crops in Ireland. The landlords of Ireland made a raid upon the grain crops and seized them and sold them for their rents, leaving the producers of those crops to starve or perish or fly the country. Thousands of families were broken up; thousands of homes were razed; I am one of the victims of those bad times. People now allude to those years as the years of the "famine" in Ireland. That kind of talk is nothing but trash. There was no "famine" in Ireland; there is no famine in any country that will produce in any one year as much food as will feed the people who live in that country during that year. In the year 1845 there were 9,000,000 people in Ireland; allowing that the potato crop failed, other crops grew well, and the grain and cattle grown in the country were sufficient to sustain three times 9,000,000 people. England and the agents of England in Ireland seized those supplies of food, and sent them out of the

35

country, and then raised the cry that there was "famine" in the land. There was no famine in the land, but there was plunder of the Irish people by the English Government of Ireland; and Coroners' juries, called upon to give judgment in cases of people found dead, had brought in verdicts of "murder" against that English Government. I will come to that time in another chapter of my recollections.

Many of the neighbors used to sit skurreechting at night at my father's fireside, and it was here I learned many matters of Irish history before I was able to read history. It was here I came to know Tead Andy, of whom I wrote thirty years ago, when I was in an English prison:

> In songs and ballads he took great delight,
>   And prophecies of Ireland yet being freed,
> And singing them by our fireside at night,
>   I learned songs from Tead, before I learned to read.

That fireside was a big open hearth; up the chimney somewhere was fastened a rod of iron about an inch thick; at the end of it below was a crook; the whole thing was called a pot-crook, and on it was a movable pot hanger to hang a pot. Then with a turf fire and a big skulb of ver in that fire that lighted the plates on the dresser below with the photograph of all who were sitting in front of it; I, standing or sitting in the embrace of one of the men, would listen to stories of all the fairies that were "showing" themselves from Carrig-Cliona to Inish-Owen, and of all the battles that were fought in Christendom and out of Christendom.

Mind now, I am, in these "recollections," taking in

the time that transpired between the years 1839 and 1845—the time I was between the age of seven and thirteen.

In the skurreechting company at the fireside was an old man who had a lot of stories about wars and battles. One story he'd tell of one battle he was in that I could not thoroughly understand at the time, nor did I thoroughly understand it either, until several years after I heard it. It was a story of some battle he was fighting, and he'd rather have the other side win the battle than his side.

One Summer's day I had my wheel-and-runners outside the door winding quills ; an old man with a bundle on a stick on his shoulder came up the street and asked me who lived there in my house. I told him. And who lives in that house opposite ? Jillen Andy. And in the next house ? Joannie Roe. And the next ? Paddy Lovejoy. That Paddy Lovejoy was the father of the rich man Stephen Lovejoy, of the Seventh Ward, New York, who died last year ; and Joannie Roe was the sister of the old man Dan Roe, who was making the inquiries of me. He was an English pensioner soldier coming home to Ireland. He had joined the North Cork Militia when a young man, just as many an Irishman joins the Irish militia to day, for the purpose of learning the use of arms for Ireland's sake ; the war of '98 broke out ; the North Cork Militia were sent into Wexford ; the battle that Dan Roe was speaking about at my father's fireside, wherein he'd rather the other side would win than his side, was the battle of Vinegar Hill.

"Oh!" he'd say, "if they had only done so and so they'd have gained the day."

Cork has got a bad name in Wexford on account of this North Cork Militia going into Wexford in '98. But the same thing could occur to-day, not only as regards Cork and Wexford, but as regards all the other counties of Ireland.

Those militia regiments are officered by the English, who live in Ireland; by the landlords of Ireland, and by the office-holders of the English Government in Ireland. In '98 the North Cork Militia were officered by the lords and the landlords of Cork; they were English; the rank and file of their command were the plundered Irish; the regiments were ordered into active service, and, under the military discipline of England the victims of England's plunder were made to fight against their brother victims in Wicklow and Wexford, who where battling against the common plunderers. 'Tis a condition of things that the Irish nationalist of to-day has to take into consideration in connection with a fight for the independence of Ireland. Every day you will hear some good Irishman say "We will have the Irish police and the Irish soldiers with us when we take the field." All right; but you must all be reasonable, too; you must first let the Irish policeman and Irishman red-coat soldier see that you are in earnest—that you mean fight—that you have fought a battle or taken a stand which will show him there is no turning back from it, and that if he turns over with you there is some chance of success.

The company of the fireside would be occasionally

recruited by some poor old traveling man or woman who had a lodging in the house that night, and seemed to be a pensioner of the family, who had known them in better days.

Looking up at the rafters and at the rusty iron crooks fastened into them, I heard one of those lady lodgers say one night, " Mo chreach! do chomairc-sa an la, na bheidheach meirg air na croocaidhe sin, air easba lon," which in English would mean " my bitter woe! I saw the day that the rust would not be on those hooks, from want of use."

The bacon-hooks had no bacon hanging on them, and were rusty. Other articles of better times were rusty, too. On the mantelpiece or clevvy over the arch of the hearth, was a big steel fork about a yard long; it was called a flesh-fork. That used to get rusty, too, and only on Christmas Days, Easter Day, New Year's Day, Shrove Tuesday and some other big feast-days would the girls take it down to brighten it up for service in the big pot of meat they were preparing for the feast.

The decay in trade and manufacture that had set in on Ireland after the Irish Parliament had been lost, had already been felt by my people. They had a Linen bleachery convenient to the town, and in a shop in the house in which I was born, we had four looms in which four men were at work. Mick Crowley and Peter Crowley had " served their time " with my father's people as apprentices to the trade; they were now " out of their time " and working as journeymen. Peter was a great singer, and every farthing or ha'penny I'd get hold of,

I'd buy a ballad for it from blind Crowley, the ballad-singer, to hear Peter sing it for me.   Peter was a Repealer, too, and I should judge his hopes for a Repeal of the Union were high, by the "fire" he would show singing:

> "The shuttles will fly in the groves of Blackpool,
> And each jolly weaver will sing in his loom,
> The blackbird in concert will whistle a tune
> To welcome Repeal to old Erin."

And I used to learn some of those songs of Peter's. I have them by heart to-day. "The Wonderful White Horse" was a great one. It evidently meant Ireland, for the first verse of it is:

> "My horse he is white, altho' at first he was grey,
> He took great delight in traveling by night and by day;
> His travels were great if I could but the half of them tell,
> He was rode by St. Ruth the day that at Aughrim he fell."

But the song about "The Kerry Eagle" is the one I used to take delight in.   Here are a few verses of it:

"You true sons of Grania come listen awhile to my song,
And when that you hear it I'm sure you won't say that I'm wrong;
It is of a bold eagle, his age it was over threescore,
He was the pride of the tribe, and the flower of Erin's green shore.

"From the green hills of Kerry so merry, my eagle took wing,.
With talents most rare, in Clare he began for to sing ;
The people admired and delighted in his charming air,
And soon they elected him in as a member for Clare.

"Then straight off to London my eagle took flight o'er the main,
His voice reached America, all over Europe and Spain ;
The black-feathered tribe, they thought for to bribe his sweet notes,
But he would not sing to the tune of their infernal oaths.

*   *   *   *   *   *   *   *

"Then back to Graniawail he set sail like a cloud through a smoke,
And told her that one of her long galling fetters was broke;
For the Emancipation the nation stood up to a man,
And my eagle in triumph united the whole Irish land.

"There was at that time a pert little bird called d'Esterre,
Who challenged my eagle to fight on the plains of Kildare;
But my eagle that morning, for Ireland he showed a true pluck,
For a full ounce of lead in the belly of d'Esterre he had stuck.

  *   *   *   *   *   *   *   *

"And now to conclude: may his soul rest in heaven, I pray,
His motto was peace, his country he ne'er did betray;
The whole world I'm sure, can never produce such a man,
Let us all rest in peace, and forever remember brave Dan."

Oh, yes; I have love-songs, too, with big rocky words of English in them, such as the song of the Colleen Fhune, of which this is a verse:

"One morning early for recreation,
  As I perigrinated by a river-side,
Whose verdant verges were decorated
  With bloom, by nature diversified;
A charming creature I espied convenient,
  She sadly playing a melodious tune;
She far transcended the goddess Venus,
  And her appellation was the Colleen Fhune."

The song that all the boys and girls in the house had, was the song of "The Battle of Ross." It was composed by John Collins, of Myross, a man of some fame as a Gaelic scholar and poet, who wrote the Gaelic poem on Timoleague Abbey. "The Battle of Ross" was fought about the year 1800. I suppose it was no regular battle, but the little boys at our side of the house used to celebrate the victory of it every July

12, and march through the lanes and streets, with twigs and rods as guns, upon their shoulders.

Most of the grown people of my day remembered the battle. At the time of its occurrence the towns of Cork were famed for their societies of Orangemen,—men who were born in Ireland, but who were sworn to uphold the foreign rule of England in their native land. They were schooled, and the like of them are to-day schooled, into believing that only for the protecting power of England, the Catholics of Ireland would kill the Protestants of Ireland. These Orangemen societies grew strong in many places, and became so aggressive and so fostered and patronized by the English governors, that they acted as if their mission was the English mission of rooting the old Irish race out of Ireland altogether. The spirit that harmonized with their education was the spirit expressed by those words painted on the gates of the town of Bandon:

"Turk, Jew or Atheist may enter here, but not a papist."

Of that it is said that some one wrote under it these words:

" Whoever wrote that wrote it well,
For the same is written on the gates of hell."

But about this battle of Ross that is celebrated in song by John Collins, I may as well let the poet tell the story of it in those words of his that are sung to the air of "The Boyne Water."

July the twelfth in ancient Ross
There was a furious battle.
Where many an Amazonian lass
Made Irish bullets rattle.

Sir Parker pitched his Flavian band
  Beyond the Rowry water,
Reviewed his forces on the strand
  And marshaled them for slaughter.
They ate and drank from scrip and can
  And drew their polished bayonets;
They swore destruction to each man
  Dissenting from their tenets.
Replete with wrath and vengeance, too,
  They drank "Annihilation
To that insidious, hated crew—
  The Papists of the nation!"
Their chief advanced along the shore
  And every rank incited;
"Brave boys," said he, "mind what you swore"—
  And what they swore recited.
"This night let's stand as William stood:
  Set yonder town on fire;
Wade through a flood of Papist blood
  Or in the flames expire."
The listening multitude approved,
  With shouts of approbation,
Of what their generous leader moved
  In his sweet peroration.
Each swore that he would never flee,
  Or quit the field of action,
Unless assailed by more than three
  Of any other faction.
They crossed the purling Rowry Glen,
  Intent on spoil and plunder;
Their firelocks raised a dreadful din,
  Like peals of distant thunder.
The Garde-de-Corps first led across;
  The rest in martial order,
And in full gallop entered Ross
  In fourteen minutes after.
The warlike women of the town,
  Apprized of the invasion,
Like Amazons of high renown,

Soon formed into a legion.
With courage scarcely ever known,
    Led on by brave Maria,
Each stood, like David with a stone,
    To face the great Goliah.
The Flavian corps commenced the fray,
    And fired a sudden volley ;
The women, strangers to dismay,
    Made a most vigorous sally.
The fight grew hot along the van,
    Both stones and bullets rattle.
And many a brave young Orangeman
    Lay on the field of battle.
Now here, now there, Maria flies,
    Nothing can stop her courses.
All instruments of death she plies
    Against the Orange forces.
Such is her speed upon the plain,
    No mortal can outpace her,
And such her valor—'tis in vain
    For any man to face her,
Great Major Hewitt, for tactics famed,
    Renewed the fierce alarms,
Celestial rays of lightning gleamed
    From his refulgent arms.
His father was of earthly race,
    His mother—once the fairest
Of rural nymphs—the stolen embrace
    Of Jove upon a " Papist."
He rushed into the virgin throng
    And put them in commotion,
But brave Maria quickly ran
    And stopped his rapid motion.
With his own pistol, on his head,
    She gave him such a wherrit
As laid him with the vulgar dead,
    Devoid of sense and spirit.
Barclay, the second in command,
    Renowned for killing number

Was by Margretta's daring hand,
  Knocked into deadly slumbers;
With a sharp saw upon his crown
  She cut so deep a chasm,
He fell, and bit the bloody ground,
  In a most frightful spasm.
The Orange banner was displayed
  By youthful Ensign Legoe,
Who was by war's sad chance soon laid
  Low as the other hero:
In this predicament he found
  Himself in no small hazard,
When a rude bullet of ten pound
  Rebounded from his mazzard
He fell upon his brawny back
  To the cold marble pavement;
The victors beat him like a sack,
  By way of entertainment.
She said, "Go, vagrant, to the shades,
  And tell Sir John the story,
How a small band of Carbery maids
  Pulled down the Orange glory."
Sir Parker, seeing his banner fall,
  His warlike troops defeated,
Under the cover of a wall
  To a small fort retreated,
Where he and all his Garde de Corps
  Lay for some time securely,
And braved the clamor and uproar
  Of th' Amazonian fury.
But while the hero from within
  Fired on a brave virago,
Who then pursued four of his men
  With vengeance and bravado,
A rocky fragment from without
  Made a most grievous rattle
Upon his cheek, his eye knocked out—
  Which finished all the battle.
Some of his men in ditches lay

To shun their near extinction;
Some from their helmets tore away
The badges of distinction;
Some in the public streets declared
Against the name and Order.
And thus our Orange heroes fared
The day they crossed the border.

I print the " Battle of Ross " not to foster the feuds
it represents, but to show the agencies that create
them; I print it because the battle occurred in my
native town; because my people were in the battle; because it was a fireside story in every house around me
when I was a boy, and because my " Recollections "
would not be complete without it. I have through life
done as much as one Irishman could do to checkmate
the common enemy's work of fostering those feuds; I
am growing into the mood of mind of thinking that I
have done more than I would care to do again could I
live my life over, because the gain of a few Protestants
or Orangemen here and there to the side of the cause
of their country's independence, is not worth the time
and trouble that it takes to convince them you want
that independence for some purpose other than that of
killing all the Protestants and all the Orangemen of
Ireland.

The poem is published in Dr. Campion's Life of
Michael Dwyer. It is from that book, sold by P. J.
Kenedy, of 5 Barclay street, New York, that I copy it
now. My childhood story of the battle is, that the
men of Ross did not engage in it at all; that martial
law was in force at the time; that the parade of the
Orangemen was only a provocation to make the Irish-

men show themselves and put them in the power of the
law, and have them either shot down or put to prison;
but, that the women of the town sallied out, and with
sticks and stones put the Orangemen to flight.   Their
leader, Parker Roche, lost an eye from the stroke of a
stone hurled at him by "brave Maria," Mary O'Mahony
(Baan), or "Mauria Vhaan," as the people familiarly
called her.

The leaders of those Orangemen were the people who
led the North Cork Militia into Wexford in '98, and
sixteen years before that, they were some of the people
that were leaders of the volunteers of '82, about whom
I think a little too much has been said in praise and
plaumaus.   I look at the names and titles of the Cork
delegates to the convention of Dungannon in 1782, and
I find them much the same as the names and titles of
those who commanded the Irish volunteers of Cork,
and the North Cork Militia, who were fighting for
England in Wexford in '98.   Just look at these names
as I take them from the history of the volunteers of
1782; by Thomas McNevin and Thornton MacMahon.
"Delegates to the Convention of Dungannon, County
of Cork, Right Hon. Lord Kingsborough, Francis Bernard, Esq., Col. Roche, Sir John Conway Colthurst,
Major Thomas Fitzgerald."

Names of the Irish Volunteers, County of Cork—
Bandon Independent Company, Col. Francis Bernard.

Carbery Independent Company, Capt. John Townsend.

Duhallow Rangers, Lieut.-Col. William Wrixon.
Imokilly Horse, Col. Roche.

Kanturk Volunteers, the Earl of Egmont.

Mitchelstown Light Dragoons, Lord Kingsborough.

Ross Carberry Volunteers, Col. Thomas Hungerford.

Carbery Independents, Captain Commanding, William Beecher.

Doneraile Rangers, Col. St. Leger Lord Doneraile.

Bantry Volunteers, Col. Hamilton White.

That Col. Hamilton White is very likely the same White who got the title of Lord Bantry, fourteen years after, for making a show of resisting the landing of the French in Bantry Bay in 1796. The whole army of those volunteers of '82 was officered by the English landlord garrison of Ireland—in every county of Ireland; and so much English were they, that they would not allow a Catholic Irishman into their ranks. Why, the great Henry Grattan himself opposed the admission of Catholic Irishmen into the ranks of the Irish Volunteers. In his opposition to a motion made in the Irish Parliament House in 1785, he said:

"I would now wish to draw the attention of the House to the alarming measure of drilling the lowest classes of the populace by which a stain had been put on the character of the volunteers. The old, the original volunteers, had become respectable because they represented the property of the nation. But attempts had been made to arm the poverty of the kingdom. They had originally been the armed property—were they to become '*the armed beggary?*'"

The words "the armed beggary" are italicized in the history I quote from. And who profited by that "beggary" of the unarmed people? The plunderers who

made them beggars, and who assembled in Dungannon
—not to free Ireland, but to fortify themselves in the
possession of their plunder.

I don't know how it is that on this subject of the
volunteers of '82, I think differently from other people.
I can't help it; 'tis my nature some way. And I'm
cross and crooked other ways, too. I remember one
day, thirty odd years ago, in The Irish People office in
Dublin, the company in the editor's room were talking
of Tom Moore, the poet. I said there were some very
bad things in his writings, and I did not care to laud
to the skies an Irishman who would tell us to

> "Blame not the bard,
> If he try to forget what he never can heal."

The editor remarked that I did not understand his
writings.

I suppose I did not. Nor do I suppose I understand
them to-day; for I cannot yet conceive how any Irishman can be considered an Irish patriot who will sing
out to his people, either in prose or verse, that it is impossible to free Ireland from English rule. Show me
that anything else is meant by the line,

> "If he try to forget what he never can heal,"

and I will apologize to the memory of Moore. That is
what England wants the Irish people to learn. That is
what she wants taught to them. And that is what she
is willing to pay teachers of all kinds for teaching
them—teaching them it is better to forget the evils
they never can heal—better forget all about Irish free-

dom, as they can never obtain it. That's the meaning of the song, and while I have a high opinion of the poetic talent of the man who made it, I cannot laud the spirit of it, or laud the maker of it for his patriotism; I incline rather to pity him in the poverty and cupidity that forced him, or seduced him, to sing and play into the enemy's hands.

CHAPTER V.

THE EMIGRANT PARTING.—CARTHY SPAUNIACH.

In the year 1841, the family of my father's brother
Cornelius, sold out their land and their house, and
went to America. In that house the priests used to
have their dinner on "Conference" days in Ross. My
uncle had recently died. His widow was Margaret,
the daughter of Daniel O'Donoghue, who belonged to
a family of O'Donoghues whom England had plundered. She had four daughters and two sons : Mary,
Ellen, Julia, Margaret, Denis and Daniel. They
settled first in Philadelphia. All the girls are dead ;
Julia died lately, a nun in a convent at Altoona, Penn.
The two boys are living in Jackson, Tenn. It is that
family started to bring out my father's family from
Ireland, when they heard in 1847 that my father died,
and that we were evicted. One incident of the time
that my uncle's family left Ross made a picture in my
mind that will remain in it forever. Sunday night a
band of musicians came from Clonakilty, and they were
playing at the house all night. It couldn't be a happy
Harvest-home festival. It was the sadder one of a
breaking up of house and home. Monday morning those
"Irish missioners" started for Cork. I joined the procession that went with them out of town. Out at
Starkey's, at Cregane, it halted. There, there was cry-

51

ing all around by the people, as if it was a party of
friends they were burying in a graveyard.

I came back home with the company. My father
was not able to go out of the house that day. He
asked me all about the parting; and when I had told
my story he commenced to cry, and kept crying for a
half an hour or so. He made me ashamed of him, for
here was I, a mere child, that was strong enough not
to cry at all, and here was he, crying out loudly, as if
he was a baby.

That's the picture I cannot get out of my mind.
But I cry now, in spite of me, while writing about it.

The English recruiting-soldiers would come to Ross
those days and take many of the boys away with them,
and then there was more crying of mothers, at having
their children join the red-coats. Some man that I did
not know was in our house for a few weeks. He remained in bed all the time. He had me at his bedside
much of the time, telling me stories and playing with
me. One dark night he came downstairs. The back-
door was opened, and out he went. I saw his shadow
going up through the hill of the Fairfield. Mary Regan was the only strange woman in the house at the
time, and she cryingly kissed and kissed the man before
he left the house.

When I grew up to manhood I occasionally visited
Ross, and Mary Regan would ullagone at seeing me,
and draw a crowd around, telling of the little child
who was the playmate of her boy when he was in the
Hue and Cry on the run, and never told any one a
word about his being for weeks in his father's house.

Her boy was Jemmie Regan, who had 'listed some time before that, and had deserted.

I saw another Ross deserter in the city of Lawrence, Mass., some quarter of a century ago. I was lecturing there one night. I was telling of Jillen Andy, whom I buried in the year 1847 without a coffin. A tall, grey-headed man in the audience commenced to cry, and came up to the platform to embrace me. I saw him in Ross when I was a child, when as a red-coat soldier he came home on furlough. He had lived next door to Jillen Andy. He was John Driscoll, the sister's son of that North Cork militiaman, Dan Roe, of whom I have spoken in a previous chapter as having been at the battle of Vinegar Hill. This John Driscoll of Lawrence had deserted from the English Army in Canada, and reached America by swimming across the river St. Lawrence.

I am writing too much about crying in this chapter. It is no harm for me to add that I must have been a kind of cry-baby in my early days, for when I grew up to be big, the neighbors used to make fun of me, telling of the time I'd be coming home from school, and how I'd roar out crying for my dinner as soon as I'd come in sight of the house.

The life of my boyhood was a varied kind of life. I had as much to do as kept me active from morning till night. Early in the morning I had to be out of bed to drive the hens out of the fields. The two town fields were bounded at the eastern side by the Rock village, inhabited mostly by fishermen. The fishermen had wives; those wives had flocks of hens, and those flocks of hens at dawn of day would be into the fields, scraping for the seed sown in springtime, and pulling down the ripening ears of corn coming on harvest-time.   No matter how early I'd be out of bed, the hens would be earlier in the field before me.   My principal assistant in chasing them out and keeping them out was my little dog Belle.   The hens knew Belle and knew me as well as any living creature would know another. But they were more afraid of Belle than of me, for when I'd show myself at the town side of the field, going toward them, they'd take their leisure leaving the field when Belle was not with me ; but if Belle was with me, they'd run and fly for their lives.

Belle and I stole a march on them one day.   We went a roundabout way to get to the rear of them. We went up Ceim hill, and by the old-chapel schoolhouse, and down through the Rock.   Then Belle went into the field and killed two of the hens.   This brought on a war between the women of the Rock and my mother, and peace was made by having the Rock women agree to muffle up the legs of their hens in lopeens, so that they could not scratch up the seed out of the ground.   It would not be a bad thing at all if the Irish people would take a lesson from me in my dealings with the hens of the Rock that were robbing my father's fields—if they would do something that would make the English put lopeens upon her English landlord scratch-robbers of Ireland.

Approaching harvest-time, the work of my care-taking was doubled by my trying to protect the wheat-field from the sparrows that lived on the Rock and in the town. They knew me, too, and knew Belle. They, too, were more afraid of Belle than of me. I could not throw stones at them, for my father told me that every stone I threw into the cornfield would break some ears of corn, and if I continued throwing stones I would do as much damage as the sparrows were doing. I had a " clappers " to frighten them away, but a flock of these sparrows, each perched upon an ear of corn, and picking away at it, cared as little about the noise of my clappers as England cares about the noise Irish patriot orators make in trying to frighten her out of Ireland by working the clappers of their mouths.

My experience with the Irish crows was much the same as with the sparrows. There was a rookery convenient in the big trees in Beamish's lawn, and flocks of those crows would come into the fields in springtime to scrape up grains of wheat, and skillauns of seed-potatoes. My father got some dead crows, and hung them on sticks in the fields, thinking that would frighten away the living crows. I don't know could he have learned that from the English, who spiked the head of Shawn O'Neill on Dublin's Castle tower, and the heads of other Irishmen on other towers, to frighten their countrymen away from trespassing upon England's power in Ireland. Anyway, the Irish crows did not care much about my father's scarecrows, nor about my clappers. It was only when a few shots were fired at them from guns, and a dozen of them left dead on the field, that they showed any signs of fear of again coming into the field.

A strange character of a man named Carthy Spauni-

ach used to travel the roads I had to travel those days.
The mothers would frightem their refractory children
by saying, "I'll give you to Carthy Spauniach." He
had the character of being a kind of madman. He
seemed to have no fixed home, he had no appearance
of a beggarman; nor did he go around our place begging; he was fairly, comfortably dressed; he walked
with a quick pace; sometimes he'd stop and ask me
who I was; then he'd tell me those fields and grounds
belonged to my people once; that they ought to belong
to my people now; but they belonged to strangers now,
who had no right to them, that they ought to be mine.
After talking that way for some time, he'd suddenly
start away from me. Sane or insane, he spoke the
truth. He was called a madman; but looking at him
from this distance of half a century, I'd regard him as
a victim of England's plunder, who embraced the mission of preaching the true faith to the children of his
plundered race. I know how men get a bad name, and
are called madmen, for speaking and acting in the true
faith regarding Ireland's rights. I have myself been
called a madman, because I was acting in a way that
was not pleasing to England. The longer I live, the
more I come to believe that Irishmen will have to go
a little mad my way, before they go the right way to
get any freedom for Ireland. And why shouldn't an
Irishman be mad; when he grows up face to face with
the plunderers of his land and race, and sees them
looking down upon him as if he were a mere thing of
loathing and contempt! They strip him of all that belongs to him, and make him a pauper, and not only

that, but they teach him to look upon the robbers as
gentlemen, as beings entirely superior to him. They
are called "the nobility," "the quality"; his people
are called the "riffraff—the dregs of society." And,
mind you! some of our Irish people accept that teaching from them, and act and speak up to it. And so
much has the slavery of it got into their souls, and into
the marrow of their bones, that they to-day will ridicule
an O'Byrne, an O'Donnell, an O'Neill, an O'Sullivan,
a MacCarthy, a MacMahon or Maguire, if they hear
him say that such and such a Castle in Ireland and
such and such a part of the lands of Ireland belonged
to his people. It is from sneerers and slaves of that
kind that the "stag" and the informer come; the
Irishman who is proud of his name and his family
and his race, will rarely or never do anything to bring
shame and disgrace upon himself or upon any one belonging to him.

Another odd character besides Carthy Spauniach
used to travel my road occasionally. His day was
Sunday. Every fine Sunday he'd be dressed up in the
height of fashion, walking backward and forward this
road that I had to walk to guard the crops from the
birds of the air and the hens of the hamlet. This man's
name was Mick Tobin; his passion was in his person;
he was a big, hearty, good-looking man, some thirty
years of age; he fancied that every girl that would
look at him couldn't look at him without falling in love
with him, and every fine Sunday he'd be walking that
strand road between the Rock and Beamish's gate, that
the Miss Hungerfords and the Miss Jenningses and the

other "ladies of quality" may see him as they were
coming from church, and that he may see them.

If I told Mick, after the ladies had passed him, that
I heard one of them say to her companion, "What a
handsome man he is?" I'd be the white headed boy
with Mick. Mick's strong weakness ran in the line of
love and self-admiration. I have often thought of him,
for in my wandering walk of life I have met men like
him, met them in the line of Irish revolution, looking
upon themselves as the beauties of creation, and imag-
ining that the whole Irish race should look upon them
as the heaven-sent leaders of the movement for Irish
freedom. God help their poor foolish heads! I bring
that expression from my mother, "God help your poor
foolish head!" she'd say to me when I'd be telling her
of the things I'd do for Ireland when I grew up to be
a man. Ah! my mother was Irish. I saw her in 1848
tear down the placard the peelers had pasted upon
the shutters, telling the people that Lamartine, in the
name of France, had refused to give any countenance
to the Dublin Young Ireland delegation that went over
to Paris with an address.

I'll speak more about that matter when I grow older.

John Dowling, of Limerick, met me yesterday in
Broadway, New York, and told me I forgot "My
Mother." I looked interrogatingly at him. "Ah,"
said he, "don't you remember the poem that was in
the schoolbooks about "My Mother"—you forgot to
say anything about it in what you wrote in the paper
last week. You're right, John, you're right, said I; I
did forget her:

Who ran to take me when I fell,
And would some pretty story tell,
And kiss the part to make it well.
My mother.

"And you also left out," said he, these two lines in the "Signs of Rain":

Low o'er the grass the swallow wings,
The cricket, too, how sharp he sings!

"Right there, too," said I. "But it shows that what I said was true—that I was quoting from memory, and that I was not looking into books to see whether my memory was right or wrong."

Oh, no, Mr. Dowling, I don't forget my mother, a tall, straight, handsome woman, when I was a child; looking stately in the long, hooded cloak she used to wear; a prematurely old, old woman when I saw her in this foreign land some years after, looking older by wearing an American bonnet instead of an Irish cloak, when I saw her Philadelphia in 1863.

I was up on the half-hatch of the door at home one day; I was looking at Lord Carbery's hounds passing by—Geary, the huntsman, sounding the bugle; the horses prancing, carrying the "quality," booted and spurred, and dressed in their hunting jackets of green and gold and orange. After they had passed, I came down from my perch on the half-hatch, and I heard my mother say of them to Kit. Brown:

"Ah! 'Ta oor la aguiv-se 'sa saol-seo, acht, beig aar la aguinne 'sa sao'l eile."

Ah you have your day in this world; but we'll have our day in the next.

This resignation to the existing condition of things
in the fallen fortunes of our people was on the tongue
of my mother. I don't know that it was in her heart
or in her spirit. I do not think it was. Our priests
preached it. I do not think it was in their heart either.
It couldn't be; they were Irish, and belonged to the
plundered race. But—but what? I don't know:
Father Jerry Molony knew as well as any priest living
how his congregation came to be poor; when the
Soupers would come to the parish to bribe the people
into becoming Sassenachs, he'd say there were people
present in the congregation whose families gave up all
they had in the world rather than give up their faith.
My family claimed the honor of that, and prided in it.
The priest had no other consolation to give, but the
consolation of religion, and, very likely, it was through
religion my father and mother learned—and tried—to
lighten the load of life, by telling us that the poorer
you are the nearer you are to God, and that the more
your sufferings are in this world the greater will be
your reward in the next.

If that be gospel truth, and I hope it is, there are no
people on earth nearer to heaven than the Irish people.

CHAPTER VI.

THE GLADSTONE BLACKBIRD.—MANY FEATURES OF IRISH LIFE.

THERE were three or four hillocks in the field near the schoolhouse, that grew nothing but bushes and briars, and in these hillocks linnets and goldfinches would build their nests. I never robbed any of these nests, and the birds seemed to understand that I would not hurt or harm them. The mother would sit there hatching, she looking at me and I looking at her, and would not fly away unless I stretched out my hand to catch her. I was great at finding birds' nests, and occasionally of a Sunday I'd go into the neighboring woods looking for them. One Sunday I went to Starkey's wood at Cregane, about a mile outside the town. I entered it, there near where the Jackey-boys lived. I went through the line of trees that run into Ownaheencha cross, till I came to another ditch. Then I leaped into a meadow, and as I leaped, a big blackbird began to screech and run fluttering, clattering and crying "chuc-chuc-chuc chuc chuc." I must have leaped on the bird's wing; I must have wounded her some way, when she could not fly; so I thought, and so I ran after her to catch her. But the rogue could fly, though she never went more than a few yards ahead of me. At the end of the field I thought I had her cor-

nered, but she rose up and flew over the ditch into the
next field. I retraced my steps to the place where I leaped
into the field. I looked to see if I would find any
feathers or any sign of my having leaped upon the bird,
and on looking I found in the side of the ditch a nest
with five young ones in it, with their mouths wide open
to receive the food they thought their father or mother
was going to give them. I did a very cruel thing that
day : I robbed that nest ; I took it away with me. On
my way home Captain Wat. Starkey met me ; Corley
Garraviagh was wheeling him in a hand carriage ; I
had the nest on my head. " Those are my birds you
have," he said. " Where did you get them ? " I didn't
mind him, but walked on.

I suppose they were his birds, for those English land-
robbers of Ireland claim dominion of " all the birds in
the air, and all the fishes in the sea."

That bird whose nest I robbed has often reminded
me of Gladstone, the Prime Minister of England, and
the prime hypocrite Governor of Ireland. Or, more
correctly speaking, I should say this Gladstone, Prime
Minister of England, in his government of Ireland, has
often reminded me of that blackbird. The ruse she
played to get me away from her nest is the ruse he has
played to get Irishmen away from the work that would
rob him of Ireland. Irishmen in the hands of English
jailers are snatched away from them in the heart of
England ; English castles are blown down ; English
governors of Ireland are slain ; there is terror in England—terror in the hearts of Englishmen. Gladstone
chuckles " chuc-chuc-chuc-chuc, I'll give you Home

Rule for Ireland." Irishmen listen to him; they follow him; he flies away from them; his eyesight gets bad, and he is blind to all his promises of Home Rule for Ireland. Irishmen are divided; the work that struck terror into the heart of the Englishman is abandoned by them; his eyesight is restored to him, and he is now writing Bible history. His " chuc chuc-chuc " is so much akin to my blackbird's " chuc-chuc-chuc " that I christen her the " Gladstone blackbird."

But the resemblance holds good only as regards the use of the cry. The objects and purposes of its use are different. The poor bird cried " chuc, chuc," to save her children from destruction. Gladstone cried " chuc, chuc," to keep the children of Ireland in the hands of their destroyer.

And how many are the storied memories that possess me now in connection with that road I traveled the day I robbed the blackbird's nest! It was on that road I shook hands with Daniel O'Connell; it was on that road Cliona, the fairy queen, used to enlist lovers; that was the road I traveled going to the fair of Newmill, and the road I traveled the day I went to Lord Carberry's funeral. I have spoken of the Jackey-boys living on that roadside. Who were they? They were boys of the name of O'Mahony, "rough and ready roving boys, like Rory of the Hill." They had a farm of land; they had a fishing boat, and they had the name of, one way or another, getting the better of any of the English garrison party that would do them a wrong. Two of them were out on the seacliffs one day, robbing an eagle's nest. A rope was tied to a pannier; one of them went into the pannier; the other let the pannier slide down till it was at the nest. The young ones were put into the pannier, and on the way up the mother eagle attacked the robber. The pannier got some jostling; the rope got jagged against the crags, and one of its strands got broken. The brother in the basket below cried out to the brother on the cliff above, " Dar fia! Shawn, 'ta ceann do na stroundee bristeh " (By this and by that, Jack, one of the strands is broken). " Coimead thu fein go socair," said the other. " Ni'l aon bao'al ort, chun go brisig an tarna strounda." (Keep quiet; there is no fear of you till the second strand breaks.)

That Starkey road is the road on which I met Daniel O'Connell. Yes; there were crowds of people on it the day he was coming from the Curragh meeting in Skibbereen, in the year 1843. Through the crowd of people, between the legs of some of them, I made my way to the carriage the liberator was in. I was raised up, and had a hearty shake hands with him.

It was the road Cliona, the fairy queen used to travel. Yes, and her fairy home of Carrig-Cliona is quite convenient to it. But I don't know whether she is living still. When I was in Ireland a year ago, it looked to me as if the Irish fairies were dead too. In those early days of mine this Cliona used to "show" herself on moonlight nights, robed in sunlight splendor. Every young man she'd meet between the cross of Barnamarrav and the Castle of Rathabharrig would be subjected to examination by her, and if she found him to her liking, he was taken to her cave, or put under an obligation to meet her a certain night in the future. Before that certain night came the young man was dead ; and, of course, the pith of this fairy story is, that the fairy queen took him away with her. She hugged to death every one she fell in love with. The Irish poets prayed for deliverance from her fatally bewitching influence. It was of her the poet, in the poem of " O'Donovan's daughter," hymned the prayer:

"God grant! 'tis no fay from Cnoc Aoibhin that woos me,
    God grant! 'tis not Cleena the queen, that pursues me."

I said that the road of Cliona's travels was the road I used to travel going to the fair of Newmill. Is there anything in that recollection that would make any kind of an interesting story? There is, and it is this.

At the fair at Newmill there used to be faction fights, and there used to be companies of policemen under the command of Gore Jones. The policemen would be encamped in a field near by—in the field next to the fair. Their arms would be stacked there. In the evening a fight would commence among the factions. The police would not stir. Gore Jones would not give them any orders to rush in and make peace while the fight was going on. But when the fight was over, he'd rush into the fair field with his men and arrest all who had any signs of blood on them. They were handcuffed and taken to the jail of Ross, and then their families and their friends were kept for days and weeks after, going around to the different landlord magistrates making interest and influence to get them out of jail. That was all a trick of the English government in Ireland, a trick to bring the people whom England had robbed and plundered, more and more under compliment and obligation to those landlord magistrates who were living in possession of the robbery and plunder. They gain their point when they can keep the people always begging and praying to them for some little favor. You now understand why it is that when I am speaking to the Irish people at home and abroad about my recollections, I consider it an interesting thing to them to speak of the fair of Newmill.

What else is that I brought in? Yes, my Blackbird road was the road we traveled the day I went to Lord Carbery's funeral. I have a purpose, too, in speaking of that. It must be some time about the year 1844. With four or five other boys, I mootched from school that day and went to Rath-a-Bharrig, or Castlefreke, as it is christened in the language of the plundering Frekes. Before the Cromwellian time, it, and the land around it belonged to the Barrys, of the Norman time.

When we got to the wake-house we did not get in; in fact we kept away from it, because as we ran away from school we did not want to let our fathers see us, so I went over to the lake to look at the swans. I found a swan's nest with three eggs in it—the largest eggs that ever I saw. I had to put my two hands around one of them, taking it up, showing it to my companions. When the bells rang for the funeral service to move, I took my position behind a big tree in view of the avenue the people would pass through. I watched for my father, and when I saw him, with a piece of white calico around his hat, I got mad, for I knew my father was mad at being subjected to such humiliation, and at being obliged to wear such a menial garb of mourning at such a funeral. The word had been sent around by the gentry that all the tenants on the Carbery estate were to attend the lord's funeral, and though my father was not paying rent directly to the Carbery lord, still, as his holding was looked upon as the Carbery property, he attended. I will give explanation on this subject by and by.

It appears to me in writing these pages that I am very anxious to get out of my childhood, and out of my boyhood days, and as I cannot get back to them once I get out, nor see any use in singing:

"Would I were a boy again,'

I will remain a boy as long as I can.

I was naturally very quiet and gentle when a boy— just as I am to-day—except when I was put to it, and when I was forced to be otherwise. I had five or six boxing bouts with schoolfellows—with Mike Crone, Micky Feen, Stephen Lovejoy, Pat Callanan and Paak Cullinane—but I never struck the first blow. Paak Cullinane and I were among the boys who went up to the Ardagh road bowling. He and I were made markers. On one occasion I thought he marked the throw of one of his friends a foot ahead of where the bowl stopped. I objected, and without his saying a word, the first thing he did was to give me a thump in the face.

He had the name of being the best boxer in the school, and could with impunity strike any one he got vexed with, but when he struck me, I struck back, and the fight had to be stopped, to stop the blood that was running from his nose. The fight with Mike Crone ended by my getting a lump on the forehead that made me give up the contest, and the other three were drawn battles.

But I never had any fight or falling-out with any of the girls of my acquaintance. They were all very fond of me, and when my mother would keep me in, to learn my lessons, I'd hear Mary Hurley and Ellen Fitzpatrick and Menzie Crone and Ponticilia Barrett come as a delegation from the girls outside, asking her to let Jer. come out to play with them.

You never saw any illuminations at the bottom of the sea. I saw them, and I used to take those girls to see them. Bounding our fields, was the strand. This strand was about a half a mile wide, every way; it had a sandy bottom, in which cockles had their home. There was no water in the strand, when the tide was out. But when the tide was coming in, or going out, and when the water would be about twelve inches deep, as pretty a sight as you could see would be to walk through that water, and see "the cockles lighting." The sun should be shining, and you should walk the strand with your face to the sun, so that your shadow would fall behind you. Then every home of a cockle would be lighted: you'd see through the cockle's chamber door,—through a little hole that a knitting needle would fill—the light down in the sand, like a little taper burning. 'Twas a pretty picture; I'd go a mile off to-day to see it again. But those days are passed and gone.

Nor, can I ever again, see the sun dancing on an

Easter Sunday morning as it used to dance when I was a boy, over the general rejoicing on that day. It was to be seen through burned glass, and on Saturday night I'd have my glass burned, ready to look at the sun next morning, if the morning was fine.

> Our Pagan sires, our strifes would shun,
> They saw their heaven, through the sun,
> Their God smiled down on every one
> In Ireland over the water.

Those are lines I wrote when in an English prison years ago. I suppose I was thinking of our Pagan fathers, who, it is said, worshipped the sun. Irish historians—historians of the Catholic church in Ireland tell us, that Saint Patrick, and other Apostles of Christianity, allowed many of the harmless habits and customs of the Irish people to remain with them; that they did not insist on the abolition of some practices that tended to the worship of a Supreme Being, and it is as reasonable as anything else to suppose that our Pagan fathers, in worshipping the sun, was only worshipping the Supreme Power that put that sun in the heavens. It was, and is to-day, the most visible manifestation of the Great God of the Universe.

On the eve of La Sowna, November day—and on the eve of La Bealtheine—May day, there are practices carried on in Ireland that must have come down to our people from times anterior to the time of Saint Patrick. I remember Jemmie Fitzpatrick taking me with him up to his farm in Ardagh one May evening, to bless the growing crops. I carried the little sheaves of straw that he had prepared for the occasion. When he came

to the grounds, he took one of the sheaves and lit it.
Then, we walked around every field, he, as one sheaf
would burn out, taking another from me, and lighting
it.   This, no doubt, is some relic that comes down to us
from those times that poets and historians tell us the
Baal-fires were lighted throughout the land.

Speaking of Patrick's day celebrations, I don't know
that I have the enthusiasm regarding them to-day that
I had in my schooldays.

Many and many a time I drew the blood from my
fingers to paint the section red part of the crosses that
I used to be making for the celebration of the day.
The green color I'd get, by gathering pennyleaves in
the garden, and bruising out the juice of them, and the
yellow color would come to me from the yolk of an egg.
If I hadn't a compass to make my seven circle cross,
I'd make a compass out of a little goulogue sprig of a
whitethorn tree—fastening a writing pen to one leg of
it.   John Cushan, the master, would not let the boys
make the crosses at school.

And often that school time of mine comes up to me,
when I hear friends in New York talking of their
schooldays in Ireland—when I hear, as I heard the
other night, Pat Egan asking Pat Cody and John
O'Connor, if they remembered the time when they were
carrying the sods of turf under their arms to school.
That was jokingly cast at them, as kind of aspachaun;
but I remember that I, myself, often carried the sods of
turf under my arm to school; and if there is any fire
in anything I write in this book, I suppose that is how
it comes.

CHAPTER VII.

THE LORDS OF IRELAND.

THE landlords of Ireland are the lords of Ireland. England makes them landlords first, and then, to put the brand of her marauding nobility on them, she makes them English lords. And they do lord it over the Irish people, and ride rough-shod over every natural and acquired right belonging to them. Whether born in England or Ireland, they must be English, and anti-Irish in spirit, in action and in religion. Some of my readers may say that some of the lords and the land-lords in Ireland at the present day are Catholics. So they are, and so were a few of them in my day, and so were the whole of them in the days preceding the time of Henry VIII. But if they were, they were English and anti-Irish all the same, and the marauding Catholic Englishman, coming over to Ireland on his mission of murder and plunder during the three hundred years preceding Martin Luther's time, murdered Irishmen as mercilessly and plundered them as ruthlessly as he has done during the last three hundred years that he is a Protestant. It is not religion, but booty, the English-man is after in this world. Of course, religion is very useful to him. It furnishes him with a pretext to enter a country and to take soundings in it,

With the Bible on his lips,
But the devil in his deeds,

71

And what is more than that, neither religion nor nationality ever stood in the way of his plundering and murdering the children of the English invader who landed in Ireland a century or so before he landed there.

The Cromwellians plundered the Strongbownians, and the English transported and murdered the Protestant Mitchels and Fitzgeralds, who resisted their plunder, as readily as they did the Catholic O'Neills and O'Donnells.

And, holy Jehoshaphat! how wholly and firmly did these freebooters plant themselves in Ireland. I stand on the top of that hill where my schoolhouse stood, and I see the lighthouse of the Fastnet Rock and Cape Clear, straight out before me in the open sea; I see the ships sailing between the Cove of Cork and America, every steamer passing showing a long trail of steam like the tail of a comet. And what else do I see before me and all around me? I see the imprint of the invader's footsteps, the steps he has taken to fortify himself in possession of his plunder, and to guard himself from assault from the victims of that plunder—for many of these victims must be wandering around the locality still. I look to the north, and I see to the right the Castle of Cahirmore, the residence of the Hungerfords. I go up the Cahirmore road (as I often went going to the home of my grandfather), and at my left hand side, for half a mile, is a wall higher than a man's height. I cannot see the grounds or anything on the grounds inside the wall, but I hear the beautiful peacocks crying out to one another.

I look to the left, and I see the Castle of Derry, the residence of the Townsends. I walk up the Derry road, and for a half a mile of that road, to my left, there is built a wall higher than myself that prevents me from seeing any of the beauties of the demesne inside.

I look to the south, and to my right, at Rowry is the Bleazby residence, walled around by a wall some fifteen feet high, with the Smith family at Doneen further south, having another wall around them equally high.

I look to the south at my left and there is Castle Freke the residence of Lord Carberry. There is a wall around the castle and demesne here, that is, I suppose, some two miles in circumference, a high wall, as around the other places around Ross.

I traveled through England, Scotland, Wales and France, and I did not see those high walls around the residences and the grounds of any of the people.

I traveled every county in Ireland and I saw them in every county. In Monaghan one day I wanted to see James Blaney Rice of Tyholland. I came out of the railway train at Glaslough station, and walked a bit into the country, taking a roundabout way to go to the house. At the left hand side of the road I walked, there was a wall some ten feet high for a long distance. I got out of humor with that wall, as it shut out from me a view of the whole country side. When I got to James Rice, I asked him who lived inside that wall; he said it was Leslie the landlord and land agent. That's in Ulster. In Connacht I walked out from Ballinasloe one day to see the grounds on which the battle of Aughrim was fought. I had a walk of about

three miles, and at my right hand side during a long
distance of that walk there was a wall higher than my
head, that hid from me the castle and the grounds of
Lord Clancarty.

In Leinster one day John Powell of Birr took me
out for a drive through Kings County. He drove as
far as the banks of the Shannon. There was the residence of Lord Rosse walled around in the castle of the
O'Carrolls; and the castle of the O'Dempseys, walled
around in the residence of Lord Bernard.

And look at the castle of Kilkenny, the residence of
the Butlers, the lords of Ormond. Around the
grounds is a wall twelve feet high. Tom Doyle of
Kilkenny told me yesterday that that wall had a circumference of four miles and that, in the neighborhood
of the city, the wall in some places was twenty feet,
and thirty feet high.

That, no doubt, was to save the plunderer inside
from fear from any missiles being aimed at him by any
of the plundered people from the housetops of the city.
Those Butlers—the Ormonds, were often fighting about
boundaries and other matters with the Fitzgeralds, the
lords of Desmond. The two families came in, in the
Strongbownian time. It is said of them that they became more Irish than the Irish themselves. That tran-
sition came on naturally. Ireland became a hunting
ground for marauding Englishmen. The Englishmen
of the thirteenth century learned that the invaders of
the twelfth century had got a "soft snap" of it in Ireland, and they tried their luck there. They trespassed
on the possessions of the Desmonds and the Ormonds;

so the Fitzgeralds and the Butlers planted in Ireland had to fight against the new English coming in. And thus it came into Irish history that some of these Butlers and Fitzgeralds have been century after century declared in rebellion against England.

The old saying has it that a guilty conscience needs no accuser. Those walls were not built around the castles of Ireland 'til the English came into Ireland.

Prendergast in his book of the "Cromwellian Settlement of Ireland," and Regnault, in his "Criminal History of England," and other historians say they were built for the double purpose of securing the claim from other plunderers who would want to dispute the boundary, and of saving the plunderer from the chance of getting a bullet or a stone or any other hostile missile or message from any of the plundered people in the neighborhood.

Those plunderers know they deserve it, and that is why they try to shelter themselves against it. That is how it is that England has passed so many laws to keep arms of all kinds out of the hands of the Irish people, and how she has passed so many laws to kill the Irish language out of their tongues. She passed those laws against the language, because wherever that language is spoken it gives the name and ownership of the castle to the old Irish owner of it. Lord Rosse's castle in Birr is to-day called by the Irish-speaking people "Caislean ui Carrooil," the Castle of the O'Carrolls; Castle Bernard, the residence of the Earl of Bandon, is called Caislean ui Mahoona; Castle Freke, the residence of the Freke Lord Carberry, is called

"Rath-a-Bharrig," the Castle of the Barrys, and so on throughout all Ireland.

The Dublin "Gaelic Journal" for the month of May, 1896, has come to me as I write this chapter. I look at it and see a few lines that naturally fit in here. These are they; "Donghall, O'Donngaile, O'Donnelly, Baile ui-Dhonnghaile, O'Donnelly's town, now called Castlecaulfield, County Tyrone."

The English name or title has not a place in the Irish language, no, nor has it caught on to the Irish tongue yet. Neither has it a place in the Irish heart. Notwithstanding all that English laws have done to blot Irish history, the Irish people, in the Irish language, still hold their own.

That is why England has tried hard to kill the Irish language. Some of my readers may think she is encouraging the cultivation of it now. She is not; she doesn't mean it; her heart is not in the professions she is making, no more than was the heart of my hen blackbird Gladstone in the professions about home rule that he was making for Ireland for the past twenty years.

Yes, 'tis twenty years now since he made that Mid-Lothian speech, in which he said "Ireland should be governed according to Irish ideas." He was out of office then. But, shortly after, he came into office, and he put thousands of Irishmen into prison for having them dare to think they ought to be governed by Irish ideas. And he kicked the Irish members out of the English House of Commons for having them dare to think Ireland should be governed according to Irish ideas.

'Tis my mother and father, God be good to them,

that had the true Irish natural feeling about those Englishmen governing Ireland.

I can see now how relieved they felt whenever they'd hear of a landlord being shot in Tipperary or anywhere else in Ireland.

It was like an instinct with them that an enemy of theirs had been done away with. That kind of instinct is in the whole Irish race to-day, and if the power that supports landlordism in Ireland could be stricken down, there would be a general jubilee of rejoicing in the land. Until it is stricken down, there is no freedom, no home rule for Ireland.

Going into the town of Bandon one day, I overtook on the road a man who had a car-load of hay. At the right hand side of the road was the demesne of Lord Bandon. I was on horseback, and was high enough to see over the wall, the mansion called Castle Bernard in the demesne. "Go d' aon caislean e sin thall ansann?" (what castle is that over there) said I. "Caislean ui Mhahoona" (O'Mahony's castle) said he. The O'Mahonys are out of it, on a tramp through the world; the Bernards are in it, and are lords of Bandon. And these are the lords that administer the English laws to the people they have plundered. Take the present day, and look at the list of grand jurors that are summoned the two seasons of the year in every county in Ireland. They are the plunderers who hold the lands and castles of the plundered people, and they sit in judgment on the children of those to whom the lands and castles belonged. And these children, in cases of difficulties with the law, have to be running after the

makers of that law for influence to get them out of the
troubles that eternally surround them.

One of the fireside stories that got into my mind
when I was a child was the story of a bill of indictment
against my people, the time of the " White boys."

These " White boys" came into the bleach-field one
night, and washed their faces in the stream that ran by
it, and dried themselves with the linen that was bleach-
ing in the field. Whatever offence the White boys
were charged with, my people were put into the indictment with them, either as participants or sympathizers,
or as assisting in the escape of criminals who had committed offences. It was considered they knew who
blackened the linen, and they should be punished as
they wouldn't tell on them. My grandfather, after using all the influence of all the friends, had got some
letters from the lords and landlords around to the grand
jury of the Cork assizes. He had them one evening,
and he should be in Cork city at ten o'clock next morning. There were no trains running anywhere at that
time. He got on horseback, and galloped to Rossmore.
He got a fresh horse at Rossmore. Then he galloped
on to Ballineen and got another fresh horse there ; then
another in Bandon, and another in Ballinhassig that
landed him at Cork city courthouse before ten o'clock
in the morning. He gave in his letters to the grand
jury, waited a few hours, and returned home with the
news that the bills were "ignored." That is ; that
the grand jury " threw out " the bills and did not follow
up the prosecution of the case against the people who
owned the bleach.

You may think that's a kind of a make-up of a story about my grandfather getting three or four relays of horses all in one night. I don't wonder you would think so. Perhaps I thought so myself when I was a child listening to it at the fireside; but, stop awhile; wait till I come to write my chapter on genealogy, and come to show you how my grandfather had family relations and connections in every corner of the county, and then you will not be surprised at what I am saying. You'll be more surprised at what I have to say yet.

The White boy indictment was before I was born. Soon after I was born, my father got into trouble with the head lord of the soil by selling to Mick Hurley, the carpenter, four tall ash trees that were growing in the kitchen garden back of the house. Lord Carberry claimed that the trees belonged to the soil—belonged to him—and that my father had no right to cut them down and sell them. My father had as much right to that soil as Lord Carberry had; he had more right to it, in fact.

One of the Irish histories I read in my youth has these words: "The O'Donovans—a branch of the Mac-Carthys—had extensive possessions in the neighborhood of Ross."

They owned all Ross, and all around it, but the turn in the world came that turned them and turned many other old Irish families upside down, and left the Englishmen on top.

CHAPTER VIII.

A CHAPTER ON GENEALOGY.

When I was a little fellow, I got so much into my head about my family, and about what great big people they were in the world before I came among them, that when I grew up to be a man, I began to trace the genealogy of that family, and I actually did trace it up the generations through Ham, who was saved in Noah's Ark, to Adam and Eve who lived in the Garden of Paradise one time. While at this work, I was for a few years in communication with John O'Donovan of No. 36 Northumberland Street, Dublin. He was professor of the Irish language in Trinity College At the college, and at his house I met him whenever business would take me to Dublin. He had then seven children —seven sons, "an effort of nature to preserve the name" as he says in one of his letters to me. I don't know—sometimes my thoughts are sad, at thinking that perhaps it was my acquaintance with those children when they were young, in the years '54, '5, '6, '7, '8 and '9, that brought them into association with me, and with my crowd of people when I came to live in Dublin entirely in the years 1864 and '65. John, Edmond, and Willie were the three oldest of the seven sons of John O'Donovan. The three of them were put to jail in Dublin charged with connection with Fenianism. John was drowned in St. Louis, Edmond was killed in Africa, and I was at the funeral of Willie in Calvary cemetery, Brooklyn. I'll come to them again. Now, I'll get back to my genealogy.

Some of my friends may say: " To Jericho with your genealogy; what do we care about it! We are here in America, where one man is as good as another." That's all right, for any one who wants to have done with Ireland; all right for the man who can say, with him who said to me in New York, one day, twenty-five years ago: "What is Ireland to me now?" "Sure I'm an American citizen!" All right for him who wants to forget all belonging to him in the past, and who wants to be the Adam and Eve of his name and race, but it is otherwise for men who are no way ashamed of those who have gone before them, and who do not want to bury in the grave of American citizenship, all the duties they owe to their motherland, while it remains a land enslaved.

It would be no harm at all, if men of Irish societies in America, in introducing other men into these societies would know who were their Irish fathers and mothers. Any man who is proud of belonging to the old blood of Ireland, will never do anything to bring disgrace upon any one belonging to him. I don't mind how poor he is; the poorer he is, the nearer he is to God; the nearer he is to sanctification through suffering, and the more marks and signs he has of the hand of the English enemy having been heavily laid upon him.

That hand has been heavily laid upon my race. I, even to-day, feel the weight of it on myself. When the lands of Rossmore were confiscated on my people, they moved to neighboring places, and were hunted from those places, till at last a resting place was found in the town of Ross Carberry. " My great-grandfather came into Ross Carberry with a hat full of gold," said Peggy Leary to me the other night, " and the family were after being outcanted from seven places, from the time they left Rossmore, till the time they settled in Ross."

Calling in to Dan O'Geary of Glanworth on my way home from Peggie Leary's, I got talking to him about old times in Ireland, and I found that Dan had a family story much like my own. " I heard my grandmother, Sarah Blake, say," said he, " that when my grandfather John Foley came into Glanworth, he had a hat full of gold."

" A strange measure they had for gold that time, Dan," said I—" a hat. I heard a cousin of my own make use of the very same words an hour ago."

" When my great-grandfather came in to Ross," said she, " he had a hat full of gold."

" It must mean," said Dan, " as much gold as would fill a hat." And so it must. That is the meaning of it in the Irish language—Laan-hata, d'ore—as much gold as would fill a hat. " A hat, full of gold " would be " hata, laan d'ore." The Irish tongue and the Irish language are not the only things that suffer by the effort to turn everything Irish into English.

That nickname " Rossa " comes to me from Rossmore, not from Rosscarberry. That great grandfather of Peggie Leary's and mine was called " Donacha mor a Rossa." The word "outcanted" that his great-grand-daughter Peggy Leary used is very likely much the same as the word "evicted" that is in use to-day.

When the Cromwellian plunderers got hold of the lands of our people, they did not like that the plundered people would be settled down anywhere near them. That is how the desire arose of having them sent "to hell or Connacht." Nor did the plunderers like that the plundered people would hold any remembrance of what belonged to them of old, and that is how it came to my notice that it is only in whispers my people would carry the name "Rossa" with them. The people would call my father "Donacha Russa"—leaving out altogether the name O'Donovan, and in signing papers or writing letters, my father would not add the name Russa, or Rossa.

I vowed to myself one day that if ever I got to be a man, I'd carry the name Rossa with me. And to-day, in the city of New York, in the face of the kind of people that govern that city, I find it as hard to carry that name as ever my fathers found it, in the face of the English governing Ireland.

Indeed it is not much amiss for me to say that it looks to me as if it was the same English Sassenach spirit that was prominent and predominant in the government of this city, and many other cities of America to-day.

My great-grandfather Donacha Rossa was married to Sheéla ni Illean :—Julia O'Donovan-Island. They had six sons. Those six sons were married into the following families: Dan's wife, an O'Mahony-Baan of

Shounlarach; John's wife, a Callanan of East Carberry; Den's wife, a McCarthy-Meening of East Carberry; Conn's wife, an O'Sullivan Bua'aig; Jer's wife (my grandmother), an O'Donovan-Baaid, and Flor's wife, an O'Driscoll—sister to Teige oge O'Driscoll of Derryclathagh.

Those six brothers had three sisters, one of whom married into the Lee family of Clonakilty, one of them into the Barrett family of Caheragh, and the other into the O'Sullivan-Stuocach family of the Common Mountain.

My grandmother Maire-'n-Bhaaid had six sisters. One of them married into the Good family of Macroom; one of them into the Hawkes family of Bandon, one of them into the Hart family of Cahirmore, one of them into the Nagle family of Fearnachountil, and the other two into some other families between Bandon and Cork It was through this O'Donovan-Baaid connection that my grandfather got the relays of horses between Bandon and Cork the time he had to make the run to the grand jury to save himself from the White-boy indictment.

Then, my grandfather, at the mother's side was Cornelius O'Driscoll of Renascreena, and my grandmother was Anna ni-Laoghaire. My grandfather had two brothers—Patrick, who was married to the sister of Florry McCarthy of the Mall, and Denis who was married into the O'Donovan-Dheeil family of Mauly-regan. There were some sisters there also—one of them the mother of the O'Callaghans of the Mall, and the other, the mother of the Noonans of Cononagh.

One of my mother's sisters is Mrs. Bridget Murray, No. 11 Callowhill Street, Philadelphia, and wanting some information for this chapter of my " Recollections," I wrote lately, asking her to answer some questions that I laid before her. These are the questions and answers :

Q.—What was the maiden name of the mother of my grandfather, Conn O'Driscoll ?

A.—Ellen White.

Q.—What was the maiden name of the mother of my grandmother, Annie O'Leary ?

A.—Ellen MacKennedy.

Q.—What was the name of my aunt that died young ?

A.—Mary.

Q.—What was her husband's name ?

A.—John O'Brien.

Q.—What was the name of the wife of my granduncle, Denis O'Driscoll ?

A.—Mary O'Donovan-Dheeil.

Q.—Had my grandfather any sister but the one that was Paddy Callaghan's mother ?

A.—Yes; Kate O'Driscoll, married to Denis Noonan.

Father James Noonan, the grandson of that grandaunt of mine is now in Providence, R. I. I had a strange family reunion with him one time. I went to Washington, D. C., to attend the funeral of Col. Patrick J. Downing. His body was taken to the Cathedral, and after the Requiem Mass, Father Noonan came on the altar to say some kind words as to the worth of the dead soldier. There I sat between the two ; the priest was the grandson of my grandfather's sister, at my mother's side; the dead man was the grandson of my father's sister. And that is how we scatter, and how we die, and how we meet in the strange land—not knowing each other.

Another strange meeting at a funeral came to my notice here in New York one time. Dr. Hamilton Williams, of Dungarvan, had me to stand godfather for a child of his. The child died, and I went to the funeral to Calvary cemetery. Dr. Williams was not long in America at the time. It was the first death in his family, and the child was buried in the plot belonging to its mother's sister. The next plot to the right hand side of it was one on which a tombstone was erected, on which was engraven, "Sacred to the memory of Denis O'Donovan-Rossa, of Ross Carberry, aged ninety years." There is my godchild, belonging to Waterford, lying side by side with my grand-uncle's son, belonging to Cork.

I often thought, while reading the tombstones of Flatbush and Calvary, what an interesting book of record and genealogy could be made from them; and from the information that could be derived from the people who own them. I often thought I would like to write such a book. I would like to do it yet, but circumstances are against the possibility of my doing so. How peacefully there, the "Fardown" rests side by side with his up-the-country neighbor, and how quietly the Connaught man slumbers side by side with the Leinster man. Neighborly, as in death, so should we be in life.

I spoke of Father Noonan at Col. Dowling's funeral;

it is no harm to let him be seen in my book, in this letter of his:

ST. ALOYSIUS, Washington, D. C.,
September 29, 1886.

MY DEAR FRIEND—Sister Stanislaus was my sister's name in Religion. I received an account of her death from one of the nuns. While I naturally regret the death of my only sister, I am consoled that she died in carrying out the end of her vocation, viz: charity to the poor and suffering. All my relations are dying out rapidly, but we mourn—not like those who have no hope. I would have answered at once, but was away from Washington when your letter reached here.

Yours most truly,
JAMES NOONAN, S. J.

If I traveled from New York to San Francisco now, and stayed a time in every city on the way, I could find a family cousin or connection in every one of those cities—scores of them in these two cities I name, among people who do not even know me. The mother of the children of Alderman Henry Hughes, of New York, was an O'Donovan-Maol; her mother was an O'Donovan Rossa, the daughter of one of my grand-uncles. The mother of Counsellor McIntyre's children, of San Francisco, is an O'Donovan-Ciuin; her father is Martin Ciuin, of Sawroo, the son of my mother's sister, Kate O'Driscoll.

I could go into any parish in the Province of Munster and find family relations and connections in it. Even in England I found relations in whatever city I entered.

In London the member who gave me a ticket to go into the House of Commons in May, 1895, was one of my Old country cousins—Ned Barry, of Newmill, one of the members for Cork County.

Then, when I went up to Newcastle-on-Tyne, a man called on me who told me he recollected seeing me at his father's house, in Dunmanway, when he was a child. He was a grandson of old Jerrie Donovan, of Nedineh, whom I met in my early days—Jer-a-Bhaaid, who belonged to the family of my grandmother, Mauria 'n Bhaaid. This New Castle Irishman was half a Tipperary man. His mother, before she married his father, Tim O'Donovan Baaid, was a Miss Doheny, the niece of Father Doheny, of Tipperary, who was a parish priest in Dunmanway.

The day before I left Chatham prison I had a visit from a man who was living outside the prison walls. He said I may want some money, and he put into my hand eight or ten sovereigns. He was Bildee Barrett, of Ross, the son of Ned Barrett, whose mother was an O'Donovan Rossa, the sister of my grandfather.

In 1894, when I was in Ireland, a double cousin of mine wrote me this letter:

THE ARCADE, Ross Carberry,
June 5th, 1894.

DEAR MR. O'DONOVAN—We regret very much not having the pleasure of seeing you in Skibbereen last evening, but we are glad to learn from James Donovan that you will visit Ross Carberry shortly, when we hope to give you a hearty welcome to your native town. If my father (Rick Donovan-Roe) lived, how delighted he would be to see you.

My husband is also a cousin of yours—a grandson of old Garrett Barry. I remain, your fond cousin,

ELLEN COLLINS.

When I think of how many ways that girl is related to me it looks like a labyrinthian puzzle to go through the relationship. I have to travel through all the bohreens of the barony to get to the end of it. Her father was Rick Roe; Rick Roe's father was Paddy Roe; Paddy Roe's wife was Margaret O'Driscoll; Margaret O'Driscoll was my godmother, and she was the sister of my grandfather, Cornelius O'Driscoll. Then that Ellen Collins' mother, Rick Roe's wife, was an O'Donovan-Island—a cousin of that Ellen Collins, though she was her mother. Ellen Collins is also related to her husband, as he is the grandson of Garrett Barry, for Garrett Barry's mother was an O'Donovan-Island, the sister of my great grandmother.

That Ellen Collins has bigger cousins in New York than I am. The Harringtons of Dunmanway are the biggest and the richest butchers in the city. I was going up Second Avenue one summer evening last year and I met Charles O'Brien, of Clare, at Forty-seventh Street. He keeps an undertaker's store. Two or three men were sitting on chairs outside the door. He brought out a chair, and invited me to sit down, which I did, for of all the O'Briens in New York, I love to hear this Charlie O'Brien speak of Ireland—he has such a pride in his name and his family, holding his head as high as the richest man who walks the earth. Among the neighbors I was introduced to, was a Mr. Harrington, about seventy-five years of age. When he spoke, and while he spoke, his tongue was sounding in my ears as if it was jingling on the hearthstone of my childhood.

" Where in the world, Mr. Harrington," said I to him at last, " were you living when you were growing up a child ? "

" I was living in Dunmanway," said he.

" I have never met you before," said I, " but your voice sounds to me as if I heard it before ; I must have known some people belonging to you. What was your mother's name ? "

" My mother's name," said he, " was Donovan ; she was a sister to Tom Donovan-Roe of Ross."

That Tom Donovan-Roe was the grandfather of my correspondent Ellen Collins, and the brother-in-law of my grand-aunt and god-mother. The sound of the voice of Mr. Harrington's mother must have sounded in my ears some of the days of my childhood. Mr. Harrington's voice is to-day—after his fifty odd years in America —as Irish as my own.

The old Garrett Barry, Ellen Collins speaks of, was the grandfather of Edward Barry, the member of Parliament who took me into the House of Commons last year, and was the rent-receiver on the Lord Carberry estate when I was a boy.

I did not satisfy the desire of Ellen Collins-Sguab-bera to see me in Ross, when I was in Ireland ; nor did I satisfy my own desire either, of seeing the spots where I had the nests of the goldfinch, and the green-linnet, and the grey-linnet, and the wren, and the robin, and

the tomtit, and the yellow-hammer, and the ladywag-
tail. I did not go into my native town. I specially
avoided going into it, because I could not go into it, as
I would wish to go. I knew I would meet many there
who were broken down in the world, and I could not
meet them in the manner I would like. I, too, like
Terrie of Derry have had my dreams in the foreign
lands:—

Still dreaming of home
 And the bright days to come,
When the boys should all
 Dub me "Sir Terrie;"
And flowing with cash
 I could cut a big dash,
In the beautiful city of Derry.

But those dreams and many other dreams of mine
have not been realized.

All this I am saying may be idle gossip, personal or
family gossip, yet it may lead to something that may
affect every one who is not ashamed of having an Irish
father and mother, and of having every one and everything belonging to him, Irish. To those who would be
ashamed of having it known who their father and
mother and their family connections were, I have nothing to say, and I heed little what they say of me for
having a little Irish family pride about me. My story
is the story of many a decent father and mother's son,
cast out upon the world—the story, alas! of many a decent father and mother's daughter too:

"Through the far lands we roam,
 Through the wastes, wild and barren,
We are strangers at home—
 We are exiles in Erin."

When Cromwell ravaged Ireland; when the cry was to the Irish people of Munster, Leinster and Ulster—"To hell, or to Connacht, with you!" there were not enough of people left in those three provinces to till the land. Then propositions were made to the plundered, exterminated people, that some of them would return, and that others of them would go back to their lands under an agreement of paying rent to an English landlord, and some who even owned the land got a foothold to remain as rent-gatherers for the Cromwellians. The Barrys owned Rathabharrig—Castle Barry. The Frekes and the Aylmers and the Evanses came in, and changed the name from Castle Barry to Castle Freke, and the Barrys got a chance of living on their own lands, by becoming rent-payers and rent collectors for the Invaders.

Old Garrett Barry was the rent-agent on the Carberry estate. It was through his friendship and influence that my father was not crushed out entirely when he cut down the trees in the kitchen garden, and sold them to Mick Hurley.

I have said in a previous chapter that although our land was on the Carberry estate, Lord Carberry was not the direct landlord who received the rent. And here I will have to notice another trick or two of those English marauding plunderers in Ireland, and notice the habits of servility and slavery into which the writers of Irish manners and customs have fallen. There is the custom of "fosterage" and there is the custom of "sponsorship" between the plunderer and the plundered.

The plunderer knows that nothing kills the wrath of the Irishman so much as trust in his honor. The Cromwellian landlord has an heir born to him, and he goes to the tenant O'Donovan and tells him Lady Carberry is in very delicate health, and would take it as an everlasting favor if Mrs. O'Donovan would take the baby from her for a short time. Mrs. O'Donovan has had a baby of her own about the same time that Lady Carberry had her baby. Mrs. O'Donovan takes the lord's baby, and brings it up with her own. The two grow up as "foster brothers." The lord had heard that O'Donovan had been plotting to kill him for being in possession of the lands of the O'Donovans. But now the lord sleeps soundly at night, for he feels O'Donovan's wrath is paralyzed by this confidence in his honor that the lord has shown in entrusting to his keeping the life of his son and heir. The young lord and the young O'Donovan grow up to be men. They are foster-brothers, "dearer to each other than full brothers," as those Anglo-Irish story-writers say, who have no conception of Irish manhood or Irish spirit, and who write as if the Irishman and his wife felt it an honor to suckle the Sassenach robber's child. No Irishman of the old stock feels such a thing as that an honor to his house, though the conditions of slavery may compel him to suffer it. That great-grandfather of mine that I have spoken of had six sons. I have named the six families into which they married. The mother of one of these families had one time nursed the young landlord of their land, and it was held to be a stain upon the name of a Rossa to make a matrimonial connection with any one who had an English landlord for a foster-brother.

How is it that you never read of the foster-brother's coming into existence by his being the Irish boy who got from the English mother the suck that did not naturally belong to him. It is—that it is the Irishman who is in the condition of slavery, and that the English breed in Ireland would consider themselves degraded and disgraced at nursing an Irishman.

The second trick of the two tricks I have spoken of is the trick of sponsorship.   The lands of the Maguires are confiscated, and are made over to an English surveyor who gets the title of Lord Leitrim.   Young Andy Maguire has the name of being a Rapparee; he is out on the hills at night.   Leitrim is afraid of him, and can't sleep the nights well.   Mrs. Maguire has given birth to a daughter, and the lord asks that he may be allowed the honor of standing god-father for the child. Then, he makes the child a present of some of the old Maguire lands that lie around the town of Tempo.

This is making a little restitution to the Maguires, and it appeases their wrath a little.   Andrew Maguire of Tempo, living at No. 242 East 14th Street, is one of the most decent Irishman living in New York City, to day. He will not say I am far astray in what I an telling you.   I said Lord Carberry was not our landlord direct in Ross.   No, the mother of Dr. Daniel Donovan was our landlord; it was for her Garrett Barry used to collect the rent, and the story I brought from childhood with me about how she became landlord is that Lord Carberry stood sponsor for one of the O'Don-

ovan-Island children, and made it a birthday present
of the town and townland of Ross. That's the childhood story that got into my head. It is, perhaps, possible to reconcile it in some shape with the following
book story that I read in "Sketches in Carberry, by
Dr. Daniel Donovan, Jr., published by McGlashin &
Gill, Dublin, 1876."

"In 1642 MacCarthy, of Benduff, captured the town
of Ross, and laid siege to Rathbarry Castle (the ancient
seat of the Barrys in Carberry), now Castle Freke."
. . . Ross was garrisoned in the time of James
II. by the Irish forces under General McCarthy, and
was reconnoitered by a detachment of William III.'s
army."

"Large military barracks were formerly erected at
Ross in close proximity to the site of St. Fachtna's
simonastery. These barracks, where so many warlike
garrisons had been stationed from time to time during
the stirring events of the last two centuries and which
changed occupants as often as the fortunes of war
veered from one side to the other, are now in a semi-
ruinous condition. Here lived formerly, after the military had evacuated the place, a branch of the O'Donovan family (the Island branch), to which the town of
Ross Carberry belonged, under a lease, from the end
of the 18th century, up to within the last ten years;
and here also was born in December, 1807, Dr. Donovan,
Senior, of Skibbereen." My childhood history is, that
Lord Carberry stood god-father for that Dr. Donovan's
mother and made her a present of the town and townlands of Ross, and it is very likely there was a com-

promise otherwise of some kind, wherein my people came
in for shelter, for, whereas they were hunted from place
to place, since Rossmore was confiscated on them, the
six sons of my great-grandfather now came into possession of about half the town and townland of Ross.   And
they must have been respected people, too, because
those six brothers got six women to marry them who
belonged to six of the best families in the barony.
That is one thing that stood to me in my battle through
life—my family record.   I never was rich; I never will
be rich; but I got some of the best and handsomest
girls in the country to.marry me—simply on account of
myself and of my name.

One little story more will end this genealogy business
of mine.

When I was in Cork city, in June, 1894, I was staying at the Victoria Hotel.   Crowds of people were calling to see me.   Councilor Dick Cronin spoke to me on
a Monday morning and said: "Rossa, I have to take
you away from these people, or they will talk you to
death, and you won't be able to give your lecture to-
morrow night.   Here, I have a carriage at the door,
and we'll drive down to Fort Camden."   I went with
him.   Passing by Ringaskiddy I told him I had some
cousins living around there, and I'd like he would inquire for them.   "Ask the oldest inhabitant, " said I,
"where is a Miss Nagle who taught school here forty or
fifty years ago."   He made the inquiry, and we found
her living under the name of Mrs. Murphy, the mother
of the present schoolmaster.   I made myself known to
her.   I was her mother's sister's grandson.   I asked

her if there was any one around living belonging to another sister of her mother, that was married near Cork
to a man named Hawkes. She said there was a grandson of hers, named McDonald, who kept chinaware
stores, on the Coal Quay, Cork. I went to McDonnell
next day. He was at his home in Sunday's Well. I
did not go further to see him. His bookkeeper gave
me this business card. "John McDonnell (late T. &
P. McDonnell), earthenware, china and glass merchants,
Nos. 58 and 59 Cornmarket Street, Cork. Established
over 50 years. (127 Sunday's Well.)"

Mr. James Scanlan, the wholesale meat-merchant of
No. 614 West 40th Street New York, is reading these
" Recollections." His grandfather was one of that
O'Donovan-Baaid family to whom my grandmother be-
longed. This is his letter:

ABATTOIR, Nos. 614 to 619 West 40th Street,
New York.

DEAR O'DONOVAN ROSSA—It is forty years since
I left Dunmanway, and did not bring with me much
news about our family relations.

When I was a boy, our friends would come to town
on market-day, and have their talk in the Irish language. It was a pleasure to hear them in their own soft
tongue—the women with the long cloak and the hood
thrown gracefully back. The times and the people all
gone now, and none to take their place!

My mother's name was Nora Donovan. She had
one sister and three brothers. All came to the United
States. One uncle lives. Their father was Pat Don-

ovan of Bauhagh, four miles above Dunmanway. He
was a Donovan-Baaid. He married a Kingston from
near Drimoleague. Both died in Dunmanway about
1846. My mother married James Scanlan. He taught
school in the town. The Teady Donovan you spoke
about is second cousin to my mother. With my best
regards for you and family, I am, yours truly,

                                    JAS. SCANLAN.

And James Donovan of 36th Street and Second
Avenue, another cousin of mine, writes me this letter,

DEAR ROSSA—The reading of your genealogical
sketches has brought many circumstances connected
with the history of your family to my mother's recollection.

Donough Mor (your and her great-grandfather)
died at Milleen, northeast of Rosscarberry, where he
lived with his eldest son Denis. Donough and his wife,
Jillen or Julia Island, were born the same year (according to the tradition of the family), lived to be over
a hundred years old, and were buried the same week,
dying in or about the year 1793. When the funeral of
Donough Mor was departing from the house, his wife
went to the door and exclaimed in Irish, "Donough,
you led a good life and had a happy death. You have
a good day and a good funeral. Good-bye for a short
time ; I will soon be with you." Before seven days had
elapsed her remains were laid beside those of her husband near the old Abbey.

A few years after, his son Denis was outcanted of
the large farm he cultivated, which embraced the

ploughland of Milleen and part of Froe. He moved
to Ross, where he erected the most commodious house
then in that town. Here he engaged in the grocery
and liquor business, with much success for many years.
In his house the monthly conference dinners of the
priests of the diocese were held up to the time of his
death, in 1823.

All the brothers combined on the manufacture of
linen with farming. Five of the brothers, Daniel,
Jeremiah, Cornelius, John and Florence, had adjoining
farms further north.

During the time of the free quarters they were
much harassed by the frequent raids of the English
soldiers who plundered and burned at will. A party
visited Daniel's house while he was absent at Cork on
business. They threatened his wife, (Breeda O'Mahony Bawn), with dire vengeance unless she revealed
where the money was hidden of which the Donovans
were reported to be possessed. Finding their threats
unavailing against the heroic woman, they set fire to
the dwelling houses, loom houses, and barns, leaving
ruin and desolation where industry and plenty reigned.
When Daniel returned and heard the story from his
wife he fell on his knees, and with uplifted hands, he
cried, " I thank God, alanna, that you and the children
are left to me."   This occurred in the summer of 1797.
The state of terrorism increased to such an extent, and
the plundering of the soldiery became so high-handed,
that the brothers, who were marked as special prey by
the marauders, to ensure the safety of their wives and
children, removed to Ross. The money possessed in

gold was sewed into the clothes of the women and children. After remaining a short time in Denis's house, the brothers resumed the linen business in houses which they built for the purpose. They were the largest employers of labor in the town of Ross Carberry, where linen-weaving was in a flourishing condition. Your grandfather had between twenty and thirty looms at work for him; he had the reputation of being an upright and honest business man, and in disposition generous, but hot-tempered.

It was a noted coincidence that your great-grandmother, Jillen Island, had six sons, Denis, Jer., Dan, Flor., Patrick and Conn, and her brother, Dan Island, of Gurrane, had six sons Jer., Dan, Rick, Flor., Patrick and Conn. Dan, the father of Jer-Dan was a great genealogist, and knew the history of all the Donovans. His sister, Aunt Nell, (Mrs. Malony of Gurrane) whom I remember very well as a straight, pleasant featured woman, was similarly gifted. Donal was the name of the father of your great-grandfather Donacha More a Rossa. That Donal had a brother Donough who was an officer in King James' Army; of him nothing was known after the Williamite wars. Yours truly,

JAMES T. DONOVAN.

That ends my childhood story days. The next chapter will get me into the movement for the Repeal of the Union between England and Ireland.

CHAPTER IX.

" REPEAL OF THE UNION."

I DID not know what " Repeal of the Union " was when I heard all the grown-up people around me shout-ing out " Repeal! Repeal!" It is no harm now to let my young readers know what Repeal meant when I was a boy in Ireland.

Before I was a boy—before you or I were in the world at all—Ireland had a Parliament of her own. Ireland's representatives met in the Parliament House in College Green, Dublin. Or, more correctly speak-ing, the English breed of people living in Ireland held Parliament in College Green. The real old Irish peo-ple, who remained true to the old cause and the old faith, had no voice in that Parliament; they had not even a voice in electing a member to it. Things were so arranged by the English that only an Englishman, or an Irishman who became a turn-coat, and changed his nature and his religion, could have anything to say or do with that Parliament. Yet, when the English-men, the Sassenachs and the Protestants, who came into possession of Ireland, came to find out that England would rob them of their rights, too, as well as she would rob the Catholics, they kicked against the rob-bery, and in the year 1782 they made a show of resist-ance, and got England to take her hands off them for

awhile. But up to the year 1800 England had had intrigued and bribed so much, that she bought over a
majority of the members, and they voted that our Irish
Parliament would be abolished; that they would not
meet in Dublin any more, but that they would have a
united parliament for Great Britain and Ireland in
London. The act by which that was done was called
the Act of Union, and it was to repeal that act that the
movement for the "Repeal of the Union," was started.

Daniel O'Connell, of Kerry, was the head man of
that movement. He was a great man at moving the
Irish people, and carrying them with him. Many of
the people thought he meant to fight, too, in the long
run, for at some of his monster meetings, speaking to
tens of thousands of people, he'd cry out "Hereditary
bondsmen! Know ye not! Who would be free, themselves must strike the blow." But he never seriously
meant fight. If he did he would, in a quiet way, or in
some way, have made some preparation for it. Those
same remarks hold good as regards the later Irish
movement of Charles S. Parnell. A great many people said he meant to fight when he'd cry out that he'd
"never take off his coat to the work he was at, if there
was not some other work behind it." But he never
seriously meant fight either. If he did, he would, in a
quiet way, or in some way, have made some preparation
for it.

But England became alarmed at O'Connell's movement, and she put him and hundreds of men in prison
in connection with it, just as she became alarmed at
Parnell's movement in the heydey of its vigor, and put

him and hundreds of men to prison in connection with
it. England gives great allowance to Irishmen in showing themselves great and patriotic in constitutional
and parliamentary agitation, but when it goes a little
too far beyond her liking, she is very quick at stopping
it.

I recollect when O'Connell was put to prison, and
when he was released from prison. I recollect the night
the bonfires were blazing on the hills throughout the
country in celebration of the release of the prisoners, and
the song that was afterward sung about it, a verse of
which is this :

> " The year '44, on the 30th of May,
>   Our brave liberator, these words he did say :
> ' The time is but short that I have for to stay,
>   When the locks of my prison shall open.
>   You'll find me as true—that the laws I'll obey,
>   And I'll always be so, till I'm laid in the clay.
>   For Peace is the thing that will carry the sway,
>   And bring parliament back to old Erin.' "

" He's fined and confined," said one of the ushers of
Beamish's school, in my hearing, to his scholars, as I
was playing ball outside the schoolhouse gate, the
evening the news of Dan O'Connell's being found
" guilty " came into Ross. And these scholars seemed
to receive the news with glee. They belonged to the
English crowd in Ireland. Four or five of them were
boys named Hickson, sons of one of the Lansdowne
agents in Kerry. Twenty years after, I met a few of
them at the races of Inch Strand, west of Castlemaine.

And what a lively time there was in Ireland those

days of the O'Connell movement! And how delight-
fully the birds used to sing! There were more birds
and more people there then than there are now. Nine
millions in 1845; four and a half millions in 1895.
And those English savages rejoice over the manner in
which they destroy us. They thank God we are gone,
"gone with a vengeance," they say. What a pity we
haven't the spirit to return the vengeance. But we are
taught to do good to those that hate us, to bless those
that curse us, and to pray for those who persecute and
calumniate us. I can't do it; I won't try to do it; I
won't be making a hypocrite of myself in the eyes of
the Lord; I could sooner bring myself to pray for the
devil first.

I have written that neither O'Connell nor Parnell
meant fight, because neither of them made any preparation for fight. While all of us talk much of fight,
and glorify in song and story those who fought and fell,
is it possible that something degenerate has grown into
us, that always keeps us from coming to the point when
the crisis is at hand! There is no doubt that we fight
bravely the battles of all the nations of the earth. But
then, we are *made* to do it. We join their armies, and
we are shot down if we don't do it. There is no power,
no discipline, to compel us to fight for Ireland, and it
is surprising the facility with which the leaders of Irish
physical-force organizations of the present day can lead
their forces into the fields of *moral* force, to obtain for
their country a freedom that they swore they were to
fight for. 'Tis desertion of that kind that made Par-
nellism; 'tis base desertion of that kind that leaves he-

roic Irishmen dead and dying in the dungeons of England to-day. I'm getting vexed. I'll stop.

Why do I make these remarks? I don't know. I have been talking of O'Connell and I have been thinking of John O'Donovan, the great Irish scholar, and what he said to me one time about O'Connell. In a letter he wrote to me, about the year 1856, he says: "There were no two men of the age who despised the Irish name and the Irish character more than did Daniel O'Connell, and the late Dr. Doyle, Bishop of Kildare and Leighlin. Dr. Miley, in whose hands O'Connell died, told me this at this table, and I firmly believe it."

John O'Donovan was intimately acquainted with Father Meehan, the author of the History of the Confederation of Kilkenny and other historical works. I met Father Meehan at John O'Donovan's house one night in 1859. I was after being released from Cork jail, and we had some talk at table about the Phœnix movement. John O'Donovan thought I was somewhat over-sanguine. "The bishops won't let the people fight," said he. Dr. Meehan never said a word. I'll now go back to my story.

I told you I shook hands with O'Connell when he was coming from the great meeting in Skibbereen, in the year 1843. I remember the morning the Ross men were going to that meeting. Some of them had white wands. I see Dan Hart having one of those wands, regulating the men into line of march. Those wand-men were the peace-police of the procession. Paddy Donovan-Rossa was prominent in command, giving out new Repeal buttons. Some years after, he was in New York with his wife and his six sons—all dead now: all belonging to him dead now, I may say. Meeting him here in the year 1863, I said to him—" Uncle Paddy, I remember you, the time you had all the Repeal buttons in Ross to free Ireland." I was sorry for saying it, for the tears ran down his cheeks. The movement I myself was connected with ended no better, and we are in no position to say anything hurtful to O'Connellites. We all turned out to be O'Connellites, or Parnellites, which is much the same ; all putting our trust in England to free Ireland for us—" without striking a blow." No, there were not ten men of the whole Fenian movement, and the whole I. R. B. movement in America, that did not turn in to the Parnell movement. That is how England feels strong to-day, and that is how she feels she can treat with contempt all the resolutions passed by Irishmen in Ireland and America, about the release of the Irish political prisoners that she holds in her English prisons. No society of Irishmen exists now that she is afraid of. She has everything in her own hands. And, until England is made afraid, she will do nothing for Ireland, or give nothing to Irishmen.

The Repeal movement, the Father Mathew movement, the Young Ireland movement, and the English-made famine movement, ran into one another, from the year 1840 to the year 1848. I was in the whole of them—not much as a man, but a great deal as a little boy. I remember on Sundays, how I'd sit for hours in the workshop of Mick Hurley, the carpenter, at the lower side of the Pound Square, listening to Patrick

(Daniel) Keohane reading the *Nation* newspaper for the men who were members of the Club. He was the best scholar in our school; he was in the first class, and he was learning navigation. And he *did* go to sea after that, and sailed his own ship for years. When last I saw him he kept shop, or kept store, as we here call it, in that part of the town where the Courceys and Crokers and Moloneys lived. And he is there yet. Won't he be surprised, if he reads what I am writing, to know that he had a hand in making a "bad boy" of me, listening to him reading the *Nation* newspaper fifty odd years ago! It is very possible it was through his reading I first heard of the death of Thomas Davis. It was in 1845 Thomas Davis died, and Patrick Keohane and I were in Ross then. It was the first of the years that are called the "famine" years; years that will require from me the whole of the next chapter.

CHAPTER X.

HOW ENGLAND STARVED IRELAND.

COMING on the harvest time of the year 1845, the crops looked splendid. But one fine morning in July there was a cry around that some blight had struck the potato stalks. The leaves had been blighted, and from being green, parts of them were turned black and brown, and when these parts were felt between the fingers they'd crumble into ashes. The air was laden with a sickly odor of decay, as if the hand of Death had stricken the potato field, and that everything growing in it was rotting. This is the recollection that remains in my mind of what I felt in our marsh field that morning, when I went with my father and mother to see it.

The stalks withered away day by day. Yet the potatoes had grown to a fairly large size. But the seed of decay and death had been planted in them too. They were dug and put into a pit in the field. By and by an alarming rumor ran through the country that the potatoes were rotting in the pits. Our pit was opened, and there, sure enough, were some of the biggest of the potatoes half rotten. The ones that were not touched with the rot were separated from the rotting ones, and were carted into the "chamber" house, back of our dwelling house. That chamber house had been specially prepared for them, the walls of it being padded with straw, but it was soon found that the potatoes were rotting in the chamber too.   Then all hands were set to work to make another picking; the potatoes that were rotting were thrown into the back yard, and those that were whole and appeared sound were taken up into the loft over our kitchen.   The loft had been specially propped to bear the extra weight.   But the potatoes rotted in the loft also, and before many weeks the blight had eaten up the supply that was to last the family for the whole year.

Then one of our fields had a crop of wheat, and when that wheat was reaped and stacked, the landlord put "keepers" on it, and on all that we had, and these keepers remained in the house till the wheat was threshed and bagged, and taken to the mill.   I well remember one of the keepers (Mickeleen O'Brien) going with my mother to Lloyd's mill, just across the road from the marsh field, and from the mill to the agent, who was in town at Cain Mahony's that day, to receive rents.

When my mother came home she came without any money.   The rent was £18 a year.   The wheat was thirty shillings a bag; there were twelve bags and a few stone, that came in all to £18 5s., and she gave all to the agent.

I don't know how my father felt; I don't know how my mother felt; I don't know how I felt.   There were four children of us there.   The potato crop was gone; the wheat crop was gone.   How am I to tell the rest of my story!

Volume upon volume has been written and printed about those "bad times" of '45, '46 and '47. I could write a volume myself on them, but as it is not that work I am at, I have only to write down those impressions made on my mind by the incidents I witnessed and experienced—incidents and experiences that no doubt have done much to fortify me and keep me straight in the rugged life that I have traveled since.

I told how our potato crop went to rot in 1845. Some Irishmen say that that was a "visitation of Providence." I won't call it any such thing. I don't want to charge the Creator of the Irish people with any such work.

I told how our wheat crop in 1845 went lost to us also. That, no doubt, was a visitation of English landlordism—as great a curse to Ireland as if it was the arch-fiend himself had the government of the country.

During those three years in Ireland, '45, '46 and '47, the potato crops failed, but the other crops grew well, and, as in the case of my people in '45, the landlords came in on the people everywhere and seized the grain crops for the rent—not caring much what became of those whose labor and sweat produced those crops. The people died of starvation, by thousands. The English press and the English people rejoiced that the Irish were at last conquered; that God at last was fighting strongly at the side of the English.

Coroners' juries would hold inquests on Irish people who were found dead in the ditches, and would return verdicts of "murder" against the English government, but England cared nothing for that; her work was going on splendidly; she wanted the Irish race cleared out of Ireland—cleared out entirely, and now something was doing for her what her guns and bayonets had failed to do. She gave thanks to God that it was so; that the Irish were gone—"gone with a vengeance"—"that it was going to be as hard to find a real Irish man in Ireland as to find a red Indian in New York,"—"that Ireland was nothing but a rat in the path of an elephant, and that the elephant had nothing to do but to squelch the rat."

What wonder is it if the leading Irishman to day, in New York or anywhere else, would do all that he could do to make a return of that "vengeance" to England! We adopt the English expression and call those years the "famine years"; but there was no famine in the land. There is no famine in any land that produces as much food as will support the people of that land—if the food is left with them. But the English took the food away to England, and let the people starve.

With their characteristic duplicity, they cried out that there was a famine in Ireland, and they appealed to the nations of the earth to help the starving people. Ships laden with food were sent from America, from Russia and from other nations, and while these ships were going into the harbors of Ireland, English ships laden with Irish corn and cattle and eggs and butter were leaving the harbors, bound for England. Ireland those three years of '45, '46 and '47, produced as much food as was sufficient to support three times the population of Ireland. What I say is historical truth, recorded in the statistics of the times. It is English his-

tory in Ireland *all* the time during England's occupation of the country.

In the year 1846, the blight struck the potato crop
in the month of June. The stalks withered away before the potatoes had grown to any size at all. There
was no potato crop. In fact many of the fields had remained untilled, and grew nothing but weeds. It was
the same way in the year 1847. The weeds had full
possession of the soil, and drew from it all the nourishment it could yield. They blossomed beautifully.
Though sad, it was a beautiful picture to look at—the
land garlanded in death. Standing on one of the hills
of our old-chapel field one day, and looking across the
bay, at the hillside of Brigatia, the whole of that hillside—a mile long and a half a mile broad was a picture
of beauty.

The priseach-bhuidhe weed had grown strong, and
with its yellow blossoms rustled by the gentle breeze,
glistening in the sun, it made a picture in my mind
that often stands before me—a picture of Death's victory, with all Death's agents decorating the fields with
their baleful laurels.

Any picture of baleful beauty like it in America?
Yes, there is, and I have seen it: seen it in the fields
of Irish patriotism.

Gladstone the English governor of Ireland is after
putting thousands of Irishmen into his prisons; his
Irish governors are killed by the Irish; his castles in
London are leveled by the Irish; his policy makes him
play hypocrite, and he talks of "Home rule for Ireland." The Irish in America dance with delight.

They get up a monster meeting in one of the finest halls of the chief city of the nation, and they get the governor of the State to preside at the meeting. The representatives of all the Irish societies, and of all the Irish Counties and Provinces are there, arrayed in their finest and best; the large platform is sparkling with diamonds; every man, every woman is a sparkling gem. The governor of the State of New York tells the world, represented there, that the thanks of the whole Irish race is there transmitted to Mr. Parnell and to Mr. Gladstone, for the freedom of Ireland. Handkerchiefs and hats are waved, and twirled in every circle that hands can motion; diamonds and rubies sparkle and dance with the electric lights of the hall; the O'Donnells of Donegal, the O'Neills of Tyrone, the MacMahons of Monaghan, the McGuires of Fermanagh, the O'Briens of Arra, the O'Sullivans of Dunkerron, the McCarthys of the Castles, the O'Donoghues of the Glens, and all the other Clans are wild with delight.

Yes, that was the other field of priseachh-bhuidhe I saw in America, that equalled in dazzling splendor the field I saw in Ireland, but it was one that was just as fruitless of food for Ireland's freedom, as the Brigaysha field was fruitless of food for Ireland's people. There was no home rule for Ireland. Gladstone, or any other Englishman, may humbug Irishmen to their hearts' content, but he is not going to give them Irish freedom until they pay for it the price of freedom. They are able to pay that price, and they are able to get it in spite of England.

It is not to vex Irishmen that I talk this way; I don't want to vex them. My faith is strong that they are able to free Ireland, but I want to get them out of the priseachh-bhuidhe way of freeing it. But I cannot blame myself for being vexed; nor should you blame me much either. Look at this proclamation that was issued against our people from Dublin Castle by the English invaders, one time:

PROCLAMATION.

By the Lord Justices and Council:

"We do hereby make known to all men, as well good subjects as all others, that whoever he or they be that shall, betwixt this and the five-and-twentieth day of March next, kill and bring, or caused to be killed and brought to us, the Lord Justices, or other Chief-Governor or Governors, for the time being, the head of Sir Phelim O'Neill, or of Conn Magennis, or of Rory Maguire, or of Philip MacHugh MacShane O'Reilly, or of Collo MacBrien MacMahon, he or they shall have by way of reward, for every one of the said last persons, so by him to be killed, and his or their head or heads brought to us as followeth, viz: For the head of Sir Phelim O'Neill, one thousand pounds; for the head of the said Sir Rory Maguire, six hundred pounds; for the head of the said Philip MacHugh MacShane O'Reilly, six hundred pounds; for the head of the said Collo MacBrien MacMahon, six hundred pounds."

Dublin Castle, Feb. 8, 1641.

> JOHN ROTHERHAM,
> F. TEMPLE,
> CHAS. COOTE.

"God save the King."

Then, forty pounds a head were offered for the heads

of some two hundred other chieftains, embracing men of nearly all the Milesian families of Ireland.

What wonder is it, if I look vexed occasionally when I meet with O'Farrells, and O'Briens, and O'Flahertys, and O'Gradys, and O'Mahonys, and O'Callaghans, and O'Byrnes, and O'Neills, and O'Reillys, and O'Keefes, O'Kanes and O'Connors, O'Crimmins, O'Hallarans, O'Flynns, O'Dwyers and O'Donnells, and O'Donovans and O'Kellys, O'Learys, O'Sheas, O'-Rourkes, O'Murphys, Maguires, and Mc'Carthys, and MacMahons and MacLaughlins, and other men of Irish stock, who will talk of having "honorable warfare" with England, for the freedom of Ireland. It is not from nature they speak so. It cannot be. There is nothing in their nature different from mine. I have heard men making excuses for me for being so mad against the English—saying it is on account of the harsh treatment I received from the English while I was in English prisons. That kind of talk is all trash of talk. What I am now, I *was*, before I ever saw the inside of an English prison. I am so from nature.

Before I was ever able to read a book, I heard stories of Irish women ripped open by English bayonets, and of Irish infants taken on the points of English bayonets and dashed against the walls; and I heard father and mother and neighbors rejoicing—"buidhechas le Dia!"—whenever they heard of an English landlord being shot in Tipperary or any other part of Ireland.

And as I grew up, and read books, didn't I see and hear big men praying curses upon England and upon England's land-robbers in Ireland. Didn't John

Mitchel say, that the mistake of it was, that *more* land-lords were not shot! and didn't he say that if he could grasp the fires of hell, he would seize them, and hurl them into the face of his country's enemy! Didn't Thomas Davis pray: " May God wither up their hearts; may their blood cease to flow; may they walk in living death; they, who poisoned Owen Roe! Didn't Thomas Moore tell us to flesh " every sword to the hilt" into their bodies! Didn't J. J. Callanan pray " May the hearthstone of hell be their best bed forever!" Didn't Daniel McCarthy-Sowney pray: " Go raibh gadhair-fhiadh Ifrion a rith a ndiadh 'n anam air Innse shocuir, gan toortog!" and " go gcuireadth Dia cioth sparabli a gcoin-naibh a n-anam!"

No, no! Irishmen don't pray for the English enemy in Ireland. If prayers would drive them to hell, or anywhere else, outside of Connaught, Leinster, Munster and Ulster, some of them would stay praying till their knees were tanned.

In the " bad times" of '46 and '47, the Donovan-Buidhe family of Derriduv were friends of my family. There were four brothers of them on the land of Derri-duv, some two miles from the town of Ross. Donal Buidhe came to our house one day. His wife and six children were outside the door. They had with them a donkey that was the pet of the eldest boy. They had been evicted that morning, and had nowhere to go for shelter. There was a " chamber" back of our house, and back of the chamber was another house called the " linney." My father told Donal to clear out the linney, and take the whole family into it. Some days

after, it may be a few weeks after, I heard my father
and my mother whispering, and looking inquiringly at
each other; the donkey was the subject of their conversation. The donkey had disappeared: where was the
donkey? The last seen of him was in the backyard,
there was no way for him to pass from the backyard
into the street but through our kitchen, and he had not
passed through it.

That donkey had been killed and eaten by Donal
Buidhe and his family. That was the decision I read
on the faces of my father and mother. They did not
think I was taking any notice of what they were whispering about. "Skibbereen! where they ate the don-
keys!" is an expressive kind of slur cast at the people
of that locality. But, 'tis no slur.

You have read, and I have read in history, how people besieged in fortresses have eaten horses, and don-
keys, and cats, and dogs, and rats, and mice; and how
people wrecked on sea, have cast lots for food, and
have eaten each other. Reading these stories when I
was a boy, I could not get my mind to conceive how any
human being could do such things, but I was not long
in English prisons when I found my nature changed—
when I found that I myself could eat rats and mice, if
they came across me. And, perhaps that prison life of
mine changed other attributes of my Irish nature too.

The year '47 was one of the years of "the Board of
works" in Ireland. Any man in possession of land—
any farmer could get none of the relief that the Poor
Law allowed under the name of "out-door relief." To
qualify himself for that relief, he should give up the

land to his landlord. But, under the Board of works
law, a farmer could get employment on the public
works. My father was so employed. He had charge
of a gang of men making a new road through Rowry
Glen. He took sick in March, and Florry Donovan,
the overseer of the work, put me in charge of his gang,
while he was sick. I was on the road the twenty-fifth
of March, '47, when the overseer came to me about
noontime and told me I was wanted at home. I went
home, and found my father dead.

CHAPTER XI.

THE BAD TIMES: THE "GOOD PEOPLE." JILLEN-ANDY:
HER COFFINLESS GRAVE.

THIS chapter that I have to write now is a very hard
chapter to write. I have to say something that will
hurt my pride and will make my friends think the less
of me. But I'll say it all the same, because the very
thing that hurts my pride and humbles me in my own
estimation, may be the very thing that has strengthened
me to fight Ireland's battle against the common enemy
as I have fought it. If the operation of English rule
in Ireland abases the nature of the Irishman—and it
does abase it—the Irishman ought to fight the harder
and fight the longer, and fight every way and every
time, and fight all the time to destroy that rule. So,
stand I to-day in that spirit. Not alone in spirit but
in deed—if I could do any deed—but action is out of
the question in a situation where the parade and show
and color of patriotism is regarded as patriotism itself.

I said my father died in March, 1847. I was then
fifteen years of age. I said, that the year before he
died, the potato crop failed entirely, and the landlord
seized the grain crop for the rent. About that time, I
heard a conversation between my father and mother
that made a very indelible impression upon my mind.
I have often thought, that if things are dark around
you, and that you want a friend to assist you out of

the darkness, it is not good policy at all to cry out to
him that you are stricken totally blind, that you are so
helpless for yourself that there is never any hope of
recovery from that helplessness. My mother was after
returning from a visit she made to a sister of my
father's, who lived some twelve miles away, and who
was pretty well off in the world. The object of the
visit was for assistance over our difficulties. My aunt
had a son-in-law, a very wise man; she sent for him;
he came to the house, and there was a family consulta-
tion on the matter. My mother was asked to candidly
tell the full situation of affairs, and to tell how much
money would get us over all the difficulties, and put us
on our legs again. She did tell. Then there was a con-
sultation, aside from my mother—the pith of which my
mother heard, and which was this: the son-in-law said
that we were so far in debt, and the children so young
and helpless, that anything given us, or spent on us to
get us over the present difficulty would only be lost,
lost forever; and that then we would not be over the
difficulty.

All along the fifty years of my life since that year
of 1847, I have often wanted help, and often got it. I
get it to-day, and maybe want it to-day; get it from
people who want no return for it; but that does not
remove the impression made on my mind, that when
you are in difficulties it is not good policy at all to
make such a poor mouth as will show any one inclined
to help you that the help given you will only be lost
on you.

One thing my father said to me one time I will tell

here for the benefit of the little children who live in the house where this book will be read. It is this: I stayed away from school one day; I went mootching. My mother was coming from Jude Shanahan's of Dooneen, and she found me playing marbles at the courthouse cross. She caught hold of me by the collar, and she did not let go the hold until she brought me in home. I was crying of course; roaring and bawling at the thrashing I was to get from my father. "Stop your crying," said he, "stop your crying; I am not going to beat you; but, remember what I say to you; when I am dead and rotten in my grave, it is then you will be sorry that you did not attend to your schooling." It was true for him.

When my father died, the hill field had been planted for a potato crop, and the strand field had been planted for wheat.

After he died, some of the creditors looked for their money, and there was no money there. Bill Ned obtained a decree against us, and executed the decree; and I saw everything that was in the house taken into the street and canted. That must be about the month of May, 1847. One Sunday after that—a fine sunny day, I was out in the Abbey field playing with the boys; about six o'clock I came home to my dinner; there was no dinner for me, and my mother began to cry. Uncle Mickey did not come to town yesterday. He used to come to the house every Saturday with a load of turf, and a bag of meal or flour straddled on top of the turf. He did not come yesterday, and there was nothing in the house for dinner.

Some years ago, in Troy, New York, I was a guest at the hotel of Tom Curley of Ballinasloe. Talking of "the bad times" in Ireland, he told me of his own recollection of them in Galway, and asked me if I ever felt the hunger. I told him I did not, but that I felt something that was worse than the hunger; that I felt it still; and that was—the degradation into which want and hunger will reduce human nature. I told him of that Sunday evening in Ross when I went home to my dinner, and my mother had no dinner for me; I told him I had one penny-piece in my pocket; I told him how I went out and bought for it a penny bun, and how I stole to the back of the house and thievishly ate that penny bun without sharing it with my mother and my sister and my brothers. I am proud of my life, one way or another; but that penny bun is a thorn in my side; a thorn in the pride of my life; it was only four ounces of bread—for bread was fourpence (eight cents) a pound at the time—but if ever I feel any pride in myself, that little loaf comes before me to humble me; it also comes before me to strengthen me in the determination to destroy that tyranny that reduces my people to poverty and degradation, and makes them what is not natural for them to be. I know it is not in my nature to be niggardly and selfish. I know that if I have money above my wants, I find more happiness and satisfaction in giving it to friends who want it than in keeping it. But that penny-bun affair clashes altogether against my own measurement of myself, and stands before me like a ghost whenever I would think of raising myself in my own estimation.

I suppose it was the general terror and alarm of starvation that was around me at the time that paralyzed my nature, and made me do what I am now ashamed to say I did.

Friday was the day on which my father died. On Sunday he was buried in the family tomb in the Abbey field. There were no people at the wake Friday night and Saturday night, but there were lots of people at the funeral on Sunday.

It was a time that it was thought the disease of which the people were dying was contagious, and would be caught by going into the houses of the dead people, the time alluded to in those lines of " Jillen Andy."

> No mourners come, as 'tis believed the sight
> Of any death or sickness now begets the same.

And as these lines come to my mind now, to illustrate what I am saying, I may as well give the whole of the lines I wrote on the burial of Jillen Andy, for this is the year she died—the year 1847 that I am writing about. I dug the grave for her; she was buried without a coffin, and I straightened out her head on a stone, around which Jack McCart, the tailor, of Beulnaglochdubh had rolled his white-spotted red handkerchief.

Andy Hayes had been a workman for my father. He died—leaving four sons—John, Charley, Tead and Andy. The mother was known as Jillen Andy. The eldest son, John, enlisted and was killed in India ; Charley got a fairy-puck in one of his legs, and the leg was cut off by Dr. Donovan and Dr. Fitzgibbons ;

Andy also enlisted, and died in the English service, Tead was a simpleton or "innocent"—no harm in him, and every one kind to him. I was at play in the street one day, my mother was sitting on the door step, Tead came up to her and told her his mother was dead, and asked if she would let me go with him to dig the grave for her. My mother told me to go with him, and I went. Every incident noted in the verses I am going to print, came under my experience that day. I wrote these verses twenty years after, in the convict prison of Chatham, England, thinking of old times. That you may understand some of the lines, I may tell you some of the stories of our people. There were fairies in Ireland in my time; England is rooting them out, too. They were called "the good people," and it was not safe to say anything bad of them. The places where fairies used to resort were called "eerie" places, and if you whistled at night you would attract them to you, particularly if you whistled while you were in bed. Then, when a person is to be buried, you must not make a prisoner of him or of her in the grave; you must take out every pin, and unloose every string before you put it into the coffin, so that it may be free to come from the other world to see you. And at the "waking" of a friend, it is not at all good to shed tears over the corpse, and let the tears fall on the clothes, because every such tear burns a burned hole in the body of the dead person in the other world.

JILLEN ANDY.

"Come to the graveyard if you're not afraid ;
   I'm going to dig my mother's grave ; she's dead,
And I want some one that will bring the spade,
   For Andy's out of home, and Charlie's sick in bed."

Thade Andy was a simple spoken fool,
   With whom in early days I loved to stroll.
He'd often take me on his back to school,
   And make the master laugh, himself, he was so droll.

In songs and ballads he took great delight,
   And prophecies of Ireland yet being freed,
And singing them by our fireside at night,
   I learned songs from Thade before I learned to read,

And I have still by heart his "Colleen Fhune,"
   His "Croppy Boy," his "Phœnix of the Hall,"
And I could "rise" his "Rising of the Moon,"
   If I could sing in prison cell—or sing at all.

He'd walk the "eeriest" place a moonlight night,
   He'd whistle in the dark—even in bed.
In fairy fort or graveyard, Thade was quite
   As fearless of a ghost as any ghost of Thade.

Now in the dark churchyard we work away,
   The shovel in his hand, in mine the spade,
And seeing Thade cry, I cried, myself, that day,
   For Thade was fond of me, and I was fond of Thade.

But after twenty years, why now will such
   A bubbling spring up to my eyelids start?
Ah ! there be things that ask no leave to touch
   The fountains of the eyes or feelings of the heart,

"This load of clay will break her bones I fear,
   For when alive she wasn't over-strong;
We'll dig no deeper, I can watch her here
   A month or so, sure nobody will do me wrong."

Four men bear Jillen on a door—'tis light,
   They have not much of Jillen but her frame;
No mourners come, as 'tis believed the sight
   Of any death or sickness now, begets the same.

And those brave hearts that volunteered to touch
   Plague-stricken death, are tender as they're brave ;
They raise poor Jillen from her tainted couch,
   And shade their swimming eyes while laying her in the grave.

I stand within that grave, nor wide nor deep,
   The slender-wasted body at my feet ;
What wonder is it, if strong men will weep
   O'er famine-stricken Jillen in her winding-sheet!

Her head I try to pillow on a stone,
   But it will hang one side, as if the breath
Of famine gaunt into the corpse had blown,
   And blighted in the nerves the rigid strength of death.

"Hand me that stone, child." In his 'tis placed,
   Down-channeling his cheeks are tears like rain,
The stone within his handkerchief is cased,
   And then I pillow on it Jillen's head again.

" Untie the nightcap string," "unloose that lace."
   "Take out that pin." There, now, she's nicely—rise,
But lay the apron first across her face,
   So that the earth won't touch her lips or blind her eyes.

Don't grasp the shovel too tightly—there make a heap,
   Steal down each shovelful quietly—there, let it creep
Over her poor body lightly; friend, do not weep ;
   Tears would disturb poor Jillen in her last long sleep.

And Thade was faithful to his watch and ward,
   Where'er he'd spend the day, at night he'd haste
With his few sods of turf to that churchyard,
   Where he was laid himself, before the month was past.

Then, Andy died a soldiering in Bombay,
   And Charlie died in Ross the other day,
Now, no one lives to blush, because I say
   That Jillen Andy went uncoffined to the play.

E'en all are gone that buried Jillen, save
   One banished man, who dead-alive remains
The little boy who stood within the grave,
   Stands for his Country's cause in England's prison chains.

How oft in dreams that burial scene appears,
   Through death, eviction, prison, exile, home,
Through all the suns and moons of twenty years—
   And oh! how short these years, compared with years to come !

Some things are strongly on the mind impressed,
   And others faintly imaged there, it seems,
And this is why, when Reason sinks to rest,
   Phases of life do show and shadow forth, in dreams.

And this is why in dreams I see the face
   Of Jillen Andy looking in my own,
The poet-hearted man ; the pillow case—
   The spotted handkerchief that softened the hard stone.

Welcome these memories of scenes of youth,
   That nursed my hate of tyranny and wrong,
That helmed my manhood in the path of truth,
   And help me now to suffer calmly and be strong.

After the burial of Jillen-Andy and Tead-Andy I
was stricken down with the fever that was prevalent at
the time. I was nine or ten days in bed. The turning day of the illness came, and those who were at the
bedside thought I was dying. My heavy breathing
was moving the bedclothes up and down. I had con-
sciousness enough to hear one woman say to my
mother " Oh, he is dying now." But it was only the

fever bidding good-bye to me, and I got better day by
day after that.   Then, when I came to walk abroad, my
eyes got sore—with a soreness that some pronounced
the "dallakeen"; but others pronounced· it to be a
kind of fairy-puck called a "blast."   An herb-doctor
made some herb medicine for me, and as my mother
was giving it to me one day she was talking to our next-
door neighbor, Kit Brown, and wondering who it could
be in the other world that had a grudge against me, or
against the family!   She was sure I had never hurted
or harmed any one, and she could not remember that
she or my father had ever done anything to any one
who left this world—had ever done anything that
would give them reason to have a grudge against the
family.

You, friendly reader, may consider that what I am
saying is small talk.   So it is.   But in writing these
"Recollections" of mine I am showing what Irish life
was in my day.   I am not making caricatures in Irish
life to please the English people, as many Irish writers
have done, and have been paid for doing; I am telling
the truth, with the view of interesting and serving my
people.   When I was young I got hold of a book called
"Parra Sastha: or, Paddy-go-easy."   Looking at the
name of the book I did not know what Parra Sastha
meant; but as I read through it I learned that it was
meant for "Padruig Sasta"—contented, or satisfied
Paddy.   The whole book is a dirty caricature of the
Irish character; but the writer of it is famed as an
Irish novelist, and died in receipt of a yearly literary
pension from the English government.   He earned

such a pension by writing that book alone. England pays people for defaming Ireland and the Irish.

And men professing to be Irish patriots, in our own day, write books defamatory of their own people. " When We Were Boys " is the name of a book written nine or ten years ago by one of those Irish patriot parliamentary leaders of to-day. It is a libel on the character of the Fenian movement in Ireland. As I was reading it I said to myself, " This gentleman has his eye on a literary pension from the English." The whiskey-drinking bouts that he records at the Fenian headquarters in the office of the Fenian newspaper had no existence but in his imagination, and the brutal murder of a landlord by the Fenians is an infamous creation of his too. If it is fated that the chains binding England to Ireland are to remain unbroken during this generation, and that the writer of that book lives to the end of the generation, those who live with him need not be surprised if they see him in receipt of a literary pension. He has earned it.

CHAPTER XII.

1847 AND 1848.

IN the summer of 1847, when Bill-Ned's decree was executed on our house, and when all the furniture was canted, notice of eviction was served upon my mother. The agent was a cousin of ours, and he told my mother it was better for her to give up the land quietly, and he would do all he could to help her. She had four children who were not able to do much work on a farm. She had no money, and she could not till the land. There were four houses included in the lease—our own house, Jack McCart's house across the street, Jack Barrett's house next door above us, and Darby Holland's house next door below. Darby Holland had died lately, and he would get her his house rent-free during her life, and give her £12 on account of the wheat crop growing in the strand field, and let her have the potato crop that was growing in the hill field. My mother accepted the terms, and we moved into Darby Holland's house.

The previous two bad years had involved us in debt; friends were security for us in the small loan banks in Ross and in Leap, and as far as the twelve pounds went my mother gave it to pay those debts. To give my mind some exercise in Millbank prison one time, I occupied it doing a sum in Voster's rule of Interest, regarding those little loan-banks. I made myself a

130

banker. I loaned a hundred pounds out of my bank one week, I got a hundred shillings for giving the loan of it; I got it paid back to me in twenty weeks—a hundred shillings every week.

I loaned it out again as fast as I got it, and at the end of fifty-two weeks, I had one hundred and forty-seven pounds and some odd shillings. That was forty-seven per cent. for my money. I wish some of my tenants on the UNITED IRISHMAN estate would now go at doing that sum in the rule of Interest-upon-Interest, and let me know if I did it correctly. 'Tis an interesting exercise to go at, if you have leisure time; you cannot do it by any rule of arithmetic; I give out a hundred pounds the first week, and get in on it a hundred shillings interest; I lend out that hundred shillings, and get in on it five shillings: I hold that five shillings in my treasury till next week; next week I get in a hundred and five shillings; I lend out five pounds, and get in on it five shillings interest; I have now a hundred and ten borrowers for the third week, and have fifteen shillings in the treasury. So on, to the end of the twenty weeks, and to the end of the year, when my hundred pounds will have amounted up to £147.

The harvest time of 1847 came on. The potato crop failed again. The blight came on in June. In July there was not a sign of a potato stalk to be seen on the land. My brother John and I went up to the hill field to dig the potatoes. I carried the basket and he carried the spade. He was the digger and I was the picker. He digged over two hundred yards of a piece of a ridge and all the potatoes I had picked after him would not fill a skillet. They were not larger than marbles; they were minions and had a reddish skin. When I went home, and laid the basket on the floor, my mother looking at the contents of it exclaimed: "Oh! na geinidighe dearga death-chuin!" which I would translate into English as "Oh the miserable scarlet tithelings."

I will now pass on to the year 1848. In our new house there was a shop one time, and a shop window. The shop counter had been put away; the window remained; that window had outside shutters to it, but those shutters were never taken down. One morning we found pasted on the shutters a large printed bill. My mother read it, and after reading it, she tore it down. It was the police that had posted it up during the night. It was an account of the unfavorable reception the delegation of Young Irelanders had met with in Paris, when they went over to present addresses of congratulation to the new revolutionary provisional government.

France had had a revolution in February, 1848. The monarchical government had been overthrown, and was succeeded by a republican government. King Louis Phillippe fled to England—as the street ballad of the time says:

> Old King Phillippe was so wise,
> He shaved his whiskers, for disguise;
> He wrap'd himself in an old grey coat
> And to Dover he sail'd in an oyster boat.

That you may understand thoroughly what I am speaking about, I quote the following passages from John Mitchel's history of Ireland:

" Frankly, and at once, the Confederation accepted the only policy thereafter possible, and acknowledged the meaning of the European revolutions. On the 15th of March, O'Brien moved an address of congratulation to the victorious French people, and ended his speech with these words :

" ' It would be recollected that a short time ago,. he thought it his duty to deprecate all attempts to turn the attention of the people to military affairs, because it seemed to him that in the then condition of the country the only effect of leading the people's mind to what was called "a guerilla warfare," would be to encourage some of the misguided peasantry to the commission of murder. Therefore it was that he declared he should not be a party to giving such a recommenda- tion. But the state of affairs was totally different now, and he had no hesitation in declaring that he thought the minds of intelligent young men should be turned to the consideration of such questions as—How strong places can be captured, and weak ones defended—how supplies of food and ammunition can be cut off from an enemy, and how they can be secured to a friendly force. The time was also come when every lover of his country should come forward openly and proclaim his willingness to be enrolled as a member of a national guard. No man, however, should tender his name as a member of that national guard unless he was prepared to do two things : one, to preserve the State from anarchy ; the other, to be prepared to die for the de- fence of his country.'

" Addresses, both from the confederation and from

the city, were to be presented in Paris, to the President of the Provisional government, M. de Lamartine ; and O'Brien, Meagher and an intelligent tradesman named Hollywood, were appointed a deputation to Paris.

"These were mere addresses of congratulation and sympathy. De Lamartine made a highly poetic, but rather unmeaning reply to them. He has since, in his history, virulently misrepresented them ; being, in fact, a mere Anglo-Frenchman. Mr. O'Brien has already convicted him of these misrepresentations."

It was that "unmeaning reply" of Lamartine's that the English government placarded all over Ireland one night in '48. It was that poster I saw my mother tear down next morning. It is that memory, implanted in my mind very early in my life, that makes me take very little stock in all the talk that is made by Irishmen about France or Russia, or any other nation doing anything to free Ireland for us. They may do it, if it will be to their own interest to do it.

My friend, Charles G. Doran, of the Cove of Cork, comes to my assistance at this stage of my writing. He sends me a full copy of all that was printed on that poster which my mother tore down. He says:

MY DEAR FRIEND ROSSA:

I was struck when reading your exceedingly interesting "Recollections," by two things, which I am sure must have struck others of your readers also—viz, that your mother must have been a very intelligent woman, and a very patriotic woman, to discern and so promptly resent the insult offered to the Irish people by the government, in printing and placarding the cowardly cringing pro-English reply of Lamartine to the thoroughly sincere and whole-hearted address of congratulation presented by the Irish deputation to the new provisional government of France. It would hardly surprise one to learn that the pro-English spirit pervading Lamartine's reply was prompted by English influence—influence that, though working in direct opposition to the establishment of the Republic, was not adverse to availing of the new order of things to give a *coup de grace* to Irish hopes for sympathy from that quarter. Almost as soon as Lamartine had spoken his wretched response, the English government had it printed in the stereotyped Proclamation form, and copies of it sent to all parts of Ireland, and posted by the police on the barracks, courthouses, churches, chapels, market-houses—public places of every description—aye, even on big trees by the roadside—anywhere and everywhere that it would be likely to be seen. And it was seen, and read, and commented on, and criticised and bitterly denounced, and no matter what may be said to the contrary, it had the effect that England desired—it disheartened and weakened the ranks of the young Irelanders. At first, the accuracy of the proclamation was doubted, but a couple of days served to dispel the doubt which gave place to dismay and disappointment, and England scored ; substituting confidence for uncertainty and uneasiness—Lamartine, her ally—not her enemy ! As there are few Irishmen living at present who have ever read that document, or, perhaps, ever heard of its existence until referred to in

your "Recollections," I have transcribed it from an
original copy, and send the transcript to you as you may
find a nook for it in your pages some time or another.

Here it is:

REPLY OF THE FRENCH GOVERNMENT
—TO THE—
IRISH DEPUTATION.

"PARIS, Monday, April 3, 1848.—This being the day
fixed by the Provisional government for the reception
of the members of the Irish deputation, Mr. Smith
O'Brien and the other members of the Irish confederation went to the Hotel de Ville to-day at half-past three
to present their address.   They were received by Mr.
Lamartine alone; none of the other members of the
Provisional government being present.   Besides the
address of the Irish Confederation, addresses were
presented at the same time by Mr. R. O'Gorman, Jr.,
from citizens of Dublin; by Mr. Meagher from the Repealers of Manchester, and by Mr. McDermott from the
members of the Irish confederation resident in Liverpool.   M. Lamartine replied to the whole of these addresses in one speech as follows:

" *Citizens of Ireland !*—If we required a fresh proof
of the pacific influence of the proclamation of the great
democratic principle, this new Christianity, bursting
forth at the opportune moment, and dividing the world,
as formerly, into a Pagan and Christian community—
we should assuredly discern this proof of the omnipotent
action of the idea, in the visits spontaneously paid in
this city to Republican France, and the principles

which animate her, by the nations or by sections of the nations of Europe.

"We are not astonished to see to-day a deputation from Ireland. Ireland knows how deeply her destinies, her sufferings and her successive advances in the path of religious liberty, of unity and of constitutional equality with the other parts of the United Kingdom, have at all times moved the heart of Europe!

"We said as much, a few days ago, to another deputation of your fellow citizens. We said as much to all the children of that glorious Isle of Erin, which the natural genius of its inhabitants, and the striking events of its history render equally symbolical of the poetry and the heroism of the nations of the north.

"Rest assured, therefore, that you will find in France, under the Republic, a response to all the sentiments you express toward it.

"Tell your fellow citizens that the name of Ireland is synonymous with the name of liberty courageously defended against privilege—that it is one common name to every French citizen! Tell them that this reciprocity which they invoke—that this hospitality of which they are not oblivious—the Republic will be proud to remember, and to practise invariably toward the Irish. Tell them above all, that the French Republic is not, and never will be an aristocratic Republic, in which liberty is merely abused as the mask of privilege; but a Republic embracing the entire community, and securing to all, the same rights and the same benefits. *As regards other encouragements it would neither be expedient for us to hold them out, nor for you to*

*receive them. I have already expressed the same opinion
with reference to Germany, Belgium and Italy, and I repeat it with reference to every nation which is involved in
internal disputes—which is either divided against itself or
at variance with its government.* When there is a difference of race—when nations are aliens in blood—intervention is not allowable. We belong to no party in
Ireland or elsewhere, except to that which contends for
justice, for liberty, and for happiness of the Irish people. No other party would be acceptable to us in time
of peace. In the interests and the passions of foreign
nations, France is desirous of reserving herself free for
the maintenance of the rights of all.

" *We are at peace, and we are desirous of remaining on
good terms of equality, not with this or that part of Great
Britain, but with Great Britain entire. We believe this
peace to be useful and honorable, not only to Great Britain
and the French Republic, but to the human race.* We will
not commit an act—we will not utter a word—we will
not breathe an insinuation at variance with the
reciprocal inviolability of nations which we have proclaimed, and of which the continent of Europe is already gathering the fruits. The fallen monarchy had
treaties and diplomatists. Our diplomatists are nations
—our treaties are sympathies! We should be insane
were we openly to exchange such a diplomacy for unmeaning and partial alliances with even the most legiti-
mate parties in the countries which surround us. We
are not competent either to judge them or to prefer
some of them to others; by announcing our partisan-
ship of the one side we should declare ourselves **the**

enemies of the other. We do not wish to be the enemies of any of your fellow countrymen. We wish, on the contrary, by a faithful observance of the Republican pledges, to remove all the prejudices which may mutually exist between our neighbors and ourselves.

"This course, however painful it may be, is imposed on us by the law of nations, as well as by our historical remembrances.

"Do you know what it was which most served to irritate France and estrange her from England during the first Republic? It was the Civil War in a portion of her territory, supported, subsidized, and assisted by Mr. Pitt. It was the encouragement and the arms given to Frenchmen, as heroical as yourselves, but Frenchmen fighting against their fellow citizens. This was not honorable warfare. It was a Royalist propagandism, waged with French blood against the Republic. This policy is not yet, in spite of all our efforts, entirely effaced from the memory of the nation. *Well! this cause of dissension between Great Britain and us, we will never renew by taking any similar course.* We accept with gratitude expressions of friendship from the different nationalities included in the British Empire. We ardently wish that justice may be found, and strengthen the friendship of races: that equality may become more and more its basis; but while proclaiming with you, with her (Great Britain), and with all, the holy dogma of fraternity, we will perform only acts of brotherhood, in comformity with our principles, and our feelings toward the Irish nation."

There is the text of the document. It is printed

with. Great Primer No. 1 type, except the underlined portions which, to attract special attention, and convey an "Aha! see now what France will do for you?" are printed with English Clarendon on Great Primer body —an intensely black thick type.

Well, friend Rossa, that cowering Frenchman is dead, and that Republic which he so zealously guarded in the interest of England—not the Republic of the present, glory to it—is dead too! Had Lamartine lived to witness the revival of Trafalgar memories a few days ago, after a period of ninety years, I believe that he would bitterly regret ever having given birth to that disheartening document.

Hoping that you and yours are well, I am my dear friend Rossa,

Ever Faithfully Yours,

C. G. DORAN.

CHAPTER XIII.

THE SCATTERING OF MY FAMILY.   THE PHŒNIX
SOCIETY.

JOHN MITCHEL, John Martin, Smith O'Brien, Terence Bellew McManus and other prominent men in the Young Ireland movement of 1848 were transported to Australia, and the movement collapsed. There was no armed fight for freedom. The Irish people had no arms of any account. England seized all they had, and she supplied with arms all the English that lived in Ireland. She supplied the Orangemen with arms, and she supplied arms to the Irish who were of the English religion. In the year 1863, John Power Hayes of Skibbereen gave me a gun and bayonet to be raffled, for the benefit of a man who was going to America. He told me it was a gun and bayonet that was given to him by the police in 1848, when all the men of the English religion who were in the town were secretly supplied with arms by the English government.

At the end of the year 1848, my home in Ross got broken up; the family got scattered. The family of my Uncle Con, who went to America in the year 1841 were living in Philadelphia. They heard we were ejected, and they sent a passage ticket for my brother John, who was three years older than I. My brother Con, three years younger than I, was taken by my mother's people to Renascreena, and I was taken by

141

my father's sister who was the wife of Stephen Barry of Smorane, within a mile of Skibbereen. Her daughter Ellen was married to Mortimer Downing of Kenmare, who kept a hardware shop in Skibbereen, and I soon became a clerk and general manager in that shop. My brother in Philadelphia sent passage tickets for my mother and brother and sister, and I was left alone in Ireland. I suppose they thought I was able to take care of myself in the old land. How much they were mistaken, the sequel of those " Recollections " may show.

The day they were leaving Ireland, I went from Skibbereen to Renascreena to see them off. At Renascreena Cross we parted. There was a long stretch of straight even road from Tullig to Mauleyregan over a mile long. Renascreena Cross was about the middle of it. Five or six other families were going away, and there were five or six cars to carry them and all they could carry with them, to the Cove of Cork. The cry of the weeping and wailing of that day rings in my ears still. That time it was a cry heard every day at every Cross-road in Ireland. I stood at that Renascreena Cross till this cry of the emigrant party went beyond my hearing. Then, I kept walking backward toward Skibbereen, looking at them till they sank from my view over Mauleyregan hill.

In the year 1863, I took a trip to America, and visited Philadelphia. It was night-time when I got to my brother's house. My mother did not know me. She rubbed her fingers along my forehead to find the scar that was on it from the girl having thrown me from her shoulders over her head on the road, when I was a child.

Nor, did I well know my mother either. When I saw her next morning, with a yankee shawl and bonnet, looking as old as my grandmother, she was nothing more than a sorry caricature of the tall, straight, handsome woman with the hooded cloak, that was photographed—and is photographed still—in my mind as my mother—

> " Who ran to take me when I fell,
> And would some pretty story tell,
> And kiss the part to make it well."

This rooting out of the Irish people; this transplanting of them from their native home into a foreign land, may be all very well, so far as the young people are concerned; but for the fathers and mothers who have reared families in Ireland, it is immediate decay and death. The young tree may be transplanted from one field to another without injury to its health, but try that transplanting on the tree that has attained its natural growth, and it is its decay and death. The most melancholy looking picture I see in America, is the old father or mother brought over from Ireland by their children. See them coming from mass of a Sunday morning, looking so sad and lonely; no one to speak to; no one around they know; strangers in a strange land; strangers I may say in all the lands of earth, as the poet says:

> Through the far lands we roam,
>   Through the wastes, wild and barren ;
> We are strangers at home,
>   We are exiles in Erin.

Leaving the "bad times," the sad times, even though they were in the happy time of youth, I must now reluctantly move myself up to the time of my manhood. From 1848 to 1853, I lived in the house of Morty Downing—save some four months of the five years. He had five children, and we grew to be much of one mind; Patrick, Kate, Denis, Simon and Dan. They are dead. The four sons came to America, after three of them had put in some time of imprisonment in Ireland in connection with Phœnixism and Fenianism. These four went into the American army. Patrick was in the war as Lieutenant Colonel of the Forty-second (Tammany) Regiment. He died in Washington some ten years ago. Denis was Captain in a Buffalo regiment, and lost a leg at the battle of Gettysburg. He had command of the military company at the execution of Mrs. Surratt in Washington; he made a visit to Ireland; died there, and is buried in Castlehaven. Simon and Dan were in the regular army and are dead. All my family were in the war and are dead. My brother John was in the Sixty-ninth Pennsylvania regiment; my brother Con served on the warship Iroquois, and my sister's husband, Walter Webb, served in the Sixty-ninth Pennsylvania cavalry.

I now go back to my recollections in Ireland. I remember the time of the passing of the Ecclesiastical Titles bill in 1851, when England made a law subjecting to a fine of £100 any Catholic bishop in Ireland who would sign his name as bishop or archbishop of his diocese. As soon as this bill was passed, Archbishop McHale defied it, and issuing a pastoral, signed

his name to it as "John McHale, Archbishop of
Tuam." England swallowed the defiance, and did not
prosecute him. The Rev. Father Perraud, a French
priest, writing on that subject says that England came
to see that the policy of arresting a bishop for such a
breach of law would not work well. Here are a few
of his words:

"It is useless to conceal the fact it is not regiments
encamped in Ireland; it is not the militia of 12,000
peelers distributed over the whole of the surface of the
land, which prevents revolt and preserves the peace.
During a long period, especially in the last century,
the excess of misery to which Ireland was reduced had
multiplied the secret societies of the peasantry. Who
have denounced those illegal associations with the
most presevering, powerful, and formidable condemnation? Who have ever been so energetic in resistance
to secret societies as the Irish Episcopacy? On more
than one occasion the bishops have even hazarded their
popularity in this way.

"They could, at a signal, have armed a million contest-
ants against a persecuting government—and that
signal they refused to give."

I remember the starting of the Tenant League movement in 1852, that movement that opened a field of
operation for the Sadliers, the Keoghs, and others who
went in to free Ireland by parliamentary agitation. It
failed, as other movements since have failed that went
in for freeing Ireland by parliamentary agitation. It
is in that English Parliament the chains for Ireland
are forged, and any Irish patriot who goes into that

forge to free Ireland will soon find himself welded into
the agency of his country's subjection to England.

I remember the Crimean war of 1853–54, and the
war of the Indian mutiny of 1857. There was hardly
a red-coat soldier to be seen in Ireland those times.
Even the police force was thinned down, by many of
them having volunteered to the seat of war, as members of a land-transport corps that England called for.
The Irish National Cause was dead or asleep those
times. The cry of England's difficulty being Ireland's
opportunity was not heard in the land.

The cry of "England's difficulty being Ireland's opportunity" is the "stock in trade" of many Irishmen
in Ireland and America who do very little for Ireland
but traffic upon its miseries for their own personal
benefit. Irishmen of the present day should work to
free Ireland in their own time, and not be shifting
from their own shoulders to the shoulders of the men
of a future generation the work they themselves should
do. The opportunity for gathering in the crops is the
harvest time, those who will not sow the seed in springtime will have no harvest, and it is nothing but arrant
nonsense for Irish patriot orators to be blathering
about England's difficulty being Ireland's opportunity,
when they will do nothing to make the opportunity.
I immediately class as a fraud and a humbug any
Irishman that I hear talking in that strain.

I remember when Gavan Duffy left Ireland. I think
it was in 1854. He issued an address to the Irish people, in which he said that the Irish national cause was
like a corpse on the dissecting table. Yet, the cause

was not dead, though it was certainly stricken by a kind of trom-luighe—a kind of "heavy-sleep" that came upon it after the failure of '48, and after the recreancy of the Sadlier and Keogh gang of parliamentary patriots. The "corpse" came to life again.

I was in the town of Tralee the day I read Duffy's address in the Dublin *Nation* newspaper.

My brother-in-law, John Eagar, of Miltown and Liverpool, with his wife, Ellen O'Shaughnessy, of Charleville, were with me.

I got the *Nation* at Mr. O'Shea's of the Mall; I came to the hotel and sat down to read it. My friends noticed that I was somewhat restless, reading the paper; I turned my face away from them, and they asked if anything was the matter with me. Next day I was writing an account of my vacation and travels to John Power Hayes, a friend of mine in Skibbereen; he was a kind of poet, and I wrote to him in rhyme. I look to my notes in my memory now, and I find the following are some of the lines I wrote:

Dear John: it's from Miltown, a village in Kerry,
I write these few lines, hoping they'll find you merry;
For I know you're distressed in your spirits, of late,
Since "Corruption" has driven your friend to retreat,
And being now disengaged for a few hours of time,
Just to try to amuse you, my subject I'll rhyme.
Well, you know I left Cork on the evening of Sunday;
I got to Killarney the following Monday;
I traveled to view the legendary places
Till Thursday came on—the first day of the Races;
Amusements were there for the simple and grand,
But I saw that which grieved me—the wealth of the land

Was, in chief, represented by many a knight,
Who was sworn on oath, for the Saxon to fight,
And to drive all his enemies into confusion,
But I thought in my heart they were cowards, while the
    " Rooshian "
Was granting " commissions of death," ex-officio,
To remain Barrack officers of the militia.
And it sickened the heart of myself who have seen
The starved and the murdered of Skull and Skibbereen,
To see those McCarthys, O'Mahonys, O'Flynns,
And also O'Donoghue, Chief of the Glens.
All sworn—disgraceful to all our traditions—
To command the militia instead of Milesians.
I also should tell you that while at the races,
I made my companions scan hundreds of faces,
To get me a view, for my own recreation,
Of one that I knew but by name in the *Nation*,
And if I, unaccompanied, happened to meet him,
With the choicest of drinks I'd be happy to treat him ;
For I swear by all firearms—poker and tongues,
By his side I would fight to redress all our wrongs.
He may be a wealthy or poor man, a tall, or
A small man, but know that his name is Shine Lalor.
Then leaving Killarney—seeing all I could see—
I wended my way the next day to Tralee ;
I inquired of a man whom I met at the station
If he'd please tell me where I'd get the *Nation ;*
He inquired of another and then told me call
To the house of one Mr. O'Shea at the Mall.
Then I went to my inn and proceeded to read,
While the others, to get some refreshments agreed.
While reading, I fell into some contemplation
When Duffy addressed " Constituents of the *Nation*,"
And then, through what agency I cannot prove,
Each nerve of my body did instantly move,
Each particle quivered, I thought that a gush
Of hot blood to my eyelids was making a rush ;
I saw myself noticed by some of the folk,
Who, if they knew my feeling, would make of it joke,

And I kindly requested that some one would try
To detect a small insect that troubled my eye.
The effort was made, with but little success.
Say, bad luck to all flunkeys, their patrons and press.

At that time the regiment of Kerry militia were out,
under command of the O'Donoghue of the Glens, and
were officered by the McCarthys, O'Mahonys, O'Flynns
and other Kerrymen belonging to the old Milesian
families. The regiment was shortly after drafted over
to England to do duty there.

That is forty-two years ago. The reader will be able
to judge from the foregoing lines of rhyme, that my
opinions at that early day of my life were the same as
they are to-day, and that I have not got into any bohreens or byroads of Irish national politics during those
forty-two years.

Two years after the time I am speaking of, a number
of young men in Skibbereen, realizing the sad state of
things, came together and started the Phœnix National
and Literary Society. I think that Society was started
in 1856. I remember the night we met to give it a
name. Some proposed that it be called the " Emmet
Monument Association." Others proposed other names.
I proposed that it be called the " Phœnix National and
Literary Society "—the word " Phœnix " signifying
that the Irish cause was again to rise from the ashes of
our martyred nationality. My resolution was carried,
and that is how the word " Phœnix " comes into Irish
national history.

Most of the boys who attended that meeting are
dead. I could not now count more than four of them

who are living: Daniel McCartie, of Newark, N. J.; Dan O'Crowley, of Springfield, Ill., and Patrick Carey, of Troy, N. Y.

James Stephens came to Skibbereen one day in the summer of 1858. He had a letter of introduction from Jas. O'Mahony, of Bandon, to Donal Oge—one of our members. He initiated Donal Oge (Dan McCartie) into the Irish Revolutionary Brotherhood. Donal Oge initiated me the next day; I initiated Patrick J. Downing and Morty Moynahan the following day; and so, the good cause spread.

In three or four months, we had three or four baronies of the southwest of Cork County organized; Donal Oge, Morty Moynahan and I became three centres of three circles. We had drillings at night in the woods and on the hillsides; the rumblings, and rumors of war were heard all around; the government were becoming alarmed; they made a raid upon our homes on the night of December 8, and the second day after, some twenty of us were prisoners in the county jail in the city of Cork.

CHAPTER XIV.

LOVE AND WAR AND MARRIAGE.

THE last chapter commenced with the arrest of the men of '48 and ran over the succeeding ten years, up to the arrest of the men of '58. Those ten years carried me from boyhood into manhood. I could very well skip them by, and say no more about them, but many men and women who are reading these "Recollections" in the *United Irishman* would not be pleased at my doing that. They have become interested in my stories of Irish life and Irish character, and, as one purpose of my writing is to make a true picture of these, I must, even at the risk of being charged with egotism, face that charge, and tell my own story.

When I came to live in Skibbereen, in 1848, there was a Father Matthew Temperance society in the town. I took the Father Matthew pledge, and I became a member of that society. I kept that pledge till the year 1857. To that circumstance I place a due share of credit for being able to go through the world with a strong and healthy constitution. It is no harm to add that the past seventeen years of my life have been with me years of temperance, as were those nine years from '48 to '57.

I had no salary in Skibbereen the first year. I was clothed and fed as one of the family. Then, my aunt's

151

son-in-law, Morty Downing, changed his residence from one house to another, and enlarged his business by adding general hardware, cutlery and agricultural seeds to his stock of ironmongery and farm implements. I was allowed a salary of two pounds a year, I was offered an indentureship of clerkship for five years, but I would not sign the indentures. I did not want to bind myself. My aunt wanted me to do it, but I would not. My employer represented to her that I was becoming too much my own master, and that for my own good, he wanted to have a stronger hand over me. Possibly he was right, but all to no use, I remained wrong, and kept my freedom. He would go to my aunt's place at Smorane—a mile outside the town—every Sunday evening; and, riding his horse " Mouse " into town one evening, he saw me riding through the street on an empty tar barrel. Next morning he was out of bed before I was up, and as I came downstairs he met me with a whip in his hand. He gave me a good thrashing. I didn't cry, I only sulked. That evening I took my supper in the kitchen. While taking supper, Kittie, the boss servant, told me that the master said I was to do her work of cleaning all the shoes next morning, and that as she would be out milking the cows I would find the shoes in the usual place. When I came downstairs next morning, Kittie was out milking the cows; there was a nice blazing fire in the grate; I got a stool and I put it opposite the grate; I got the shoes and boots and put them on the stool; I got the water can, and I filled the boots and shoes with water. There I left them, and left the house and went home to my mother in Ross. She had not then gone to America; she was living in the house that was left to her rent-free during her life for giving up peaceable possessions of the farm.

That week, the wife and children of our cousin, Paddy Donovan in New York, were leaving Ross for America. My godfather, Jerrie Shannahan, was the car-man who was taking them to Cork. I went to Cork with them. When they sailed away I came back to Ross with my godfather. We left Cork on Saturday evening, and were in Ross on Sunday morning. Our horse had no load coming back but the two of us.

During the few days I was in Cork, I went around, looking for work. I had with me a good character certificate that I got from my parish priest. These were the words of it—" I know Jeremiah O'Donovan, of this parish, to be a smart, intelligent young lad. His conduct, up to this, has been good and correct. I recommend him as one who will prove honest and trustworthy.—Michael O'Hea, P. P., Ross Carberry."

With that, I went on board a ship in the river Lee, and offered myself as cabin-boy, or any kind of boy. The mate liked me; but as the captain was not on board he could not, in his absence, take me.

Then, I knew that Andy-Andy lately 'listed, in Ross, and that he and his regiment were in barracks in Cork. I went up to the top of Cork Hill. I inquired at the barrack gate for Andy Hayes of Ross. I was told he was detailed on guard duty at the County Jail. I made my way to the County Jail, and there, inside the gate—in the guard-house, between the inside gate and

the outside gate—I met Andy-Andy, in England's red-
coat uniform—as fine a looking man as you'd meet in a
day's walk—six feet two or three in height.   Three or
four years before that day, I buried his mother, Jillen,
without a coffin—

> Then Andy died a-soldiering in Bombay,
> And Charlie died in Ross the other day ;
> Now, no one lives to blush, because I say
> That Jillen-Andy went uncoffined to the clay.

And eight or nine years after the day that I met
Andy-Andy in the guard-room of the County Jail of
Cork, I thought of him as I stood handcuffed in that
same guard-room, going in to that Jail a Phœnix
prisoner.

And what strange connections I find myself making
in these Recollections of mine!   Last week Daniel
O'Donovan, the shoe manufacturer of Lynn, made a
visit to my office.   "Rossa," said he.   "You spoke of
an uncle of mine in that book of prison life that you
wrote ; you remember the man, Jack McCart, that gave
you the handkerchief to roll around the stone that
pillowed Jillen's head—that man, John Dempsey-
McCart, was the brother of my mother."

> "Hand me that stone, child !" in his hand 'tis placed ;
> Down-channeling his cheeks are tears like rain ;
> The stone within his handkerchief is cased,
> And then I pillow on it Jillen's head again.

And how can I help thinking of the wreck and ruin
that come upon the Irish race in the foreign land!
One in a hundred may live and prosper, and stand to
be looked at as a living monument of the prosperity,

but ninety-nine in a hundred are lost, never to be heard of. The six O'Donovan brothers that I saw sail out from the Cove of Cork—the sons of Patrick O'Donovan-Rossa and Mary O'Sullivan-Buadhaig—came to be known as men in the First Ward of New York a few years after—Den, Dan, Jerrie, John, Conn and Florrie Donovan; all of them dead; one only descendant belonging to them, living at the present day.

And what a change came in my own life and in my own character during the six or seven years that transpired after those cousins of mine left Ross. The day they left, my parish priest, Father Michael O'Hea, gave me a good character, as a "smart, intelligent young lad," recommending me to the world as one who would be found "honest and trustworthy." Seven years after, the two of us were living in Skibbereen, and he, as Bishop O'Hea, turned me away from his confessional, telling me not to come to him any more. I had become a Fenian; his "smart, intelligent young lad" had turned out to be a bad boy. Such is life. As this is jumping ahead of my story a little, and rushing into the cross part of my "Recollections" I will jump back again, and tell how I got on after I came home from Cork.

My mother had a message before me from Morty Downing, telling me he wished I would go back to him again, and that all my bad deeds would be forgiven and forgotten. I went back to him, at my £2 a year salary. The first investment I made out of that salary was to purchase the whole stock in trade of Eugene Daly, a book-seller, who hawked books around the town

and country. I bought his entire stock at one penny
a volume, and they came just to £1—240 volumes.
Then he bought a pound's. worth of knives and scis-
sors and razors and small cutlery in the shop, and the
price of them was put against my salary.

That box of literature, as I call it—for I bought box
and all—very soon brought me to grief—well, not exactly that, but it very soon got me into trouble. My
bedroom was not the very best room in the house. It
was a kind of garret, in which were stored lots of old
newspapers. Mr Downing had been one of the Young
Irelanders, and he had stored in my room all the Repeal and Young Ireland newspapers of the previous
five or six years. As soon as I'd get to bed at night I'd
read in bed, and I'd fall asleep reading, leaving the
candle lighting. Some little fire accident occurred that
Kittie reported to the governor—some of the bedclothes
had burned holes in them, and Kittie got orders not to
give me any more candlesticks going to bed. Another
accident occurred : I had two nails driven into the partition, above my pillow. I kept a lighted candle between the two nails. I fell asleep reading. When I
awoke I was in a blaze. The partition had burned in
it a hole that I could run my fist through. I had to
make an open confession this time, and to solemnly
promise I would never again read in bed.

My employer got into the wool, cotton, and flax
business, and occasionally had contracts for supplying
those materials to the Poor Law Unions of Skibbereen,
Bantry, and Kenmare. In connection with those contracts I, a few times, visited the Poor Law Boards of

Kenmare and Bantry. In Kenmare I was the guest of my employer's brother, Dan Downing of the Washington Hotel. He was married to the sister of William Murphy, the architect, who kept a hotel in Bantry. Oh! they're all dead now. And I suppose those handsome Kerry girls that played their nettlesome-night joke on me that night, are dead too. They could find no bedroom candlestick to give me; they showed me the bedroom, telling me the door was open. I went to bed, and as I rolled the clothes around me I found myself imbedded in nettles. At the breakfast table next morning, Mrs. Downing hoped I had a good night's sleep. I asked her which of the girls was the chambermaid, and I saw they had the laugh on me.

And very likely all the Kenmare men of that day are dead also. And good Irishmen they were:—John Fitzmaurice Donnelly, Patsy Glanney, Long Humphrey Murphy, Myles Downing, Paddy the Gauger, and others of that company. Stewart Trench, the land-agent of Lord Lansdowne, was that time in his glory—evicting the Lansdowne tenantry. The stories I heard of him moved me to parody that Robinson Crusoe poem, about him. Here are a few of the verses:

> He is monarch o'er all he can sway,
>   His right there is none to dispute;
> Thro' Kenmare and along by the sea
>   He is lord of the man and the brute.
>
> *   *   *   *   *   *
>
> O, Kerry! where now is the spirit
>   That ever distinguish'd thy race.
> If you tolerate Trench you will merit
>   A stigma of shame and disgrace.

Persecution by law he can preach.
  He can nicely "consolidate" farms;
He can blarney and lie in his speech,
  And exterminate Irish in swarms.

An invader, himself and his clan,
  'Tis a maxim comprised in his belief,
To coerce and evict all he can
  For the plund'ring invaders' relief.

The hum of contentment or peace
  In those valleys and glens can't be heard
Till we manfully look for release.
  From the tyrant, by rifle and sword.

No hope for a comfort in life
  While crouchingly quiet and obedient
The weal of your child and your wife
  Is to Trench the tyrannical agent.

The Kenmare men asked me to get printed for them
some slips of what I wrote about Trench. I got them
printed, and sent them to the Kerry men. Trench got
hold of one of them, and was mad to find out who was
the writer; he said it was inciting the people to murder him—for, the word "trench" has that meaning in
Kerry. But the Kerry men did not give me away.

This Trench had earned for himself the reputation of being a most expert hand at getting rid
of what the English landlords called "the surplus
population" on their Irish estates. He was well known
in the barony of Farney in the County of Monaghan,
where he was after having gone through his work of
depopulation on the Shirley estate.

And strange! this day that I am writing—some
forty-five years after I wrote the lines about Trench—

the "Dundalk *Democrat*" of November 21, 1896, comes on my desk, and I see in it an account of a Land League meeting in Carrickmacross, presided over by Dean Bermingham, the priest of the parish. The subject of the speeches at the meeting is the evictions on this Shirley estate—and this, after all the Tenant-right bills that England has passed for the tenantry of Ireland during those past forty-five years! I quote from the "*Democrat*" these few passages:

"On Thursday last a meeting was held in Carrickmacross, called nominally to support the claim for a reduction of rent made by the Shirley tenantry, and for the restoration of the evicted tenants on that estate.

"Dean Bermingham, who was moved to the chair by Mr. Peter Dwyer, V. C., P. L. G., seconded by Mr. A. Mohan, P. L. G., took as the text of his speech the resolutions recently forwarded to Mr. Shirley and the curt reply received. These resolutions, which we have already published, called for an abatement in the rents owing to the bad prices and partial failure of the harvest, and requested the landlord to take advantage of the new Land Act to have the evicted tenants on his estate reinstated. Dean Bermingham sent a courteously-worded letter to Mr. Shirley with the resolutions; but the only reply received was an acknowledgment from Mr. Gibbings, the agent, a gentleman referred to by Mr. Daly, M. P., in his speech as 'a mere day-servant, a fellow employed at thirty shillings a week.' The Dean trenchantly described the answer as cold, curt, callous, and heartless. He humorously suggested that though Mr. Shirley might not be expected to treat with courtesy the parish priest of Carrickmacross, he might have shown a little politeness to a brother land-lord. He (Dean Bermingham) is not the owner of as many broad acres, but he is the owner of as fine a cas-tle—the ancient residence of the Earl of Essex, from whom the Shirleys are descended, and from whom they inherit their Farney estate. He got that castle hon-estly—he didn't get it from old Queen Bess; and he was proud of owning the ancient stronghold of the Mc-Mahons, and having converted it to a better use than ever it was put to before. The Rev. chairman referred to the fact that while he threw open Bath walk to the public, admission to the Shirley demesne is by ticket, which people have to go to the agent to procure; and when he recently went and asked for this permission for the convent children for one day, he was bluntly re-fused."

That is enough to show my readers, that notwith-standing all the Tenant-right bills that England has passed for Ireland during the past fifty years, England, and England's lords hold Ireland to day with as tyran-nous a control as they have held it—every day of the past seven hundred years.

And by the bye, 'tis no harm to remark here, that whatever differences there may be between the Fe-nians and the priests, the priests don't forget to remind us occasionally of our history, and of how we were murdered, plundered and pauperized by the English robbers. Whenever they preach a good sermon on the life of the Church in Ireland, they have to remind us of this. Some of us blame the priests for not taking up the sword and fighting against England. 'Tis *our* place to do that. 'Tis their place to do as they are doing. But *we* shirk our part of our duty, by going around the world preaching against England, on the anniversary of every day on which Englishmen murdered Irishmen.

If we were the men that we ought to be, we would be doing something to have " vengeance wreaked on the murderer's head," instead of hugging to ourselves the satisfaction that we are doing all that belongs to Irish patriots to do, by celebrating those days, in singing " High Upon the Gallows Tree," and " The Glories of Brian the Brave."

But I have not done with Kerry yet. I was speaking of it when Father Bermingham's speech about the Essex-Shirley invasion took me into the northern County. Another of those invaders of the time of Queen Bess got into the southern County. His name was Petty. He came in as an English government surveyor, and when he had done his work, he had surveyed into his own possession all the lands of the O'Sullivans, the O'Conners, the O'Connells, the O'Moriartys, the O'Donoghues, and other Irish clans. From that Petty comes to us this Marquis of Lansdowne, who has his English title to the town of Kenmare and all the townlands around it. The Lansdowne of my day, hearing of the " good " work that Trench was able to do, brought him from Monaghan to Kerry, and gave him *carte blanche* to go on with his " improvements " there. Trench went at his work with a will. He thought the people were too numerous in the land,

and commenced rooting them out. Cromwell, two hundred years before that, brought ship-masters from England; shipped the Irish, men, women, and children, to the Barbadoes, and had them rented out, or sold as slaves. Trench brought his ship-masters from England, and shipped the Kerry people to the Canadas —in ships that were so unfit for passenger service that half his victims found homes in the bottom of the sea.

Then, to boycott the Scriptural permission to "increase and multiply," he issued orders that no people should marry on the estate without his permission; that holdings should not be divided, nor sub-divided; that any son to whom he gave permission to marry, and whom he recognized as the tenant in possession, should not give shelter to his father or mother, or to the father or mother of his wife. What wonder is it that the Kerry people regarded Trench with a holy hatred? What wonder if they would be glad that somebody would "trench" him?

In reading the history of France, and of what the "nobles" of France were for some centuries preceding the time of Napoleon, I couldn't help thinking of the kinship in manners and mind that seemed to be between them and the English "nobles" in Ireland. French history says, that the French noble would come home from a day's hunting; his boots would be wet; his feet would be cold; he would order that one of his retainers be slain, and his body slit; then, he would put his naked feet into the bowels of the dead man that they might get warm there. Also that the French

"noble" on many estates claimed the right of honey-
moon with every woman who got married on his estate.
I am not saying that Trench or his "noble" Lansdowne went so far; but there was one of those English
"nobles" slain in Leitrim or Donegal a dozen years
ago, whose character came very near the mark, and to
which account his death is credited.

I now come back to Skibbereen for a while. During
a few seasons of my time there, I used to take a hand
at making what are called Skellig lists. These are
rhyming productions that are gotten up in the south-
western towns of Ireland after Ash-Wednesday—de-
scriptive of the pilgrimage to the Skellig rocks of the
young people who were eligible for marriage, but who
didn't get married the preceding Shrovetide. On
Shrove-Tuesday night the little boys go around to the
houses with tin whistles, kettle drums, and baurauns,
drumming them away to Skellig's, making much such
a racket as the youngsters make in America on New
Year's night or Thanksgiving night. For dabbling in
the idle diversion of making those Skellig lists I got
the name or fame of being the poet-laureate of the locality.

And yet I cannot leave my 'box of literature' without
saying something more about it. It became the library
of my boyhood days and nights. There were all kinds
of books in it; books of piety, books of poetry, books of
love, languages, history, war, and romance. "Hell Open
to Sinners—Think Well On It," was a terror-striking
book. "The Glories of Mary," must be a touching
book; reading it used to start tears to my eyes.

One Good-Friday night every one in the house went
to the chapel to the Office of Tenebræ. I was left at
home to mind the house; I cried enough that night
reading my " Glories of Mary." Twenty-five years ago
I was living in Tompkinsville, Staten Island. John
Gill of Tipperary was a neighbor of mine; he was a
member of an Irish society there; he asked me to join
that society. I told him I would. He afterward told
me he had proposed me and that I was elected. He
appointed a night for me to be initiated. I attended at
the ante-room of the society rooms that night. I could
hear some noise inside. I was not called in to be initiated. Next day John Gill told me that some one
had started the story that my mother was a Protestant.
I can say that neither my mother, nor my father, nor
any one before me, back to the time of St. Patrick, was
anything but a Catholic; and the tradition in my house
is, that my people gave up all they had in the world
rather than give up the true faith. With such ante-
cedents, I can afford to care but very little about what
any one may say about my losing my soul because I do
all in the world I can do to wrest from the English
robbers what they robbed my people and robbed my
country of.

We had a dancing school in Skibbereen that time
too, and I went to it. Teady O' (Teady O'Sullivan)
was the dancing master. I learned from him ten
shillings worth of his art—two steps; the first one, the
side step, and the second one, an advance-and retire
step; and, though I am past practising them now,

I can travel back in memory with those I hear singing —

> Oh! the days of the merry dancing;
> Oh! the ring of the piper's tune;
> Oh! for one of those hours of gladness—
> Gone, alas! like our youth—too soon.

With that ten shillings worth of Teady O's dance I
went pretty well through the world—so far as dancing
through it is concerned. I used it to my amusement,
as well as to my punishment on one occasion in prison.
I was in chains in a cell in Portland one day; my legs
near my ankles were circled with chains; my waist was
circled with a chain, and from the waist chain to the
ankle chains there were other chains connecting, down
between my legs. In my £1 library of my early days
was a book I had read, called "Schinderhannes, or The
Robber of the Rhine." In that story was a rapparee
character named Carl Benzel. Carl was often put to
prison, and in his prison he used to amuse himself by
dancing in his chains. I thought of him when I was in
chains in Portland Prison, and I commenced dancing
'in my cell that side-step I learned from Teady O'. By
and by, the warders were shouting out at me to stop
that noise. I would not stop; so, to get rid of the
noise that was going from my cell through the corridor,
they put me in the black-hole cell.

The one great book of my early-day library was a
a book by the name of "Colton." It was a collection
of many of the sayings of the great writers. One
paragraph in it stuck fast in my mind, and it is in my
mind still. It is this: "That head is not properly

constituted that cannot accommodate itself to whatever pillow the vicissitudes of fortune may place under it."

That sentence seems to light up in my head whenever the clouds of " hard times " hover over me—and that is often enough. That is how it lights up before me at present.

Morty Downing, of Skibbereen, was a Poor Law Guardian; and, in connection with his business, I got acquainted with every one connected with the Skibbereen Poor Law Union. Neddie Hegarty, the porter at the main gate, was the man I skurreechted most with. He had most to tell me about the starvation times of the years that had just passed by. The Chairman of the Board, during most of those times, was Lioney Fleming, of Oldcourt, a small landlord magistrate. He was a pretty fair specimen of the English planter in Ireland, who considers that Ireland was made for England, and that all the people to whose fathers Ireland belonged are better out of it than in it. Sheep and oxen were tenants more welcome to Lioney's estate than Irish men, women, and children; and the faster the men, women and children in the poorhouse would die, the oftener would Lioney thank the Lord. "When we were burying them in hundreds every week," said Neddie to me one day, "the first salute I'd get from Lioney, when he'd be coming in, every board-day, would be: 'Well, Hegarty, how many this week?' and if I told him the number this week was less than the number last week, his remark would be: 'Too bad; too bad; last week was a better week than this.'"

An inmate of the workhouse named Johnnie Collins
was Neddie Hegarty's messenger boy. He was lame;
he had been dead and buried, but had been brought
back to life by a stroke of Rackateen's shovel. Rackateen was the name by which the poorhouse undertaker was known. The dead were buried coffinless
those times. Rackateen took the bodies to the Abbey
graveyard in a kind of trapdoor wagon. He took
Johnnie Collins in it one day, and after dumping him,
with others, into the grave-pit, one of his knees pro-
truded up from the heap of corpses. Rackateen gave
it a stroke of his shovel to level it down even; the
corpse gave a cry of pain, and the boy was raised from
the pit. That lame man—whose leg had been broken
by that stroke of the shovel—used to come into my
shop every week; and we used to speak of him as the
man who was raised from the dead.

Lioney Fleming was chairman also of the Skibbereen
board of magistrates. I strolled into the courthouse
one court-day, about the year 1855. The police had
George Sullivan up for trial, on some charge of assault.
He had employed McCarthy Downing as his attorney.
I sat on the seat behind the attorney. A large pocket
knife was produced, which was found on George when
he was arrested. Lioney took hold of it, and touching
one of its springs, it brought to the front a pointed
bolt of iron that made the article look like a marline-
spike—an instrument very handy to sailors and farmers
for putting eyes in ropes. Lioney asked George where
did he get that knife; George told him he bought it in
O'Donovan Rossa's shop. "The man who would **sell**

such a murderous weapon as that," said the magistrate,
"ought to be prosecuted." Touching McCarthy Downing on the shoulder, I whispered to him—loud enough
to have Lioney hear me—" Tell 'his honor' to look on
the big blade of it, and he will see that the manufacturer of the knife is Rogers, of Sheffield, England. 'Tis
he should be prosecuted for trading such murderous
weapons as that to the peaceable people of Ireland."
You should see the black look Lioney gave at me, and
the white smile I gave at him.

Now, I will take myself and my readers to Bantry
Bay for a while.

In discharge of my duty of attending to the taking
of contracts for my employer, I went to see the
Guardians of the Bantry poorhouse one day, with some
samples of wool and cotton. I had to wait a while, till
they were ready to receive the tenders. In the waiting
room was Alexander M. Sullivan, who became so active
in Irish politics, some years after, as Editor of the
Dublin *Nation*. He was then a Relieving-officer of the
Bantry Union. It was after the *coup d' etat* of Louis
Napoleon, in December, 1851, when coming on the
termination of his four years' presidency of the Republic. I find that time and circumstance alluded to this
way in one of the American school-books:

" In December, 1851, a plot formed by the Ultra or
Red Republicans, for the overthrow of the government,
was discovered by the president, who caused all the
leaders to be arrested, on the night preceding the out-
break." After that " the president became emperor by
a majority of several millions of votes."

Mr. Sullivan came in for a warm place in my memory that time. I was in the waiting-room of the Bantry Union board-room : he was there with other officers and Guardians. The conversation was about the late *coup d' etat* in Paris; he spoke warmly on the subject, and said that that tyrant Napoleon deserved to be shot, and that he himself could volunteer to shoot him for destroying the Republic. His feelings, as expressed, harmonized with my own feelings, and I held him in my mind as a thorough good Irishman. It was not without considerable pain of mind, seven or eight years afterward, that I found myself obliged to have a newspaper quarrel with him about Irish revolutionary affairs.

In those visits I made to Bantry I got acquainted with William Clarke, who kept a hardware store and a dry-goods store there. He told me he would give me a salary of ten pounds a year, if I came into his hardware store as clerk, and increase that salary if I deserved the increase. I told him I would bear the matter in mind. I did bear it in mind; and coming in to the year 1853 I wrote to Mr. Clarke telling him I would go to Bantry.

I did go to Bantry, and I spent three months with him. He had, in two stores, nine or ten clerks. I ate, drank, and slept with them. Every one of them remained to his dying day, a bosom friend of mine. Yes, they are all dead.

> The world is growing darker to me—darker day by day,
> The stars that shone upon life's path are vanishing away.

The name of one of these clerks was Eugene O'Sul-

livan.   He was from a place called Ross-MacOwen, at
the Berehaven side of Bantry Bay.   I used to call him
Eoghain, O Ross-Mac-Eoghain.   Here is where I want
to make a point in a matter of Irish history.   Historians who have written on the siege and surrender of
the Castle of Dunboy, say it was a man named Mac-
Geoghegan that set fire to the barrel of gunpowder,
that blew up the castle, at the time of the surrender.
Some of them write the name "MacGehan," "Mac-
Geoghan," "MacEggan," and "MacGeohan."

There are no people of the name of Geoghegan or
MacGeoghegan in that district.   But, there are lots of
MacOwens or MacEoghans there ; and their surname
is O'Sullivan.   Owen or Eoghan is Irish for Eugene, and
Eugene is a name in the family of every O'Sullivan-
Bere.   I am strongly of opinion that the man who blew
up the Castle of Dunbuidhe was an O'Sullivan and not
a Geoghegan ; that he was the son of Eugene or Owen
O'Sullivan, that he was known as MacEoghain ; but
that the historians who first wrote up the history—
being ignorant of the Irish language—took the pronun-
ciation of "MacEoghan," and wrote it MacGeoghan ;
and that blunder was followed up by pronouncing that
middle "g" in the word Geoghan—a "g" that is always
silent before the letter "h."   Thus comes into Irish
history the error of having the defender of Dunboy
Castle a MacGeoghegan instead of a MacEoghan O'Sullivan.

And so it happens in one of Charles Lever's novels
of romance.   The name of it is "Tom Burke of Ours."
It should be "Tom Burke of Ower."   Ower is the name

of a townland in the Parish of Headford, County Galway. It is owned by the Burke family. They are known all around Connaught as "the Burkes of Ower." They generally took service with the English. It was one of them was killed by the Irish, in the Phœnix Park, Dublin, in the year 1882, the day he was sworn in with Lord Cavendish, to govern Ireland for the English. The book publishers should also correct that error in Lever's book, and print the name of it " Tom Burke of Ower," instead of " Tom Burke of Ours."

I think there is another mistake in connection with the Irish language, in Irish national poetry, that spoils the sense of one of Davis's poems. That Irish line—

> " Is truagh gan oighre na bhfarradh,"

should be—

> " Is truagh gan oighre na'r bhfarradh."

He is lamenting the death of Owen Roe O'Neill, and lamenting there is not an heir of his among us at the present day.

The words "na bhfarradh" in the first line mean "with them"; the words "na'r bhfarradh" mean "with us," and that is what the poet meant. Some publisher of Davis's poems should make the correction.

The time I spent in Bantry was a pleasant time enough. I had a bedroom in the hardware store, and I could sleep there, or sleep with the clerks in the drapery store, whichever I liked best. I think I spent most of my nights in the hardware store. William Clarke had a brother who was a '48 man. He was dead; but all his books were in the house I had **charge** of, and as all the old "*Nation*" newspapers, and other interesting papers were here, I spent many of my nights reading them.

I took my meals at the other house. Mrs. Clark would occasionally preside at table. She was a grave, stately lady. I was somewhat afraid of her. I knew she had heard some way that some of the other boys used to call me "Jer. droll," but I would say nothing in her presence to let her think there was anything droll about me. I was proud of my name and proud of my family. She was of a good family too, for she was one of the O'Donovans of Clounagoramon, and I knew she did not think the less of me for tracing my descent from princes and lords of Carberry of the olden time.

Another lady used to preside at the tea-urn occasionally. She was a family friend—a Miss Brown of Enniskean, who was on a visit to the house. When I was bidding good bye to Bantry, I called to bid her goodbye, and she shed tears at our parting. Poor dear girl; I never saw her after. May the Lord be good to her! And the local poor "characters" of the town made a kindly acquaintance with me too, and took a permanent place in my memory. Jack Leary—Shaun-a-dauna —a poor simpleton, had a most intimate acquaintance with me. Down the Lord Bantry road, one Sunday evening, the boys wanted him to go out boating with them. He wouldn't go on sea at all; they took hold of him to force him into the boat, and he cried out to me, "Oh, Jerrie a laodh! na leig doibh me bha."—"Oh, Jerrie dear, do not let them drown me."

I had from my family the information that in old
times, a brother of my great-grandfather, named Joe
O'Donovan Rossa, went to Bantry, became a currier,
and had a tannery there.   Con O'Leary had in my day
the only tannery that was in Bantry.   I went to that
tannery one day, and found that a man named Donovan was foreman there.   His father was living, but
was sick in bed.   I went to his bedside, and found him
to be the grandson of my great-grandfather's brother.
That brother was the first tradesman that was in our
family.   So said my people, when I was picking up my
genealogical lessons from them.   You see, in those old
times, when the Irish clans owned their Irish lands—
before the English robbed them of them—the clansmen
did not care about learning trades.   But when the
plunderers came down upon them with fire and sword,
they had to realize the necessity of changing their opinions, and changing their way of living.

When I met Billy O'Shea of Bantry in Cork Jail in
1859, I asked him was Tim O'Sullivan-Coyraun dead
or alive.   He said he was dead.   Tim often told me
the story of the French fleet coming into Bantry bay
in 1796.   He was a young man then, and saw it all.
His death was in the Bantry poorhouse the time of the
Crimean war.   The priest prepared him for death.
"Father," said Tim, "I have a dying request to ask
you: tell me what news is there from the Crimea; how
are the English there?"   The priest told him there was
a terrific battle fought at Balaklava, and the English
were terribly cut up, and defeated.   "Thank God," said
Tim, "that I have that news to take with me.   Now I

can die happy." He turned in the bed, as if settling himself for a good sleep. Half a minute more, and he was dead. Other memories of Bantry picture my mind. I have spoken of Billy O'Shea. It was there I first made his acquaintance—

> With fearless Captain Billy O'
> I joined the Fenian band,
> And I swore, one day to strike a blow
> To free my native land.

Billy O' spent seven or eight months with me in Cork Jail in the year 1859. I was in my store in Madison street, New York, in the month of July, 1863. It was the day, or the second day after the days of the battle of Gettysburg. A carriage came to the door; it had a wounded soldier in it—his uniform begrimed, as if he had been rolling in earth. He asked me to go to a hospital with him; I went with him. The hospital was somewhere at the west side of Broadway, near the Cooper Institute. He wrote his name on the Register as William O'Shea, Captain Forty-second Tammany Regiment. I went to the ward with him, saw him stripped, and examined by the doctor. He had four wounds in his body. One bullet had struck him under the left breast, and went clear through his body; another struck him in the wrist and came out at the elbow. He remained a few weeks in the hospital; rejoined his regiment at the seat of war, and was shot dead in the next battle.

But I have to leave Bantry. During my time there, I could not well get Skibbereen out of my head. There was a young woman in that town who appeared to be fond of me, and who was telling me that Skibbereen seemed lonesome to her without me. I left Skibbereen, having had some kind of a falling-out with her. I was in her shop one Sunday evening; friends and neighbors were coming in; and as they came in, they would go into the parlor back of the shop; sit down and have their talk. By and by, every one was in the parlor except myself; some one closed the parlor door, and I was left alone in the shop. There was one man in the company who had a bank-book, and I knew he was always showing the bank-book to the girl who was fond of me—to let her see how well he was providing for the future. The noise of the laughing and the joking in the room inside came to my ears outside, with a kind of madness, and I walked out into the street— leaving the shop to take care of itself. Next day two of the men who were in the room came into Morty Downing's store; sat down, and commenced talking to each other, as it were confidentially, in the Irish language. I was inside the counter; I could hear all they were saying—and they meant I should hear it, but they did not pretend so. They talked of Miss Eagar and the man with the bank-book, and concluded that the match was settled. I did not pretend to hear them; I was mad. Those two rogues—Peter Barnane and Charles the Colonel—God be good to them!—carried out their joke well. For two months after that, I did not go into Miss Eagar's shop. One moonlight night I was passing by her house; she was standing in the door; I did not salute her; she stepped out after me and took the cap off my head—taking it into the shop with her. I went in after her—for my cap. She asked what was the matter with me. I asked why did she leave me alone in the shop that Sunday evening. She said—because she thought no one had a better right to mind the shop than I had. I told her I had arrangements made to go to Bantry to live. She said I could go if I liked; but she liked me better than she liked any one else. I did go to Bantry; but I came back in three months' time, and we got married on the 6th of June, 1853.

CHAPTER XV.

AFTER my marriage, my late employer moved into a new house he had built. I rented the house in which I had lived with him the previous four or five years, and I carried on the business of hardware and agricultural seeds merchant. I prospered, pretty fairly, every way. I had my advertising bills and posters printed in the Irish language. One side of the house fronted a square, and on that side, I had painted the words:

> "Here, honest value you will find
> In farm seeds, of every kind;
> If once you try, so pleased you'll be,
> You'll come to buy again from me."

The business-language of the shop was mostly Irish, as that was mostly the business language of the farmers around who dealt with me. The first Irish-language book I came to read was a book of Irish poems with translations by Edward Walsh. I was able to read these Irish poems without any previous book-study of the language. The man who gave me the book was John O'Driscoll—a grandson of the Irish poet, John Collins, of Myross. When O'Driscoll was a national school-teacher, he had been up in Dublin in the training school, and brought the book home with him.

When Fenian times came on, O'Driscoll was put in prison; he lost his school-mastership; came to America, and got married in Rutland, Vermont. The last day I spent with him was the day of John Boyle O'Reilly's funeral in Boston. He died shortly after that. God be good to him! he was a proud, manly Irishman—too manly to live long and prosper in this world.

In chapter xiii., I took myself, a Phœnix prisoner into Cork Jail in 1858.

The readers of the *United Irishman* in which I am printing these "Recollections" do not seem satisfied that I should make such a skip as that in my life, by leaping from 1853 to 1858 without saying anything particular in those four or five years.

There is nothing very particular to say about Ireland's cause those years—for that cause was apparently dead.

It was dead during the Crimean war, '54-'55, and during the war of the Indian Mutiny, '56-'57. But as many writers have written books and pamphlets about the origin of the movement that is now called Fenianism—writers, too, who evidently knew little or nothing about its origin, it may be no harm for me to put on record what I am able to say on the subject. Any historical pith that may be in it may be picked from the rest of this chapter.

The Crimean war was going on '54. There was not a red-coat soldier left in Ireland ; there was not a stir in Ireland against English rule. Charles Gavan Duffy left Ireland, telling the people the Irish national cause was like the cause of a corpse on a dissecting table.

The Crimean war ended, and then came on the English war of the Indian mutiny, '56–'57. There was not a red-coat soldier left in Ireland. Some of the young men in Skibbereen came together and started the Phœnix Society. The phœnix is some fabled bird that dies, and from its ashes rises into life again. We had some forty or fifty members in that Phœnix Society. Our first meetings were in the rooms at the back of the drug store of Doctor Jerrie Crowley.

We read in the newspapers one day in the year 1857 that some Tipperary rebel had drawn on a wooden gate in the town of Carrick on-Suir the picture of an English soldier with an Irish pike through his body, and that the Town Commissioners of Carrick had offered a reward for the capture of the artist, and had called for subscriptions to increase the reward. We got a "rasper" farthing, and we sent it with a tearful letter to the Carrick Commissioners. Some days after, we had a letter from Doctor O'Ryan (Doctor Anthony O'Ryan I think) telling us that there was a rumor that we had sent such a subscription to the Commissioners; but that the flunkeys had concealed it from those who were not flunkeys, and asking us to send him a copy of our communication. We sent it to him.

Doctor Jeremiah Crowley! I have spoken of him; I will speak more of him. He was one of these Irish doctors of the "famine" times—one of these Irish doctors who never grow rich at any time in Ireland; for always in Ireland there is distress—and ever will be while England is in it. And where there was distress and sickness and death, Doctor Jerrie was there, without

fee or money reward. He died shortly after giving us
his rooms for the Phœnix Society meetings. I was at
his wake. About midnight, twelve young girls dressed
in white came into the room and cried around his
coffin. The women cried, and the men in the room
and in the house cried—and cried loudly. A more
touching picture of Irish life and Irish death is not in
my recollection. I wrote some lines about it at the
time: they were published in the Cork *Herald;* I will
try and remember them here:

DOCTOR JERRIE CROWLEY.

With sorrowing heart my feelings tend
To paying a tribute to a friend;
But friendship is too light a name
By which to designate the flame
Of holy love that filled his mind—
That which endeared him to mankind.
Skibbereen now mourns his spirit fled,
For Doctor Jerrie Crowley's dead.
Each hill from Skea to Clashatarbh
Cries out "Ta Doctuir Jerrie marbh."

How much—how many, I can't say
That tidings grieved that dismal day.
Far from the town, with lamentation
They "waked" him—in imagination;
His house—the poor man's hospital,
Received whoever chose to call,
And townsmen flocked in countless numbers
To "wake" him from unearthly slumbers.
If ever cries aroused the dead,
That corpse would lift its lowly head
When twelve young maidens dressed in white
Approached his bier about midnight,

Shed tears, and raised in solemn tone,
An unaffected ullagone;
The women joined, the men by and by
Were forced to swell this Irish cry,
Until the house, from door to door,
Was naught but mourning and uproar.
Nor quietness reigned, 'till head and voice
Succumbed to nature—not to choice.
A hearse next day its presence showed
To take him to his last abode—
Brought forth amid an ullagone,
The public claimed him as their own,
And said, no hearse should bear his weight
From thence unto the Abbey gate.
The Abbey gate is reached, and there
Eight mourning townsmen did appear
Who worshipped God a different way,
Requesting earnestly that they
Alone would be allowed to lay
The body in its mother clay.
Ten priests in tears read obsequies;
The grave is closed 'mid deafening cries,
And there, that honest, loving heart
Ere long, of dust will form a part.
The sod is laid, the poor remain,
And loudly call his name—in vain.
Some recollect when at his door
At midnight hour they called before.
Some recollect the pressing hurry
Be smart; go on for Doctor Jerrie,"
No matter at what hour I mention,
The humblest call had his attention.
Tho' storm howled and swelled the ford;
Tho' lightning flashed and thunder roared;
Thro' hail and rain, and piercing blast,
He made his way in anxious haste,
And never took a poor man's fee,
But left one—where was poverty.

> Thus, for his family the worse,
> His heart was larger than his purse.
> A widowed wife and orphans four
> In mourning sad his loss deplore.
> Skibbereen, for whom he ever toiled,
> May pay some tribute to his child
> By educating him, to gather
> A knowledge worthy of the father.

The doctor had four children. The eldest of them was a boy, and the suggestion in the last four lines was the subject of conversation at the wake—that it would be a good thing to get up a testimonial to the widow that would enable her to send the boy to college and have him educated for the medical profession.

A few other lines in verse may be noted:

> Eight mourning townsmen did appear
> Who worshipped God a different way,
> Requesting earnestly that they,
> Alone, would be allowed to lay
> The body in its mother clay.

There was at that time somewhat of a distant feeling between the Catholics and the Protestants of the town. Some few years before that, the Ecclesiastical Titles bill was passed in Parliament, that made it an offense for a Catholic bishop to sign his name to any paper or pastoral as "bishop of his diocese." Some of the Protestants of the town had privately sent a petition to Parliament praying for the passage of the bill. Some member of Parliament got the names of those who signed that petition, and sent them to Skibbereen. The Skibbereen men had them printed and placarded on the walls, and from that sprang the cold feeling I allude to. The Protestants, at Doctor Jerrie's funeral, stood at the graveyard gate of the Abbey field, and asked us who were bearing the coffin, to do them the favor of letting them bear it from the gate to the grave. We granted them the favor, and there were the ten Catholic priests reading the Catholic prayers, and the eight Protestants, bearing the coffin through the graveyard.

John Tierney, of Kings County, is reading those "Recollections" of mine, and he sends me a communication which I will make a place for here, as the subject he alludes to had place about the time I am now speaking of—the year 1857. This is his note.

No. 635 West 42d Street, New York.

DEAR SIR—I like best the books I brought with me from dear old Ireland; though, like myself, they are sadly the worse for the wear.

I send you Charles J. Kickham's story of "Sally Cavanagh." He speaks of you in the preface. Well —well—the figure of the world, for us two anyway, "passeth away." Still, "while every hope was false to me," and also thee, there is pride and comfort in such testimony from such a whole-souled Irishman as Kickham, who knew not how to favor or flatter, any more than your old friend, JOHN TIERNEY.

The following are the words of Kickham to which Mr. Tierney refers:

"As I have spoken of so many of my fellow laborers at No. 12 Parliament street, I must not forget the

most devoted of them all. His name was first brought
under my notice in this way: It was the end of the
year 1857, a sketch of the poet Edward Walsh appeared in the *Celt*, a national periodical established by
my lamented friend, Doctor Robert Cane, of Kilkenny.
The poor poet's story was a sad one, and it was mentioned that his widow was then living in an humble
lodging in Dublin, hardly earning her own and her
children's bread, as a seamstress. This moved some
generous-hearted persons to write to her, proffering pe-
cuniary assistance; but the poet's widow was proud,
and she wished it to be announced in the *Celt* that she
could not accept money. Mrs. Walsh sent me one of
the letters she had received, and here it is:

"SKIBBEREEN, Xmas morning, 1857.

"DEAR MADAM—I hoped to spend a happy Christmas
Day; but before sitting down to breakfast, I took
up the last number of the *Celt*, and read the conclusion
of the memoir of your husband, by some kind writer.
I now find I cannot be happy unless you will do me
the favor of accepting the enclosed pound note as a
small testimony of my sympathy for the widow of one
of our sweetest poets. I remain dear madam,
"Yours, Sincerely,
"J. O'DONOVAN ROSSA."

I felt a strong desire to know more of this Mr.
O'Donovan (Rossa), who could not sit down to his
Christmas breakfast after reading an "o'er true tale"
of suffering, till he had done something to alleviate it.

And when, some months after, I saw his name in the
list of prisoners arrested in Cork and Kerry, on a charge
of treason-felony, I was not surprised. The first of
these " Phœnix prisoners placed at the bar, Daniel
O'Sullivan-agreem, was convicted and sentenced to ten
years penal servitude. But before the trials proceeded
further, there was a change of government, and Thomas
O'Hagan, now lord-chancellor, the eloquent advocate
of the prisoners, was made attorney-general. O'Donovan (Rossa) and the rest were prevailed on to go through
the form of pleading guilty, having first stipulated that
Daniel O'Sullivan should be set at liberty. By this
step they relieved the new attorney-general of the
awkward duty of becoming the prosecutors of his
clients. The prisoners were released on their own recognizances to come up for judgment when called upon.
It is needless to say that the fact that he could be at
any moment consigned to penal servitude for life, or
for any number of years the government pleased without the form of a trial, had no effect whatever upon
the political conduct of O'Donovan (Rossa). After
this I saw his name again in the newspapers as a can-
didate for the situation of Relieving Officer to the
Skibbereen Union. In his letter to the Guardians he
said in his manly way : ' If you appoint me, notwithstanding my political opinions, I shall feel proud. But
if you refuse to appoint me on account of my political
opinions, I shall feel proud, too.' It is to the credit
of the Board of Guardians that he was unanimously
elected ; and the fact shows, too, the estimation in
which the indomitable rebel was held by all who knew

him personally, irrespective of class or creed. The scenes of misery with which he was brought into closer contact while discharging the duties of this office intensified his hatred of foreign misrule. Mr. O'Donovan was the manager of the *Irish People*, and while on his business tours through Ireland and England, one of its ablest correspondents. He also contributed to its leading columns, and even to the ' poet's corner.' "

When I come to the years 1859 and 1862 I will have something to say about that "pleading guilty " and that " Relieving Officership of the Skibbereen Union."

After the death of Dr. Jerrie Crowley, the Phœnix men moved from the rooms they had occupied back of the drugstore into other rooms that they rented from Morty Downing—not the Morty I have spoken of before, but another Morty who was called Morty the Second.

On the 2d of January, 1858, we had an anniversary celebration in those new rooms. We had a supper, and after the supper we had speech-making. Daniel O'Crowley, now living in Springfield, Ill., was, I think, the secretary of the meeting at that time. Denis McCarthy-Dhoun, who afterward died in London, was the chairman at the supper. We were subscribing for the Irish National journals at the time. I sent a report of the meeting to the *Dundalk Democrat*, and I sent with it a pound note, asking the editor to send me a pound's worth of the papers.

The speeches were published in the *Democrat*, and from the *Democrat* they were published in other papers —in French papers and American papers. It was from those circumstances that that which is now called Fenianism took the start.   James Stephens was in Paris at the time, and I think John O'Mahony was in Paris, too.   Anyway, they were in communication with each other, or got into communication with each other. The report of the Skibbereen meeting showed them that the old cause was not dead; that the seed of national life was in the old land still.   They agreed to start into action.   James Stephens was to act in Ireland, and John O'Mahony was to act in America. Thus it came to pass that James Stephens visited Skibbereen in the summer of 1858, and planted the seed of the Irish Revolutionary Brotherhood there, as I have already said in chapter xiii.; and thus it came to pass that John O'Mahony started the "*Phœnix*" newspaper in New York in the year 1859, when many men in Skibbereen, Bantry, Kenmare, Killarney and other places had been arrested and put to prison, under the name of Phœnix men.

How do I know all that? you may ask.   Well, I know it this way : After the Phœnix scare had subsided, Jas. Stephens was living in Paris, and he wrote to Skibbereen expressing a wish that Dan McCartie and Patrick J. Downing would visit him there.   They did visit him; not the two together, but one at a time. Dan McCartie returned to Skibbereeen; Patrick J. Downing was sent to America.   I met the two of them since, and it is from them I learned all I have stated relative to the start of Fenianism.   Patrick J. Downing went through the American war; he was a Colonel of the Forty-second (Tammany) Regiment; he learned his drill on the hill sides of Ireland; he became our drill-master after Owens (Considine, whom James Stephens had sent us), left us; he died in Washington some years ago. Dan McCartie is living in America as I write—and long may he live.

I was in the town of Dundalk, Ireland, in the year 1894. I gave a lecture there. The chairman of the meeting was Thomas Roe, the proprietor of the *Dundalk Democrat*. I asked him had he a file of the paper for the year 1858. He said he had. He went to the office and got the issue of the paper in which was the report of the Phœnix Society meeting of January 2d, 1858. I got him to re-publish it; and it is from the *Dundalk Democrat* of August 18th, 1894, that I now publish this speech I made in Skibbereen thirty-nine years ago.

"In his lecture at the town hall, Dundalk, last week, O'Donovan Rossa referred to the fact that the first speech he ever delivered—at a commemoration of the anniversary of the Phœnix National Society, Skibbereen, in the beginning of 1858—was sent by him to the *Democrat* and published by this journal. On turning to the file of 1858, we find the report of the speech amongst those delivered on the same occasion, and it is both interesting and instructive at the present time. We reproduce it here:

PHŒNIX NATIONAL AND LITERARY SOCIETY, SKIBBER-
EEN.

"On the 2d instant the members of this society

celebrated the first anniversary of its formation by dining together. Mr. D. McCarthy presided. When ample justice had been done to the good things provided by Mrs. Downing, the following toasts were drunk with enthusiasm and responded to:

" 'OUR COUNTRY.'

" Mr. Jeremiah O'Donovan (Rossa) in response to this toast spoke as follows: Mr. Chairman and gentlemen. At your call I reluctantly rise, for I am badly prepared and ill qualified to speak to the toast of Our Country; but should that country ever have a call on the services of her sons during my existence, I trust I will be found more willing to rise and better prepared to act than I am now to speak for it. Too much talk and too little action have been the characteristics of Irish patriotism during a large portion of the last half century; and as we are supposed to learn from experience, it is believed that less of the former and a corresponding increase of the latter will, in the future, serve our country's cause best and our enemy's cause least. I don't know whether or not the committee who prepared our toasts took this view of the matter when they wrote down this land to be toasted as *our* country, when it is an established fact that *we* have no country. We are the most cosmopolitan race in the whole universe; but Irishmen *should* have a country; they have a right to the country of their birth. By the use and aid of one steel—the pen—our committee have taken possession of that right, and as their title one day may be disputed, I trust they will be able and willing to prove it by the aid of another steel—the sword (loud cheers). I have heard an anecdote, which I will repeat to you, concerning Dr. Croke of Mallow. When a young man, he was traveling through France, and in a village there he had his seat taken on a Diligence, but having forgotten something at the time, he went for it and on his return found his place occupied by another. In consideration of the loss of his seat he received some impertinence, which he resented; a dispute arose, the disputants appealed to the authorities, and their names were taken down to appear before a tribunal of justice next morning. He gave his name as Thomas Croke, of Ireland, but for reasons that you can plainly understand, he was called next morning as Thomas Croke, Englishman! Feeling the indignity to his country, he never answered till pointed out by one of the officials, and when he stated he was Thomas Croke, Irishman, and not Thomas Croke, Englishman, he was only sneeringly laughed at for presuming to think that he had a country. Thus was this Irishman reminded of the loss of his country; he had no country; we Irishmen are slaves and outcasts in the land of our birth. What a shame! What a disgrace! Yes; disgraceful alike to peer and peasant—Protestant, Catholic and Presbyterian. Thus may foreign nations believe this country is not ours, and I am sure you will not be surprised that England is particularly positive on this point. She has made all possible efforts to convince us of it. She has broken the heads of many Irishmen trying to hammer this opinion into them. For seven long and dreary centuries has she been trying to force

it on us; and against her during all this time have the
majority of Irishmen protested. Yet has she dis-
regarded every protestation, every claim, and every
petition, and instead of treating us as human beings
or subjects, she has made every effort that pen, fire and
sword could make to extirpate our race. She has
stained almost every hearthstone in the land with the
heart's blood of a victim; and the other day, in savage
exultation at the idea of her work being accomplished,
she cried out, 'The Irish are gone, and gone with
a vengeance' (groans). But the mercenary Thunderer
lies. I read it in your countenances. The Irish are
not gone; but part of them are gone, and in whatever
clime their pulses beat to-night, that 'vengeance' which
banished them is inscribed on their hearts, impregnates
their blood, and may yet operate against that oppressor
who, by his exterminating and extirpating laws, deprived
them of a means of living in the land of their fathers (hear,
hear, and cheers). I don't now particularly confine
myself to the last ten or twelve years. If I go back
centuries, the same language will apply to England.
In the seventeenth century she issued the following instructions to Lord Ormond, and as the Eastern monarch said, I now say, 'hear and tremble':—'That his
lordship do endeavor, with his majesty's forces, to
wound, kill, slay or destroy, by all the ways and means
he may, all the said rebels, their adherents and relievers;
and burn, waste, spoil, consume, destroy and demolish
all the places, towns and houses where the said rebels
are, or have been relieved or harbored, and all the hay
and corn there, and kill or destroy all the men inhabit-

ing there capable of bearing arms.'   When I reflect on this and the other innumerable instruments made and provided for the destruction of the Irish, I begin to doubt my indentity as of Milesian descent.   Many of you possess similar doubts or feelings, for assuredly our ancestors were none of the favored class, and nothing but the miraculous intervention of Providence could have preserved our race from utter extinction. Again, hear what the following historians say :—Carte writes :   'That the Lord Justices set their hearts on the extermination not only of the mere Irish, but also of the old English families who were Catholics.'   Dr. Leland says that :—' The favorite object of the Irish Governors and the English Parliament was the utter extermination of all the Catholics of Ireland.'   Clarendon writes that :—' They have sworn to extirpate the whole Irish nation ; ' and the Rev. Dr. Warner says that :— ' It is evident that the Lord Justices hoped for an extirpation not of the mere Irish only, but of all the old English families who were Catholics.'   I give you these extracts without wishing to be sectarian.   The old Irish Catholics were fighting for their nationality, and if the old Irish Protestants were to fight for the same to morrow, it is proved that the tyrant would treat them similarly if she had the power.   When will Irishmen cease from doing the work of the enemy ? When will they ponder on their present degraded condition ?   When will the sunshine of unity dispel the clouds of dissension and distrust that hover over their understanding, and make them blind to the interests of their common country ?   If it be advantageous for

Irishmen to make their own laws, to govern their own country—if they are qualified to do so—why allow another people to think and act for them? Why not Irishmen prefer the interest of their own to that of another country? Can I attribute the motives to love or fear? Are we so pleased with the fostering care and protective kindness of our masters, that we do not care about changing our condition? Or can it be that we are so much afraid of the power of England, that cowardice alone prevents us from properly claiming and obtaining the rights of free men? The time is gone when England could create fear; under present circumstances she has still the power over Ireland in consequence of all her internal elements of discord, disunion and disorganization, but not over any united or enlightened people. Russia has proved this. America and Naples insult and defy her, and India grasps her by the throat and cries: 'Robber, stand and deliver up your booty' (prolonged cheers). In her humility, she is truly a most gullible creature. She now calls for our sympathy and aid. I don't for a moment deny the Saxon interest is strong amongst us; yet who will wonder at it? And who will be surprised if Lord Mayors and Town Scoundrels, official invaders and castle traders; lunatic, militia, stipendiary, detective, expectants, and all other innumerable officers and satellites of vicious and vice-royalty should forward an address of commiseration and condolence, accompanied with a few *lacs* for the comfort and relief of their task masters (cries of 'they want it') The poor struggling tenant-at-will will pay for all; he can starve

his family a few pounds more, and he can fatten the
master's pigs proportionately, and then when he can't
do any more, he will get Indian tenant right, what he
richly deserves when he fails to take the proper steps
to right himself. If every farmer in the country had
a proper supply of agricultural implements, one of
which is a pitchfork, and if all combined then and
petitioned Parliament, stating they were determined
to improve their holdings and positions, and praying
to the House to consider their situation, it is my firm
conviction they would not be long without tenant right,
and the remnant of our race would not be forced into
exile. England has never given us anything through
a love *for us* or a love of justice. She has ever spurned
our petitions when they were not backed by the sword
or a firm determination, and whenever Irishmen de-
manded an instalment of their rights by the pen alone,
they were only mocked and laughed at, and sometimes
favored with additional fetters. Wellington and Peel
granted emancipation through fear; they admitted it
was not safe to refuse it longer; and Grattan would
never have repealed the Sixth of George I., passed in
1720, to confirm 'and better secure the dependence of
Ireland,' only that the English government knew that

> "Swords to back his words
> Were ready, did he need them.

But that treaty of '82 was broken as perfidiously as
was the treaty of Limerick, and every other treaty or
compact that was ever made between the two peoples.
As a prelude, Ireland was incited by the enemy to pre-

mature rebellion; and as Archbishop Hughes, of New York, said when delivering a lecture on Irish starvation in '46—' Martial law for the people—a bayonet or a gibbet for the patriot who loved Ireland—a bribe for the traitor who *did not*—led to that act called the Union, in which the charter of Irish nationality was destroyed—I trust not forever.' Irishmen have since experienced the happiness of being an integral portion of the *disunited kingdom ;* they have been relieved from the cares and troubles of native manufactories and internal bustle, and they are now such an important people as to be saddled with an ' integral' portion of a thousand million pounds, as a national debt. If we were able to pay this debt for England, Ireland may have some chance of becoming a separate portion of this kingdom ; but whoever would seriously endeavor to make her so without any stipulation, may experience the blessings of the ' Glorious British Constitution' through the agency of the halter, the dungeon, the convict ship, the gibbet or the jail. When I speak of these instruments of our tyrants, thoughts of blood and fiendish deeds connected with '98 and the succeeding years visit my memory. The two Thomas-street murders, within a few years and a few yards of each other, forcibly and brilliantly reveal to us the charms of that constitution, and particularly that circumstance connected with the murder of Lord Edward, where the bloodhounds pursued his spirit to the other world, and after the Universal Judge in heaven had passed sentence on him either as a traitor or a martyr, they retried him, and by a packed jury robbed and plundered his widow and orphan children. Excuse me, Mr. Chairman and Irishmen, for trespassing so far upon the property of my successor, who is to speak of the men of '98. I have digressed much from my subject, but it is more of the heart than of the mind. A few other remarks and I will have ceased from tiring you farther. You will understand that I am not one of those individuals who believe in the regeneration of my country through the agency of a viceroy or vice-*reine*, through the propagation of high-blood cattle and the cultivation for their support of mangel-wurzel and yellow-bullock; the latter would be very well in their proper time and place, but I would reverse the order of things, and the comforts of human creation would be with me a primary consideration to the comforts of the brute species, or as my friend and neighbor, Michael Burke, says, I would rather see 'stamina' in the man than in the animal (laughter). To effect this, the existing relations of Irishman and Englishman should undergo a change, and now should be the time for the Irish nation to agitate for this change, and strive to obtain it by every proper means, so as to prevent a recurrence of the national disasters of '46 and '47, when England allowed thousands of our people to starve, and blasphemously charged God Almighty with the crime, while the routine of her misgovernment compelled the cereal produce of the country to be exported. A curse upon foreign legislation. A domestic government, no matter how constituted, would never have allowed it; even this terrible evil might have been averted, had the leaders in '48 profited by the past history of their country; they ought to have known that an enemy never paid any attention to moral force, when not backed by physical force, and had the Repealers followed the example of the '82 men, and had they presented their petitions with pikes and swords instead of with magic wands and brass buttons, the issue would have been different with them, and instead of injuring the cause of their country, they would occupy as prominent and proud a place in her future history as Grattan and his compatriots. To obtain a name and a position for our country, and the restoration of our plundered rights, we will need such an organization as that of '82—nay such a one as '48, if you will. Had Irishmen, or *any one* class of Irishmen, been united, bided their time, and embraced their opportunity, the future would be ours—no matter though there may be many difficulties before men who seek to establish a name and position for their country amongst the nations of the earth. But let me say, that as Irishmen here to-night—we have no foe—no enemy amongst any class or creed of our countrymen; politically speaking, the man who looks upon us, and men of our political profession, as his enemy, is our enemy. He *must* be a man who would have his country forever under the yoke of the foreigner; or, he *must* be a man who has profited by the plunder, or who is supported by the plunderer. I now conclude, thanking you for the honor you have done me, and the kindness you have shown me, assuring you wherever I am cast by fortune, it shall ever be my pride to stand, as I stand here to-night, amongst men who are prepared to assist in any and every agita-

tion or undertaking to obtain their rights, or an instalment of their rights, which may ultimately result in
qualifying them to write the epitaph of Robert Emmet."

It isn't that I say it—that wasn't a bad speech at
all, at a time when Ireland was dead or sleeping. People who write about the origin of that particular movement called Fenianism—knowing nothing about that
speech, or about the Phœnix Society men, know nothing as to what they write about. If the license of a
little pleasantry may be given me, I may say that several of my early-day acquaintances would often lament
that I would not bind myself to the speech-making
business, to free Ireland.

CHAPTER XVI.

THE START OF FENIANISM.

In these times preceding the Phœnix arrests—from 1852 to 1858—the time of the Sadlier and Keogh Tenant Right movement, the time of the Crimean war, and the time of the Indian mutiny; the Irish National cause was in a swoon. But England was playing one of her tricks, endeavoring to get the people to put trust in Parliamentary agitation and petitions to Parliament, for the redress of their grievances. Men who had no faith in these petitions would join in, saying, "We will try once more; but this is to be the last." I suppose a dozen Tenant-Right bills have been given to Ireland since 1852; but to-day (1897), England and England's landlords have the right to root out the Irish people still, and mercilessly do they exercise that right—so much so, that the population of Ireland is two millions less to-day than it was in 1852.

When James Stephens came to Skibbereen in May, 1858, and started the Irish Revolutionary Brotherhood, we commenced to work in that line of labor, and we were not long working, when a great change was noticeable in the temper of the people. In the cellars, in the woods, and on the hillsides, we had our men drilling in the nighttime, and wars and rumors of wars were on the wings of the wind. The lords and the landlords were visibly becoming alarmed. No wonder, for their tenants who used to flock to Tenant-Right meetings cared very little about attending such meetings now. It has been said—it is said to-day by some men of the cities, that the farmers were opposed to the movement. I could not say that; I could say to the contrary, because I enrolled into the movement many of the most influential farmers in the parishes of Kilcoe, Aughadown, Caheragh, Drimoleague, Drinagh, Kilmacabea, Myross and Castlehaven. Dan McCartie and Morty Moynahan, two other "Centres" did the same. We set our eyes on the men who could carry their districts, in case of a rising—just as England sets her eye on the same class of men to-day, and swears them in as "New Magistrates." It is to counteract this Fenian work of ours that England is now giving the "Commission of the Peace" to the sons and brothers of the men that we had in the Fenian organization. I could here name a dozen of these new magistrates that I met in Ireland a few years ago, whose fathers and whose brothers were with us in the Fenian movement of thirty odd years ago. I will not name them, as it may be said I was unwarrantably saying something to their injury. But England knows them, and knows with what aim she swore them into her service. She knows that Pat and Jerrie Cullinane were in prison with me in the Phœnix time, and she knows why it is that she makes their brother, Henry, a magistrate. She knows that William O'Sullivan, of Kilmallock, was put to prison by her in the Fenian times, and she knows why it is that she makes a magistrate of his son, John, who pre-

sided at my lecture at Kilmallock two years ago.
And, sad I am to-day (July 12, '98,) as I am reading
this proof-sheet, to read in the Irish newspapers,
that John O'Sullivan of Kilmallock died last week.
English work of this kind I found all over Ireland when
I was over there lately. In the district of Belfast I found
eleven of those new magistrates whose families, thirty
years ago, gave volunteers to the Fenian movement. I
do not say they are worse Irishmen now than they were
thirty years ago; but England has sworn them into her
service; has "bound them to the peace." It is not for
love of them, or love of their race or religion she has
done so. She has done it to wean them away from the
National movement, and to paralyze that movement.
"Beware of the cockatrice! trust not the wiles of the
serpent; for perfidy lurks in his folds "— So spoke the
Bishop of Ross, when the Sassenach was hanging him
at Carrigadrohid. But we are taking little heed of his
advice; the Sassenach is getting the better of us every
way. I will now return to my story.

Every Sunday, Morty Moynahan, Dan McCartie and
myself would drive to some country chapel, and attend
mass. After mass we got into conversation with the
trustworthy men of the place, and we generally planted
the seed of our mission there. One Sunday, going to
Clonakilty, we fell in with Father Tim Murray, of
Ross, who was going to say mass at the chapel of
Lissavard. We went to mass there. We were in the
gallery. Father Tim was preaching in Irish. I was
startled, as a man sitting by me, said in a loud voice,
"Anois, athair Teige, ni doith liom gur ceart e sin "—

"Now Father Tim I don't think that's right." The priest had to address him personally, and tell him he'd have to go out in the yard to hear mass unless he held his tongue. He was a harmless simpleton, well known in the parish. After mass, McCartie, Moynahan and I went to Clonakilty. I had made an appointment to meet a farmer from the country, a cousin of mine. I settled matters with him. There are magistrates in his family now. Then, there were in the town two of the men of '48 we meant to call upon—John Callanan and Maxwell Irwin. We went to John Callanan's house, and he was not at home; we went to Maxwell Irwin's, and he was not at home; he had gone to Crookhaven to attend the auction of a cargo of a shipwreck; so the little girl told me who came to the door after I had telephoned on the bright brass knocker outside. She was a pretty little girl, too, about twelve years of age, with twinkling eyes, and red rosy cheeks and coal-black hair. She is my wife to-day. Five or six years afterward, I met Mr. Irwin's entire family—not for their welfare, I fear, as the boys of it found their way to prison and to exile through acquaintance with me.

Clonakilty is twenty miles distant from Skibbereen. That visit I made there with Dan McCartie and Morty Moynahan to start the I. R. B. Organization was in 1858. Thirty-six years after, in 1894, I was invited to give a lecture there. Dan O'Leary, one of the new magistrates, presided at the lecture. He, too, died a few weeks ago. After the lecture there was a big supper at the hotel. That cousin of mine whom I initiated into the I. R. B. movement in 1858 **sat**

near me at the supper table. We talked of old
times of course, but the old times are changed; one
of his family is also one of the new magistrates. In
those old times the magistracy was a monopoly in control of the Cromwellian plunderers of the Irish people,
such as the Beechers, the Townsends, the Frenches,
the Hungerfords, the Somervilles, the lords Bandon,
Bantry, and Carbery, with a few of the Irish themselves
who became renegades to race and religion, and thus
came into sole possession of some of the lands of the
clans—such as the O'Donovans, the O'Gradys, the
O'Briens and others, who became more English than
the English themselves. I remember old Sandy O'Driscoll, of Skibbereen; he was a Catholic, but he had the
character and the appearance of being as big a tyrant
as any Cromwellian landlord in the barony of Carbery.
That much is as much as need be said at present on
that subject.

On the subject of Fenianism I have heard many
Irishmen in America speak about the large sums of
American money that were spent in organizing the
movement in Ireland, England and Scotland. I traveled these three countries in connection with the organization of the movement from 1858 to 1865, and I can
truthfully say, that in the early years of our endeavor,
"the men at home," spent more of their own money out
of their own pockets than was contributed altogether
by the whole Fenian organization of America. Hugh
Brophy, one of the Dublin "Centres" is in Melbourne;
John Kenealy, one of the Cork "Centres," is in Los
Angeles—two extremely distant parts of the world—

they will see what I say, and they can bear testimony to the truth of my words.

Now, I'll get out of this cross bohreen I got into, and get back again to the main road of my story. As a funeral was passing through Skibbereen to the Abbey graveyard one day in '58, I saw two men whom I thought would be great men in our movement; they were looked upon as the leaders of the clan O'Driscoll and clan McCarthy, of the parishes of Drinagh, Drimoleague and Caheragh. I got into the funeral procession and talked with them the mile of the road out to the Abbey field, and back again. We went into my house and had some dinner. In my bedroom I pledged Corly-Batt, McCarthy-Sowney to work for the cause; somewhere else I gave the pledge to Teige Oge O'Driscoll, of Doire-gclathach. Each of them was about sixty years of age at the time. Teige Oge's wife was a McCarthy-Sowney, and Teige Oge's sister was the wife of Finneen a Rossa, the brother of my grandfather, Diarmad a Rossa. Then I met Teige Oge's eldest son, Conn, and I swore him in. Some dozen years ago I met him in Natick or Holliston, Massachusetts, the father of a large family of hearty sons and daughters.

The McCarthy-Sowney family are a noble Irish family; thoroughly hostile to English rule in Ireland, however they are, or wherever they are.

If you are "on the run" from England in Ireland, no matter what you are hunted for, you have shelter, and protection, and guardianship in the house of a Mc-Carthy-Sowney. Corly-Batt had a grinding mill on the bank of the river, by the main road, between

Drimoleague and Bantry; in this mill was Johnnie O'Mahony, a grandson of his, about seventeen years old; he swore in the grandson; and that grandson swore in all the farmers' sons who came to the mill with wheat and oats and barley. That Johnnie O'Mahony is living somewhere around Boston now.

In the year 1864 I was living in Dublin, I came down to Skibbereen on some business. As I was passing by Drimoleague —it was a fair-day there—I went up to the fair field on the Rock, and as I got within the field, a fight commenced. I knew all the men around, and all the men around knew me. The two leaders of the fight were inside in the middle of the crowd; they had a hold of each other; the sticks were up; I rushed in; I caught hold of the two men—" Here," said I, "this work must stop; 'tis a shame for the whole of you to be going on this way." I glanced around as I spoke; the sticks were lowered, and the crowd scattered.

That was one good thing the Fenian organization did in Ireland in its day—it in a great measure broke up the faction-fights and the faction-parties, and got the men of both sides to come together and work in friendly brotherhood for the Irish cause. That, as much as anything else, greatly alarmed the English government and its agents.

CHAPTER XVII.

IN the Autumn of 1858, Patrick Mansfield Delaney and Martin Hawe were arrested in Kilkenny, and Denis Riordan was arrested in Macroom. While they were in jail, the Kilkenny men came in numbers into the farm of Mr. Delaney, and harvested all the produce of the land for his family. Denis Riordan died in America. Patrick Mansfield Delaney died in America. I met Martin Hawe at his home in Kilkenny in the year 1894. In those early years of my life—embracing the Tenant-Right movement, and the start of the I. R. B. movement, the Parliamentary people were getting up petitions to Parliament every year, everywhere, and the speech-makers were declaiming their opinions on platform meetings.

I was young then—too young to have a voice on the platform—and I'd often say to myself, "If I could speak on that platform, how differently I'd speak of Ireland's wrongs and rights!"

I am old enough to-day to speak on a platform, but the leaders of the meetings do not want me to speak.

One of those leaders said to me a few days ago:— "Rossa: you should have been on the platform at that meeting the other night, but if you were called upon to speak, we could not depend on you—that you would not say something which would destroy the purpose of the whole meeting."

Some years ago I got a platform ticket to go to one of those meetings in New York City, and as I was going with others in the ante-room on to the platform, one of the ushers accosted me, and expressed a wish that I would sit in the body of the hall. I made a note of the circumstance in my notebook that day, and I here transcribe it:

"Tuesday, April 10, 1883. I bought a ticket from O'Neill Russell to go to the Gælic Irish entertainment at Steinway Hall. Then, I was given two platform tickets and two hall tickets by one of the Irish-class men of Clarendon Hall. I gave in one of the platform tickets, and was going up the steps to the platform, when one of the ushers said, 'I beg your pardon, sir; for various reasons, I wish you would sit in the body of the hall.

"I make this note—to see if the world will change."

The world hasn't changed much during the fourteen years since I made that note. Now I'll go back to Ireland.

Besides killing the spirit of faction-fighting in Ireland, the Fenian organization did another good thing— it killed the evil spirit that set county against county, and province against province—an evil spirit that worked mischief even in America, up to the advent of Fenianism. But now that is all dead, and we can sing—

> Hurrah! for Munster, stout and brave,
>   For Ulster, sure and steady;
> For Connaught rising from the grave,
>   For Leinster, rough and ready;

The news shall blaze from ev'ry hill
    And ring from ev'ry steeple,
And all the land with gladness fill—
    We're one united people.

There are, to-day, in America, many county organizations, but they do not foster the inimical spirit of the
olden time; though I would not much mind if there
was among them a little rivalry as to who or which
would do most to drive from the old land the savage
enemy that rooted them out of it.

My mind is full of little incidents connected with
the start of the movement in Ireland in 1858. We
had our drillings in the woods and on the mountains
that surrounded Skibbereen. On Sunday summer even-
ings our camping ground was generally on the top of
Cnoc-Ouma, where Thomas Davis must have stood one
day of his life, if he saw those hundred isles of Carbery
that he wrote about in his poem, "The Sack of Baltimore "—

"Old Inisherkin's crumbled fane looks like a moulting bird,
    And in a calm and sleepy swell, the ocean tide is heard."

From no other spot but this camping ground of ours
on the top of Loughine hill could any one see the picture that the immortal Irish poet shows in that verse
of his. Next year, at the Summer Assizes in Tralee, a
revenue officer from Barlogue—a coast-guard station
between Loughine and the sea—came on the witness
table when Dan O'Sullivan-agreem was on trial, and
swore, that with his spy-glass he saw men drilling on
the top of Cnoc-Ouma—Dan O'Sullivan-agreem was
not there; but we were there; and what was sworn

against us was taken as evidence to convict the Kerry man to ten years' penal servitude, as the charge against him was "conspiracy." Sullivan-goula, the informer, swore that the society Dan Agreem belonged to in Kerry, was the same society that we belonged to in Cork, and what we did in Cork, was used in Kerry to convict Dan Agreem, who never saw us, or knew us. Such is English law in Ireland.

Returning with a few comrades from our midnight drill in Loriga wood one night, a voice rustled through the trees, praying, " Buadh Dia libh, a bhuachailidhe." —The victory of God be with ye, boys. The prayer came from an " Unfortunate " who had been hunted out of town by the good-government society. She had twined herself a shelter-bohawn in the thicket, and must have heard some of the command-words of our drill-master. When the arrests were made, a few months after, Attorney Everett, who was employed by the stipendiary magistrate to hunt up evidence against us, offered her a large amount of money to swear against us; but she spurned it; she knew nothing about drilling, or about any one drilling in Loriga wood; and if she did, she was not going to disgrace herself by taking blood-money.

God be good and merciful unto you Kit Cadogan, and " God's wrath upon the Saxon " that wrought the wreck and ruin of the millions of the men, women, and children of my land and race.

Rumors were rife in the land, of those drillings in the woods and mountains; the police were most active trying to find them, and the boys played those police many tricks to harass them. The girls played them tricks too—for the spirit of the women of Ireland was with us in the work of organization. I have known many girls to refuse to continue acquaintance of courtship with young men who would not join the Society. Poor Driscoll of Kilmacabea, the Crimean soldier, comes to my mind here. He was out of his mind. He was in the Crimean war; he was wounded in the head, and he was discharged from the army, with a pension of ninepence a day for twelve months. Then he became a strolling beggarman. He was what was called an "innocent"; quite harmless, and wouldn't hurt or harm any one; his dress was a bundle of tatters of various colors, with the proverbial straw "sugawn" tying them around his body—even tying his shoes. At the side of my residence, a stream called the Caol ran into the Ilen river. This stream was arched over and made a kind of square on which some of the goods of my shop would be displayed. Mary Regan was one of the servants; she was sweeping this square one morning. Driscoll the soldier was there, and after sweeping she began to joke Driscoll with being discharged from the army for not knowing his drill. Driscoll took hold of the sweeping brush, and using the handle of it for a gun, put himself through all the military evolutions, giving himself the words of command, etc. The police came up and stopped Driscoll from drilling. He was an Irishman—his tongue was Irish. I was at the shop door looking on; he came over to me after giving up the broom, and said, "Oh Jerrie a laodh! nach truadh na bhfuilim a m' tarbh—mar a rithfin triotha a's futha, a's cathfain anairde san aor liom a'ircaibh iad."—" Oh ! Jerrie, dear ! what a pity that I am not a bull—how I'd run through them and under them, and throw them up in the air with my horns." And saying that, he'd lower his head, and hump his back, as if he was the bull running through them. There was the poor, insane Irishman, with the instinct of sanity still alive in him against the enemies of Ireland ! Poor Driscoll ! I often think of you. The Mary Regan I speak of is living to-day in West Brighton, Staten Island—Mrs. Mary Walsh. She had her wedding in my house.

Coming on to the end of the year 1858 the Irish newspapers were speaking of drillings going on in the South of Ireland, and some of the ministers of religion seemed to have caught the alarm. On that Sunday in November when the gospel of the day tells us to " render unto Cæsar what belongs to Cæsar, and unto God what belongs to God," the priest that preached the sermon in Skibbereen as much as told us we owed allegiance to England. England's head was on the coins I had in my pocket, but I knew those coins did not belong to her, as well as I knew that the lands of my people all around me that England's land-robbers held, did not belong to them. As this is a vexed question, that is all I need say on the subject.

The English government in Dublin Castle had been preparing to put us to prison, at this time. A stipendiary magistrate named Fitzmaurice had taken up his residence in the town. He had been sent to the South from the North of Ireland, where he had won his spurs in the English service by trapping many Ribbonmen into prison.

At this time too there came to Skibbereen from Kerry a man named Dan Sullivan-goula; he took lodgings at the house of a Kerry man named Morty Downing, from whom we had rented the rooms of the Phœnix Society. Morty had two children, and I used to see this Sullivan-goula fondling the eldest of those children on his knee, and calling her his Kerry pet. He at that time was swearing her father into jail. Irish history records a similar incident in the case of the children of one of the Sheares brothers, whom a Captain Armstrong swore to the scaffold in '98.

Morty Moynahan had a letter from a correspondent in Kenmare who knew Sullivan goula, cautioning him to beware of the fellow; that he was suspected; that he had been taken in to the organization at a fair, by a Bantry man who did not know the bad character he had in his own locality in Kerry; that none of his Kerry neighbors would think of taking him as a member; and that no one knew what business he could have in Skibbereen, only bad business. But Fitzmaurice the stipendary had laid the plans for him, and had instructed him before he came to Skibbereen to write to McCarthy Downing, the attorney in Skibbereen, asking for a position of clerk in his office. Morty Moynahan was chief clerk in McCarthy Downing's office, and had the care of all his letters; and when Morty got the warning letter from our Kenmare friend he put against it the other letter of Goula's application for employment; and thought that that would in some measure account for his being in town amongst us.

One morning as I was going to the news-room in North street, I saw Goula walking the sidewalk before me. After turning the corner from Main street into North street, he suddenly turned around and walked back against me. I walked on, and saw Fitzmaurice walking down against me. Goula had seen him before I saw him, and that is why he made the sudden turn back. A week after that, I was in Cork Jail.

During that week I had a letter from Lord Colchester, the Postmaster-General, telling me an application I had made for the postmastership of Skibbereen had been received by him—that the office was not yet officially declared vacant, and when it would be declared vacant I would hear again from him. As my readers want me to give them a little light reading occasionally in these "Recollections" I may as well tell how my correspondence with Lord Colchester originated.

Some day in the month of November, 1858, Owen Leonard, the postmaster, called me in to his private office and told me that in consequence of some mistake in the management of his business, a man was sent down from Dublin to make an examination, and that the man advised him to send in his resignation. He accordingly was sending on his resignation that day. He advised me to make an application for the position; he was sure I could get as many to back me as were necessary—the endorsement of Deasy and McCarthy, the members for the County, and a few others. I did not take the matter very seriously, but as it gave me an opportunity to

write something funny to one of the lords of the land,
I rhymed the following letter to Lord Colchester, the
Postmaster-General:

> Most noble, influential lord,
> I hope some time you can afford
> To read a modest application—
> To grant an humble situation.
> The old postmaster of Skibbereen
> Disqualified has lately been,
> And many a strong and long petition
> Is filled to gain his lost position.
> I see each office-seeking creature:
> Him of the low, and lofty stature,
> And every idle, luckless wight
> All rushing by me as I write,
> Their pockets filled with paper white,
> Enough to tail a flying kite.
> And Alick seems in highest spirit —
> He learned, all would go by merit,
> And from his high qualification
> He'd get it, at examination.
> And this and that and th' other wrote,
> Unto the County members, both —
> Why, just, in fact, the whole agree
> That there's no chance at all for me.
> Ennobled, as to name and birth,
> And great your character and worth
> I know your Honor never can
> Condemn my writing as a man,
> And trust you'll give consideration
> To this my modest application.
> Though, for support, I too could stand
> Before some good, and great and grand,
> I scorn to travel through the land
> For signatures, with hat in hand,
> Demean myself, and send my party
> To beg to Deasy and McCarthy.

No; " starveling " first shall be my name
Ere I will sully thus my fame,
While I have leave to state my case
On this, before your Lordship's face.
And now, my lord, to tell you all
Relating to me—*personal* —
Like bards of high and low **degree**:
Of amative propensity ;
I married, just at twenty-one,
Since then four years are past and **gone,**
And every year that passed me o'er
An Irishman came on my floor.
I, with these youths, my time beguile,
Half-idle in my domicile,
Which in a large and central street,
For a post office would be meet.
I trust I'll meet with no disaster
Till you address me as " Postmaster."
Excuse, my lord, the wish most fervent
I have to be your lordship's servant.

Some days after I mailed that letter, I had a letter from Lord Colchester, telling me the position was not yet officially declared vacant, but, when it would be so declared, I would hear from him again.

I made no secret of getting that letter. Every one was sure I was booked for the postmastership. But I never got it, and never heard from Lord Colchester since. I suppose there was a very good reason for that; because five days after, I was a prisoner in the hands of the law.

CHAPTER XVIII.

A STAR-CHAMBER TRIAL.

On the evening of December the 5th, 1858, there was an entertainment at my house in Skibbereen in compliment to Dan McCartie, the brewer, who was leaving town, to accept the position of brewer in some Brewery in the County Galway. The company did not separate till about two o'clock. I went to bed, and was soon aroused from sleep by a thundering knocking at the hall door. When it was opened a dozen police-man rushed in and took charge of me and of every one in the house. Then every room was ransacked for papers, and for everything contraband of war—contra-band of peace or war, I may say. I stood in the draw-ing-room under arrest. The sergeant-in-command was smashing the drawers of the chiffonier in search of documents. My wife rushed toward him, crying out not to break the drawers, as she would get him the keys. He rudely shoved her away. One of the police-men near me was making a rush at him, but I caught him and pushed him back. He was a Kerryman named Moynahan; he is not living now, so I do him no harm by mentioning his name. Tom O'Shea was a guest at the entertainment, he lived at the Curragh, some dis-tance from the town. As there was an "eerie" place at the Steam-mill Cross, on his way home, where the 'good people" used to show themselves, I told him it was better for him to sleep in one of the rooms than to risk getting a "puck" by traveling that road at the dead hour of the night. He was occupying one of the bedrooms when the police ransacked the house. They made a prisoner of him, and he was taken with us to Cork Jail, though he never was a member of the Phœnix Society. He was simply a friend of mine and a friend of Dan McCartie, and was at the entertainment as such. 'Tis one of those misfortunes that come upon good people on account of keeping bad company. Some twenty men were arrested in Skibbereen that night. We were lodged in the police barracks till clear day in the morning. Then, with two policemen in charge of every one of us—every one of us handcuffed to a policeman—we were taken through the towns of Rosscarbery and Clonakilty, to Bandon, where we arrived about seven o'clock in the evening. We were put into the jail of Bandon that night, and put into cells that were flooded with water. We met here Jerrie Cullinane, Pat Cullinane, Denis O'Sullivan, and William O'Shea, who had been arrested in Bantry that morning. Next morning we were taken by train to the county jail in the city of Cork. We were two weeks in this jail, without any trial or any charge of any kind being made against us. Then, two stipendiary magistrates came into the jail, and opened court in a room in the jail, and charged us with treason of some kind to something belonging to England. We had McCarthy Downing for our attorney. Sullivan-goula was there to swear that we belonged to the Phœnix so-

ciety; that he saw us in the rooms of the society, and
that he saw me drilling three hundred men out near
the New bridge one night. He never saw such a drilling; there never was such a drilling took place; he
never saw a drilling of any kind amongst us anywhere.
'Tis true, that he saw many of us at the rooms of the
Phœnix Society, for he was lodging in the house where
those rooms were. We, having word from Kenmare,
that he was a suspicious character, and maybe sent
among us as an English spy, went in some numbers to
the rooms that night, out of curiosity, to see him. We
told Morty Downing to bring him in to the room, that
we may have some talk with him. In his sworn information against us, he swore against every man that
was in the room that night—swore that they were all
among the three hundred men that I was drilling out
at the New bridge that same night. He didn't leave a
single one of the company escape, that would be able
to contradict his perjury. Fitzmaurice, the stipendiary
magistrate, knew well that he was swearing falsely.
In fact, it was Fitzmaurice that made the swearing for
him; and made the plot for him. Davis, the stipendiary magistrate, knew well he was swearing falsely;
Davis belonged to Roscommon, and seemed to have
more of a conscience than Fitzmaurice, for he used to
occasionally address Goula, when McCarthy Downing
was cross examining him, and say " Oh, you unfortunate man! Remember you are testifying on your oath
before your God; " but 'twas all to no use; Goula
went along with his perjuries. Sir Matthew Barring-
ton, the Crown Prosecutor, was down from Dublin to

assist Goula in this star-chamber prosecution. To provide some kind of testimony that would make a corroboration of Goula's testimony, he put on the witness table one of the Skibbereen policemen, who swore that he saw Denis Downing marching through North street, Skibbereen "with a military step." In the cross-examination of this policeman, our attorney asked him, " Who was walking *with* Denis Downing ? " The policeman said, "No one was walking with him, but he was stepping out like a soldier." And so he was a soldier—by nature and instinct—as many an Irishman is ; he is the Captain Denis Downing who lost a leg at the battle of Gettysburg in America, and who had charge of the military company that were present at the execution of Mrs. Suratt in Washington, America. He was released from Cork Jail that day of the examination there ; but his brother Patrick—who afterward came to be in command of the Forty-second (Tammany) Regiment in the American war—was detained in jail till an appeal was made to the Queen's Bench for his release on bail. About half the number arrested in Bantry and Skibbereen were so released at this first examination in Cork Jail. The other half were kept in prison, and would not be released on bail. Then, an application for "release on bail" was made to the Court of Queen's Bench in Dublin, and all were released, except Billy O'Shea, Morty Moynahan, and myself.

The Tralee Assizes came on in March, 1859, and Dan O'Sullivan-agreem was convicted and sentenced to ten years' penal servitude. The Cork Assizes came on a week afterward. Our attorney came to us in

Cork Jail and told us that if we allowed our counsel
to put in a plea of "guilty" we would be released
without any sentence of punishment being passed
against us. "Plead guilty!" said we, "and confirm
the sentence on Dan Agreem, and put the stamp of
truth on all the perjuries Sullivan-goula swore against
us! No, we would not do it."

Patrick's Day came on; it was the day the Assizes
opened in Cork. Morty Moynahan, Billy O'Shea and
I were placed in the dock. Patrick J. Downing and
others who were out on bail were put in the dock too.
Patrick was telling us he had a grand time of it last
night down at Cove, in company with Poeri, and other
Italians, who had escaped from a convict ship in which
they were being transported to a penal colony. Those
are the Italian convicts about whose prison treatment
England's prime minister Gladstone shed rivers of tears
—that same prime boy who afterward treated Irishmen
in England's prisons far worse than King Bomba
treated Poeri and his companions. Gladstone starved
me till my flesh was rotting, for want of nourishment;
Gladstone chained me with my hands behind my back,
for thirty-five days at a time; Gladstone leaped upon
my chest, while I lay on the flat of my back in a black
hole cell of his prison. Poeri didn't experience such
treatment as that in the Italian prisons. Yet the great
Englishman could cry out his eyes for him. No wonder
those eyes of his got sore in the end!

(This chapter of my "Recollections" was published
in the *United Irishman* newspaper of May 8, 1897. I

am, this fourth day of June, 1898, revising all the chapters for publication into book form. The telegrams of the day announce that this Mr. Gladstone was buried in London this week—Rossa.)

That Patrick's Day, in the dock in Cork Jail, I was ready for trial; my companions were ready for trial; we had our witnesses ready; the people of my house were in court, to swear truly that I was in and around my house the hour Goula swore he saw me drilling 300 men one night. Our counsel also declared they were ready for trial. The Crown Counsel whispered with Keogh, and then Keogh announced that our trial was postponed to the next assizes; that the prisoners who were out on bail could remain out on bail; but that the prisoners who were brought into the dock from the jail, should be taken back to jail. Bail was offered for us by our counsel, but no bail would be taken. Morty Moynahan, Billy O'Shea, and I were taken back to the County Jail, where we remained till the following July.

A second application for release on bail was made for us to the court of Queen's Bench, in April, but it was refused. The Tory ministry, under Lord Derby as prime minister, were then in office. They were outvoted in parliament on some division; they "made an appeal to the country," and there was a general election. I was a voter of the County Cork, and I took it into my head to write to the English Lord Lieutenant of Ireland in Dublin Castle, telling him it was against the Constitution to hold an innocent voter in jail at such an important crisis, and keep him from recording

his vote on election day; that English law proclaims
every man innocent until he is adjudged guilty. I told
him he could have me taken to Skibbereen in charge of
his jailers, to record my vote on election day, or let me
out on parole that day, to return to jail the second next
day. I haven't that letter in my head. It was published in the newspapers afterward. The London
Spectator wrote a leading article about it. When I was
in London in 1895, I went into the *Spectator* office and
bought a copy of the paper of the date of May 14, 1859.
The following is the article it contains:

"THE GENEROUS PRISONER."

For a genuine love of freedom commend us to the
Irish gentleman (we should not like to apply any lower
title,) who being imprisoned in the county jail of Cork
on a charge of sedition,—he was a member of the
Phœnix Society—wished, nevertheless, being an elec-
tor, to record his vote at the late county election. He
addressed a petition to the Lord Lieutenant to this effect, and it certainly is a prize specimen of prison literature. We must premise that Jeremiah O'Donovan—
for this is his highborn name—is not a convicted prisoner; he is waiting for trial. He thus argues his case,
in a letter dated:

"COUNTY JAIL, CORK, April 30th.

"Need I remind your lordship how unconstitutional
it would be to deprive an innocent man of his voice in
this important crisis; and, such a deprivation of right
may entail the most disastrous results. For instance,

my lord, my support may be instrumental in returning an honorable and independent man to the Imperial
Parliament; the support of this honorable and independent man may be instrumental in maintaining Lord
Derby in office, and the retention of Lord Derby in
office may be the means of preventing the shedding of
oceans of blood, by affording him time and opportunity
for bringing the troublous affairs of Europe to a speedy
and pacific termination; whereas, opposite and most
disastrous results may follow from my inability to attend the polls."

He adds, with the most clinching logic:—"Your
lordship will perceive at a glance that mine is no ordi-
nary case." In counting up the Liberal and Derby-
ite gains and losses, we must admit at least that Lord
Derby, through adverse circumstances, lost one ardent
supporter, and if a war follows his lordship's resignation, we shall remember this new prophet Jeremiah.
How pleasantly the captive insinuates the excellent
use he will make of his vote, as the prisoner at Norfolk
Island, asking for the removal of the prohibition against
talking, said to the Governor, "Double if you will the
chains on our legs; increase the amount of our daily
work; reduce our rations even below the present mini-
mum, but do not, at least, deprive us of the power of
confessing to one another the justice of the punishment
we undergo." "Transport me if you will for sedition,"
cries O'Donovan, "but let me at least give one vote for
Lord Derby."

Blanqui, the imprisoned Republican, was released by
Napoleon, because he uttered generous sentiments; in

this country, we fear that even this good Tory must be tried, but at least he ought to be defended by Mr. Philip Rose, and his counsel feed out of the Carlton Club fund. He admits in the latter part of the letter, that an application for bail is pending, and that the Lord Lieutenant may, therefore, not like to interfere, but he continues with a kind considerateness that might hardly have been expected —

"Granting me permission would be much more convenient than the postponement of the election. Skibbereen is my polling place, so, as the distance is fifty miles from here, your Lordship will please have the "pass" made out for not less than three days, as it is a day's journey. To prevent any unnecessary trouble on my account, I will require no guard; my parole to return in three days, or for the time specified, will, I am sure, be sufficient guarantee for my safe keeping."

The Lord Lieutenant "has no power to comply with the petition." Such was the substance of the grave official reply. Red tape cannot laugh; but we feel kindly toward the pleasant fellow, light-hearted enough to poke fun at a viceroy from behind prison bars. We hope he will be proved innocent, and thus record his vote at the next county election as a real freeholder.

"Light-hearted enough to poke fun at a viceroy from behind prison bars," says the London man. Well, I did try to keep a light heart through all my prison days and nights. I got into my head, from one of the books in that library of my boyhood, that "that head is not properly constituted that cannot accustom itself to

whatever pillow the vicissitudes of fortune may place
under it." My pillow was hard enough many times,
and it was sometimes made a little harder by reproofs
from some of my companions for not behaving myself
more gravely in penal servitude. But I carried myself
through those hard times more in the spirit of that
poet, who sang :

> " Let me play the fool
>   With mirth and laughter, so let wrinkles come
>   And let my visage rather heat with wine
> That my heart cool with mortifying groans.
>   Why should a man whose blood is warm within
>   Sit like his grandsire, cut in alabaster
> Sleep when he wakes, and creep into the jaundice,
>   by growing peevish !
>
> " I tell thee what, ' O'Leary ! '
> There are a class of men
>   Whose very visages do cream and mantle like a
>   standing pond,
> And do a wilful stillness entertain,
>   On purpose to be dressed in an opinion
> Of wisdom, gravity, profound conceit,
>   As who should say :   ' I am Sir Oracle,'
> And when I ope' my mouth, let no dog bark."

And, to the fact that I did carry myself that way,
under prison difficulties, and have carried myself so,
under worldly difficulties—almost as harassing as the
prison ones—do I, under Providence, attribute my
good fortune that I am not entirely bald-headed at the
present time.

The Cork summer assizes were coming on at the end
of July. Our attorney was not sure that we would be
tried then either, or let out on bail, but might be kept

in prison till March, 1860, if we did not satisfy the now "liberal" government, and plead guilty. This again, we positively refused to do. A member of this new liberal government was Thomas O'Hagan who defended Dan O'Sullivan agreem, at the March Assizes in Tralee, and who afterward was raised to the peerage, with the title of "lord" or "baron" of Tullyhogue. He had had briefs for our defence, and he knew well that most of what was sworn against us was false. But he was now sworn in to work for England, and he should do his duty. It was before him Captain Mackey was tried in Cork City some years after. Our Irish parliamentary patriots affect to believe that it is better for the Irish people to be governed by English Liberals than by English Tories, but there is very little difference between them, so far as Ireland is concerned. Daniel O'Connell said that the Whigs were Tories when in office, and the Tories were Whigs when out of office. Dan was right. John Mitchel was right, too, in his dislike of having his friend, Thos. Francis Meagher run for member of Parliament in his native city of Waterford. This is what he says on the matter in his "Last Conquest of Ireland:"

If Mr. Meagher were in Parliament, men's eyes would be attracted hither once more; some hope of justice might again revive in this too-easily deluded people. The nobler his genius, the more earnest his zeal, the more conspicuous his patriotism, just the more mischief would he do, in propping up through another session, perhaps through another famine, the miserable delusion of a Parliamentary party."

Those expressions of men who moved in Irish national politics fifty years ago, and a hundred years ago hold good to-day. I have them in mind when I hear Irishmen talking of the great good it is to send good men to that London parliament.

In July, 1859, I got this letter from our attorney, McCarthy Downing:

(*Private*)   July 2, 1859.

DEAR SIR—A proposition has been again made to me, that if you all plead guilty, you will be released on your own recognizances. I am not at liberty to use this yet; but I have replied to say, that you have before rejected a similar offer from the late government, and that you would do the same now. Either on Saturday or Monday some decision will be come to. I have little hope of your being admitted to bail.

Yours truly,
MCCARTHY DOWNING.

I have the original of that letter, in the handwriting of Mr. Downing in my possession. When I visited America in May, 1863, I brought all my Fenian letters with me. When I was returning to Ireland in August, '63, I left those letters with John O'Mahony. When I came to America from English prisons in 1871, I got them back from him. That is how I am able to produce this letter now, and many other Irish letters.

A few days before the opening of the Cork Assizes Mr. Downing visited us in prison and told us that he had made terms for the release of the Kerry man by our pleading guilty. We told him it was a disgraceful

thing to do, anyway. He thought we should not consider ourselves better patriots than Arthur O'Connor,
and Thomas Addis Emmet, and Doctor McNevin, and
the other '98 men who pleaded guilty. He told us he
would call up to the jail to-morrow again, and, in the
meantime, we could talk the matter over among ourselves.

When he left us, Morty Moynahan, William O'Shea,
and I discussed the subject. They are dead. I will, in
justice to their memory, say, that they left the decision
to me; they were willing to do what I decided to do—
to stay in jail or get out of jail.

My business in Skibbereen was ruined; the creditors
came down on the house after my arrest; the ownership of the house got into law; the landlord whom I
had it rented from got beaten in the lawsuit, and the
other man, Carey, was declared the rightful owner.
He had to get immediate possession; and my wife, with
four young children, had to move into another house.
Letters from friends and neighbors were telling me it
was not a proper thing for me to remain in jail under
such circumstances—while I could get out of jail if I
wished.

But I had the cause of Ireland in my mind as well,
and to do anything that would hurt or injure that
cause anyway was not in my mind to do.

On that side of the situation, the Cork City men,
William O'Carroll and others who were in communication with us, gave us to understand that James Stephens had left Ireland after our arrest, that he was in
France, that no word was received from him, that the

work seemed dead, and that we may as well accept the
terms of release that were offered us. I have read the
"Memoirs of Fenianism," by Mr. John O'Leary. He
says word was sent to us *not* to plead guilty. I can
say, and say truly, that no such word ever reached us,
and that we were obliged to conclude that the work, or
the cause for which we were put in jail, was dead or
deserted. So, we decided to accept the terms of release offered, and we were let out of prison on the 27th
of July, 1859.

It was three months after, before Dan O'Sullivan-
agreen was released, and not until I had written a
strong letter to McCarthy Downing, telling him I
would write a letter to the newspapers charging
the government with another "breach of treaty" in
keeping the man in prison for whose release we had
stipulated.

Looking over some books and papers connected with
the terms of release made by the '98 men, I see there
was a breach of treaty in their case also. They stipulated for the release of many men who were arrested in
March and April, 1798 — before the "Rising." And,
after signing the papers, some of those men were
hanged, and more of them were kept in prison until the
year 1802.

Looking over the books and papers concerning the
'98 times, and the books and papers concerning our
own times, I do not see much change in the spirit of
England and Englishmen regarding Ireland and Irishmen. Those who are reading what I am writing will
not, I hope, consider I am doing much amiss in em-

bodying in "Rossa's Recollections," some of the experiences of Irishmen who were fighting against English rule in Ireland a hundred years ago, and comparing England's treachery and duplicity a hundred years ago, with her tyranny, treachery and duplicity to day. I find myself much in feeling with William Sampson, one of the '98 men, when he says, "If a man be injured, you add to his injuries by extorting false protestations from him, which must aggravate his feeling or wound his honor."

Those words from the grave strike the chords that hold me in life. England's holding me in prison from assizes to assizes, and not releasing me until I would acknowledge as true the perjuries that were sworn against me, has planted in my nature an ineradicable desire for personal satisfaction, and "If I could grasp the fires of hell to-day, I would seize them and hurl them into the face of my country's enemy." These words are the words of John Mitchel.

William Sampson of Antrim, arrested on the 12th of February, '98, in his "Memoirs" says:

"After several months of cruel and secret imprisonment, a Mr. Crawford, an attorney, was first permitted to break the spell of solitude, and enter my prison door. This gentleman had been employed in defence of Mr. Bond, Mr. Byrne, and others, for whose fate I was much interested."

At the time of that visit the rising had taken place and the fight was going on. From all the information the prisoners were allowed to get, they were led to believe that their people were getting the worst of it;

that aid which they expected had not come; that to
continue the fight was useless. The paper presented
to them to sign, amounted to an advice to the insur-
gents to submit and give up their arms, on stipulation
of general amnesty and the release of some seventy men
who were in prison on charges of high treason.

Sampson says, "Upwards of seventy prisoners, against
whom no evidence appeared, had signed an act of self-
devotion, and peace was likely to be the result. . . .
One day, as we were all together in the yard of the
bridewell, it was announced that the scaffold was erected
for the execution of William Byrne, the preservation of
whose life had been a principal motive for the signature of many of the prisoners to the agreement."

That was the famed Billy Byrne, of Ballymanus.

Sampson, after making some bitter remarks on the
tyranny that will imprison an innocent man, and keep
him in prison until he will sign a paper saying his jailers
were justified in doing all they did, says:

"If a man be injured, and knows and feels it, you
only add to his injuries by extorting false protestations
from him, which must aggravate his feeling or wound
his honor."

This book of Sampson's that I am quoting from was
printed by George Forman, at No. 24 Water street, Old
Slip, New York, in the year 1807. I have also before
me, as I write, the Dublin *United Ireland*, paper of
May 8, 1897, and I see in it the following passage that
bears on the subject of this chapter:

"It may not be generally known that the United
States Minister to London in 1798, was guilty, in con-

junction with his government, of one of the meanest
pieces of servility ever placed to the account of any
plenipotentiary or diplomatist.   When Arthur O'Connor, Thomas Addis Emmet, Dr. McNevin, and the
rest of the United Irish Leaders, who had brought the
Pitt Ministry to terms which honorably secured their
lives, were about to be released on condition of departing to America, an extraordinary obstacle presented
itself.   Rufus King, the American Minister, waited on
the English Ministry, and declared on behalf of his
government that the United States could not consent
to receive upon its soil men who had instigated the
recent dreadful rebellion in Ireland ! !

" In consequence of this action by these Anti-Irish
Yankees, the United Irish Leaders, instead of being
immediately released, were detained in confinement in
Scotland, in Fort George, until the year 1802."

It is surprising how, even up to the present day,
England can fashion into instruments of meanness and
servility the kind of men that America sends to represent her in London.   The one enemy in the world that
America has is England.   But then, England is the
great land of Christian civilization, and it may not be
a thing to be much wondered at that our Americans
whom we send to represent us in London become in a
short time somewhat civilized, and learn to love those
who hate them, bless those that curse them, and do
good to those that persecute and calumniate them.   All
very well, so long as that civilizing influence is confined to England and to our representatives to the government of England; but when that influence creeps

into the government of America, it is quite another thing.

This telegram from the seat of government that appeared in the morning papers of New York this day I am writing, shows it is creeping in ;—

WASHINGTON, May 26.—The approach of the Victorian Jubilee served as the theme for an eloquent invocation to-day by the blind chaplain of the Senate, Rev. Dr. Milburn.

" The long and illustrious reign of the gracious lady, Victoria, wife, mother, as well as sovereign," he said, " has shrined her into the hearts and reverence of true-hearted men and women around the world.

" May her last days be her best and happiest. Guide the councils of that realm and of our own beloved country, that, hand in hand, they may tread the path of conservative progress to the goal of Christian civilization."

Of toadyism of that kind, and of the kind that is introduced into the public schools of New York City in getting little children to vote to send their teachers to the Queen of England's jubilee celebration, the New York *Sun* says :

" Every American citizen who subscribes to the proposed preposterous tribute to Queen Victoria should be a marked man. His should be the fate of those Tories of the revolutionary epoch, who, for the betrayal of their country and shameful subservience to George III., were branded, ostracized, and eventually hounded out of their native land."

CHAPTER XIX.

COMING on the year 1860, the men of Skibbereen
took up the threads of the organization that were let
slip through the arrest of the Phœnix men in '58. We
met James Stephens in Bantry, and Mr. Dan McCartie, Morty Moynahan, and I, with the Bantry men, Denis
and William O'Sullivan, Pat, Jerrie and Michael
Cullinane, and some others, went in Denis O'Sullivan's yacht to Glengarriffe, where we had dinner at
Eccles' Hotel. Stephens paid for the dinner. Sailing
through Bantry bay, Stephens was smoking a pipe. I
remember his taking the pipe in his hand, and saying
he would not give the value of that dudeen for the
worth of Ireland to England after the death of Queen
Victoria; that she, in fact, would be the last English
reigning monarch of Ireland.

I don't know if he is of that opinion to-day. I do
not know did he speak that way that day in Bantry
bay, from the strong faith he had in the success of his
own movement. Anyway, the way he always spoke
to his men seemed to give them confidence that he was
able to go successfully through the work that was before him, and before them. That was one of his strong
points, as an organizer.

About the beginning of the year 1861, a letter from Jas. O'Mahony, of Bandon, announced to us that he and John O'Mahony would be in Rosscarbery on a certain day. Dan McCartie, Morty Moynahan and I went to Ross in Moynahan's coach. We met them; they had come to town in Banconi's long car. James O'Mahony returned to Bandon, and John O'Mahony came on to Skibbereen in our coach. He remained in town a few days. We called in from the country some of the most active workers we had in the organization, and introduced them to him. He was very much taken with the McCarthy-Sowney Centre, who told him he would not be satisfied with getting back his lands from the English, without getting back also the back rents that the robber-landlords had been drawing from his people for the past two hundred years.

That was the first time I met John O'Mahony. He made the impression on me that he was a man proud of his name and of his race. And I liked him for that. I like to see an Irishman proud of his people. It is seldom you will find such a man doing anything that would disgrace any one belonging to him. In my work of organizing in Ireland, I felt myself perfectly safe in dealing with men who were proud—no matter how poor they were—of belonging to the " Old Stock." I trusted them, and would trust them again.

Three years ago, in the summer of 1894, I was traveling with Michael Cusack, John Sarsfield Casey (since dead), and some others, by the Galtee Mountains, from Mitchelstown to Knocklong. We stopped at a village called Kilbehenny. We strolled into the graveyard,

and there I saw a large tomb, on the top slab of which
were cut the words:

"THIS IS THE TOMB OF THE O'MAHONYS."

That was the tomb of John O'Mahony's family.
Some days after, I stood within the walls of the ruins
of Muckross Abbey in Killarney, and there I saw another tomb (just like the one in Kilbehenny) on which
were graven the words:

"THIS IS THE TOMB OF THE O'DONOGHUES."

That was the tomb of the family of the O'Donoghue
of the Glens. That showed me that in old Irish times
John O'Mahony's family had the same standing among
the people as the other family. In those graveyards, I
thought of that Shane O'Neill of Tyrone who, when
offered an English title, said he was prouder of the
title of "The O'Neill" than of any title England could
give him.

In the year 1861 came on the funeral of Terence
Bellew McManus in Ireland. He was one of the '48
men who died in San Francisco. His body was brought
to Ireland. I had a letter from James Stephens asking
me to be one of the delegation who would accompany
the remains from Cork to Dublin.

The funeral procession in Cork City was on a Sunday. There was an immense gathering of people.
Passing along the quay, a ship in the river was flying
the English flag, and a little boy caused a little com-
motion by running and clambering up the ship's ropes
and poles, and tearing down that flag.

Coming on nightfall we were on board the train for Dublin. The delegation having charge of the coffin were in the train compartment next to the coffin. We were armed with pistols, as it was rumored that there might be some necessity for using them. Some men were, it seems, in favor of making the funeral the occasion of a " rising "; they thought it would arouse the country if the remains were taken to Slievenamon or some such historic place on the way between Cork and Dublin, and the people called upon to rally around, for God and for country. James Stephens was averse to that being done, and this is why he thought it well to have an armed guard to prevent its being done. I saw, a few nights after, that one of the men who favored the project, was James Roche, of Monaghan, who came from New York to Ireland the time of the funeral. The delegation from America and some others went to the Shelburne Hotel in Dublin to see William Smith O'Brien on some matter. Smith O'Brien was not in when we called. We were waiting in the coffee-room ; the subject of the " rising " came to be spoken of, Maurice O'Donoghue, of Kilmallock, one of the Dublin Centres, charged James Roche with being the prime mover in the project of the " rising." Hot words passed between them. Maurice moved angrily toward Roche ; Roche drew a cane sword. Some of us rushed between the two angry men, and matters were soon quieted down.

But on the railway route between Cork and Dublin, something occurred that I may make note of. When the train came to the Limerick Junction, there was a

stop there of several minutes.   A large crowd was on
the platform.   If there was an attempt to be made anywhere to take away the body, it was thought that
would be the place most likely for it.   James Stephens
was in the coach with us.   He had previously given
orders that the men of Tipperary town be there to prevent such a thing being done.   As the premonitory
bell rang for the starting of the train, Stephens called
on the men to kneel down and say a Pater and Ave
for the dead ; and, while the whole crowd was on their
knees, the train rolled out from the depot.

Arriving in Dublin before daybreak, the city seemed
ablaze with torch lights.   The remains of McManus
were taken in procession to the Mechanic's Institute,
where they lay in state until the following Sunday,
when, by a public funeral they were laid to rest in
Glasnevin.

During this week in Dublin I attended a banquet
given to Colonel Smith, Colonel O'Reilly, Colonel Doheny, Michael Cavanagh, Jerrie Cavanagh, and Captain Frank Welpley, the members of the American
delegation, and I called upon some friends I had been
in correspondence with.   The dinner had been at Cof-
fey's or Carey's Hotel in Bridge street.   Father Conway, of Mayo, who was staying at the hotel, attended
it.   When the toasts and speech-making commenced, he
was called upon to speak.   He spoke of the sad state
of his part of the country, and said that he was then
traveling on a mission to collect funds for some parishioners of his who were under sentence of eviction—
dwelling particularly upon one case, that of a man and

his wife who had eight young children. "Put my name down for ten pounds," said Michael Doheny. The priest taking his notebook, commenced to write. "Hold," said Doheny. "The ten pounds is to buy a gun, powder and ball for the man who is to be evicted, that he may shoot whoever comes to put him out of his house." The priest shut up his notebook.

I had been for five or six years previously in correspondence with Professor John O'Donovan, the Irish scholar, and I called in to Trinity College to see him. In the room with him was Professor Eugene O'Curry. I had a long talk with them. John O'Donovan asked me to tea next night at his home, No. 136 North Buckingham street; "and you," said he to O'Curry, "you try and come up." "No," said O'Curry, "but let Rossa come to my house the night after." I told him I would not be in Dublin the night after, as I should leave for home. O'Curry was a big, stout man, over six feet tall. O'Donovan was a small man. Those two men were dead, one year after that day I was speaking to them. They were married to two sisters of the name of Broughton—"of Cromwellian descent," as John O'Donovan says to me in one of his letters, wherein he speaks of the mother of his seven sons—Mary Anne Broughton.

I went to John O'Donovan's house that evening, and met there Father Meehan, the author of that book called "The Confederation of Kilkenny." We talked of Fenianism, or of the cause for which I had been lately in Cork Jail. I, as well as I could, justified my belonging to that cause—not that my host or the priest said anything in condemnation of the cause—but I was surprised when I heard John O'Donovan say in the priest's presence—" *the priests won't let the people fight.*" The priest said nothing.

About twelve o'clock a coach came to take him home. I went in the coach with him, and he let me down at my hotel in Lower Bridge street. His chapel in the parish of Sts. Michael and John is near that street.

I had been at John O'Donovan's house on some other occasions on which I visited Dublin before this time of the McManus funeral. The seven sons would be around us. He would send John and Edmond to the library to bring some rare Irish books to show me. "Are those boys studying the Irish language?" said I. "No," said he. "I cannot get them to care anything about it, though they are smart enough at Greek and Latin." I fear that my early acquaintanceship with those boys had something to do with disturbing the serenity of their lives in after years; because when I came to live in Dublin in 1863 I used to visit their house, and they used to come to the *Irish People* office to see me. They got initiated into the I. R. B. movement, and got into prison the time of the arrests. John, the eldest was drowned in St. Louis; Edmond, the second, the famed war correspondent, was lost in Asia or Africa; and I saw William, the third son, buried in Calvary Cemetery, New York.

I have among my papers twenty or thirty of the letters of John O'Donovan, that I received from him between the years of 1853 and 1863. They are among my old papers. I cannot get them now. I may get

them before I put these " Recollections " in book form.
If I do, I will print a few of them in the book. One
letter in particular has some passages in it that I cannot thoroughly understand. It speaks of the Irish people and the Irish cause ; of Daniel O'Connell and of
Doctor Doyle, and it says :

" There have been no two Irishmen of this century
that despised the Irish race and the Irish character
more than did Daniel O'Connell and the late Doctor
Doyle, bishop of Kildare and Leighlin. Doctor Miley,
in whose hands O'Connel died, told me this at *this*
table, and I firmly believe it."

Now, the puzzle to me is : Why was that so ? Why
did they despise the Irish race and the Irish character ?
I make many guesses at answering the question, and
the only answer reasonable to myself, that I can get,
is, that the Irish people made it a sin to themselves
to do anything that could be done in the way of
striking down English rule, and striking down everything and every one that belonged to English rule in
Ireland.

The McManus funeral tended very much to increase
the strength of the Fenian movement. Men from
Leinster, Ulster, Munster and Connaught met in Dublin who never met each other before. They talked of
the old cause, and of the national spirit in their respec-
tive provinces, and each went back to his home,
strengthened for more vigorous work. England's eyes
were somewhat opened, too, to the increasing danger to
her rule in Ireland, and shaped herself accordingly. In
the policy of government she is not blind to what passes

before her eyes; she knows how averse to the interests of her rule it is to allow the people to come together and understand each other, and hence, those many Convention or anti-Convention laws that she passed for Ireland in her day. In the days of the *United Irishmen*, secret committees of the Houses of Lords and Commons were appointed to make inquiries into the state of Ireland. A committee of the Lords sat in 1793, and a joint committee of Lords and Commons sat in 1897. They summoned before them every one they thought could give information, and every one who refused to answer their questions was sent to jail.

On the 17th of May, 1797, the English governors at Dublin Castle issued a proclamation in which they said : "Whereas, within this Kingdom a seditious and traitorous conspiracy, by a number of persons styling themselves United Irishmen exists, and whereas, for the execution of their wicked designs, they have planned means of open violence, and formed secret arrangement for raising, arming, and paying a disciplined force, and, in furtherance of their purposes, have frequently assembled in great and unusual numbers, under the colorable pretext of planting or digging potatoes, attending funerals and the like," etc. "And we do strictly forewarn persons from meeting in any unusual numbers, under the plausible or colorable pretext as aforesaid, or any other whatsoever."

So, that while James Stephens, for his side of the house, saw the good and the necessity of bringing his chief men together at the McManus funeral, the other side of the house, with all the experience of government they have on record, were pretty well able to give a good guess at what it all meant.

Not that England doesn't know that the mass of the Irish people are always discontented, disaffected and rebellious—and have reasons to be so—but that they would be organized into a body actively preparing for fight is what strikes terror to her heart. The Irish Revolutionary Brotherhood were so preparing, secretly preparing, but circumstances connected with the necessity of receiving a promised or expected assistance from America—that was not received—which circumstances I will show further on—developed things so, that the organization soon became as much a public one as a private one. We were assailed publicly in many ways and by many parties, and we had to defend ourselves publicly, and thus show ourselves to our enemies as well as to our friends. Twenty-five years ago I wrote a book called " O'Donovan Rossa's Prison Life." I see in it some passages in relation to those times of 1861, 1862 and 1863, and I cannot do better than reproduce them here. After that, I will introduce some letters, I have, written by John O'Mahony, James Stephens, and others, that give a very fair idea of the difficulties that beset the Irish Revolutionary Brotherhood in Ireland, and Fenianism in America, at the starting of the movement.

Rossa's book says:

" I found the people under the impression that if any kind of military weapon was found with them they would be sent to jail. Is was hard to disabuse them of this, and I took a practical method of doing it.

"I was in possession of an Enfield rifle and bayonet, a sword, and an old Croppy pike, with a hook and hatchet on it, formidable enough to frighten any coward, and these I hung up in a conspicuous part of my store; and yet this would not even satisfy some that they could keep these articles with impunity, and I had many a wise head giving me advice. But when I have satisfied myself that a thing is right, and I make up my mind to do it, I can listen very attentively to those who, in kindness, would advise me, for the purpose of dissuading me from a course inimical, perhaps, to my own interests, while at the same time I can be firm in my resolve to have my own way as soon as my adviser is gone. The arms remained in their place, and on fair days and market days it was amusing to see young peasants bringing in their companions to see the sight. "*Feuch! feuch!* Look! look!" would be the first exclamation on entering the shop; and never did artist survey a work of art more composedly than would some of those boys leaning on their elbows on the counter, admire the treasured weapons they longed to use one day in defence of the cause of their father-land.

"At the end of a few years the people were fully persuaded that they could keep arms in defiance of the police. It would answer the ends of government very well, if the authorities by keeping the people scared could keep them unarmed without the passing of arms acts and other repressive measures, that look so very ugly to the world. If England could keep her face clean—if she could carry the phylacteries—if she could have the Bible on her lips and the devil in her deeds, without any of the devil's work being seen, she would be in her glory.

"My pikes were doing great mischief in the community it seems, and rumors were going around that others were getting pikes, too. Tim Duggan, whom I spoke of as being in Cork Jail was employed in my shop. Tim should always be employed at some mischief, and taking down the pikes one day to take some of the rust off them, no place would satisfy him to sit burnishing them but outside the door. This he did to annoy a very officious sergeant-of-the-police, named Brosnahan, who was on duty outside the store. Next day I was sent for by my friend McCarthy Downing, who was Chairman of the Town Commissioners, and magistrate of the town. He told me that the magistrates were after having a meeting, and had a long talk about what occurred the day before. Brosnahan represented that not alone was Tim Duggan cleaning the pikes, but showing the people how they could be used with effect—'what beautiful things they were for frightening exterminating landlords and all other tools of tyranny. Mr. Downing asked me if I would deliver up the arms, and I said, certainly not. He said the magistrates were about to make a report to the Castle of the matter. I said I did not care what reports they made; the law allowed me to hold such things, and hold them I would while the district was not 'proclaimed.'

"Now," added he, "for peace sake, I ask you, as a personal favor, to give them up to me; I will keep them for you in my own house, and I pledge you my

word that when you want them, I will give them to
you."

" Well," replied I, "as you make so serious a matter
of it, you can have them."

" I went home ; I put the pike on my shoulder, and
gave the rifle to William (Croppy) McCarthy. It was a
market day, and both of us walked through the town,
and showed the people we could carry arms, so that we
made the act of surrender as glorious as possible to our
cause, and as disagreeable as it could be to the stipen-
diaries of England.

" These are small things to chronicle, but it is in small
things that the enemy shows a very wary diligence to
crush us. Inch by inch she pursues us, and no spark
of manhood appears anywhere in the land that she has
not recourse to her petty arts to extinguish it.

" In the spring of 1863, the Poles were struggling
against their tyranny, and we conceived the idea of
having a meeting of sympathy for them in Skibbereen,
and carried it out. We prepared torchlights and republican banners, and we issued private orders to have
some of our best men, in from the country. The authorities were getting alarmed, and they issued orders
to have a large force of police congregated in the town
on the appointed night. During the day the ' peelers,'
as I may inoffensively call them, were pouring in, and
as they passed by the several roads, the peasantry
crowded in after them. The rumor went around that
we were to be slaughtered, and men from the country
came to see the fun. The town was full of ' peelers '
and peasants ; and, to have another stroke at the ' big

fellows' we got Landbills stuck off, calling upon the people not to say an offensive word to any of the police; that they were Irishmen, like ourselves, and only obliged from circumstances to *appear* our enemies. We posted these bills, and got boys to put them into the hands of police. There were six magistrates in the town; and the stipendiary one, O'Connell—a member of the 'Liberator's' family—was in command of the forces. They thought to intimidate us from carrying out the programme of our procession, and we felt bound to maintain the confidence of our people by proceeding according to our announcement. They recognized in our meeting of sympathy for the Poles a meeting of organized hostility against England; they knew that bringing the masses together, and allowing them to see their strength and union would create confidence, and that is what they wanted to kill. And, to be candid, it was necessary for us to humor the peculiarities of our people some way. They are ever ready to fight; ever impatient for the 'time,' and when the time is long coming, they are drooping and restless without stimulants.

"The officers of arrangement moved from the committee-rooms. The committee were armed with wands, and marched in front, toward the place where the vast assembly of people were formed in line of procession with torches in their hands.

"The wives of the police, and the police themselves, had been sent to the mothers of young men on the committee, telling them that the police had orders to fire on us; and the mothers implored us, on their knees, to give up our project. We went on; and, as we proceeded to move, the magistrates came in front of us, with the police behind them, and stopped the route of our march. The Castle agent O'Connell addressing himself to Brosnahan, asked —

"Who are the leaders of this tumult?"

And the police sergeant answered —

"Here, they are sir; Dan McCartie, Mortimer Moynahan, Jerrie Crowley, Con Callahan, O'Donovan Rossa, James O'Keefe, etc."

O'Connell—"I order this assembly to disperse."

Committee—"For what?"

"For it is disturbing the peace of the town."

"It is you who are disturbing the peace of the town. We are peaceful citizens, met here to demonstrate our sympathy for a people struggling against tyranny. Do you say we have no right to do so, or that we must not walk the streets?"

"You are meeting in an illegal manner; I will now read the Riot Act, and if you do not disperse before fifteen minutes, you have only to take the consequence."

He read the Riot Act; after which we asked —

"What do you see illegal in our procession?"

"That red flag," pointing to an equilateral triangle banner.

The Committee—"Take that flag down. Now, Mr. O'Connell, do you see anything else illegal?"

O'Connell—"Those transparencies, with the mottoes."

Committee—"Take away those transparencies. Do you see anything else illegal, Mr. O'Connell?"

"Those torchlights."

Committee—"Put out those torchlights. Do you see anything else illegal?"

"You had better disperse."

Committee—"Do you tell us, now, that you came here with your authority and your armed force to tell us that we must not walk through the streets of Skibbereen?"

"I do not."

The committee ordered the band to play up "Garryowen" and march on. The boys did so; the magistrates moved aside; the police behind them opened way, and the procession marched twice through the streets, and ended the demonstration by the reading of an address.

The marriage of England's Prince of Wales, in '63, came on a few nights after we had the Polish sympathy meeting in Skibbereen, and some of the loyal people of the town illuminated their houses. There was a public newsroom in the "Prince of Wales' Hotel," and as the loyalists had paid the proprietor seven pounds for illuminating the house, those of them who were members of the newsroom held a private meeting, and passed a resolution that the windows of that room be illuminated too.

So they were illuminated. But some of the committee of the Polish procession were members of the newsroom, and when they heard that it was aflame with loyalty, they went to the room; called a meeting; pointed to one of the rules which excluded politics from the place, and denounced those who held a hole-and-corner meeting to introduce them there that day. A crowd was outside the hotel listening to the fight inside; they cheered and groaned, according as the several speakers spoke. One of the loyalists inside said it was "a mob meeting" they had in the room. "Then we may as well have mob law," said I, and making for the windows, I tore down the transparencies, the fil-dols and the English flags, and threw them into the street.

The I. R. B. movement generated a spirit of manhood in the land that the enemy could not crush, and cannot crush, if we do not prove ourselves dastards. Acts of hostility, similar to those I speak of, were occurring everywhere; and if the people only had arms to back their spirit, they would do something worthy of them.

The Gladstones know this, and use all their ingenuity to keep the dangerous weapons from the people, "lest," as one of them said lately, "the people would hurt themselves." But, "beg, borrow or steal" them, we must have arms before we can have our own again.

After those occurrences in Skibbereen, the Stipendiary Magistrate O'Connell, and Potter, the Police Inspector, came to me, and said they had instructions to give me notice that if I " did not cease from disturbing the community," I would be called up for sentence, pursuant to the terms of my "plea of guilty." I told them they should first show that I violated any of those terms; that they should prove me guilty of the practice of drilling, and of the other things sworn against me at the time of my imprisonment; but while to their eyes I was acting within their own law, I did not care about their threats.

CHAPTER XX.

THE STRUGGLE AGAINST THE ENEMY.

DAN HALLAHAN, John O'Gorman, Willie O'Gorman, William McCarthy, Jerrie O'Donovan, John Hennigan, Jerrie O'Meara and others who had charge of the flags the night of the Polish demonstration, took them to my house. They went up to the roof and planted them on the chimneys. That was more high-treason. But I let the flags fly, and would not haul them down—much to the alarm of the men of the English garrison who had "charge of the peace" of the community. McCarthy Downing, trying to reason me out of any rebellious propensities those days, told me what a strong '48 man he was—how affectionately he cherished the possession of a green cap the '48 men gave him when they were "on the run," and how he himself would be the first man to handle a pike—if *he thought 'twould be of any use.* But with England's strong army and navy, it was nothing but folly for us to think we could do anything against her wonderful power. That is the kind of talk that is of most use to England in Ireland; particularly when it comes from men who have the character of being patriots. And we have many such patriots among us to-day; not alone in Ireland, but in America, and in every other land to which the Irish race is driven—patriots who

251

will do anything to free Ireland but the one thing that MUST be done before she is freed. And to say that she cannot be freed by force is something that no manly Irishman should say—something he should not allow a thought of to enter his mind, while he has it in his power to grasp all these resources of war, or "resources of civilization" that England has at her command for the subjugation of Ireland and other nations. England knows well that Irishmen have it in their power to bring her to her knees, if they fight her with her own weapons, and that is why she labors so insidiously to put the brand of illegality, infamy, and barbarity upon such instruments of war in their hands as in her hands she calls "resources of civilization." "England," said Gladstone to Parnell, "has yet in reserve for Ireland the resources of civilization." Ireland has such "re-sources" too; and, when it comes to a fight—as come it must—the Parnells must be sure to use them in England as the Gladstones will be sure to use them in Ireland. Then, may there be an eye for an eye, a tooth for a tooth, and blood for blood—with an opening for Macauley's New Zealander in London. When I was in Ireland three years ago, I got a letter from Father John O'Brien of Ardfield, Clonakilty, inviting me to spend some time with him in memory of old times in Skib-bereen. He was a curate in the town in my time there. The boys in the shop told me one day that Father O'Brien was in looking for me, and left word to have me call up to his house. I called up; in answer to my knock on the rapper, Kittie the housekeeper opened the door. "Kittie," said I, "is Father O'Brien in?" "Yes," said he, speaking from the head of the stairs, "Is that Rossa? Come upstairs." I went upstairs: sat with him for two or three hours; had lunch with him, and lots of talk upon the questions of the day. The question of the day at that time was Fenianism, and we talked it over. "Why is it," said I, "that I can go to confession and get absolution, and that Dan Hallahan and Simon Donovan and others will be turned away from the confessional unless they give up the Society?" "Oh," said he, "in that matter the Church has a discretionary power which it uses according to its judgment. The historical experience of the Church regarding political secret societies is, that no matter how good the purpose for which such societies are started, the control of them generally gets into the hands of men who use them against the Church, and not in the interest of any good purpose in the name of which young men are drawn into them. Where we meet a man who, we think, cannot be used against the Church, we use our discretionary power to admit him to the sacraments; when our judgment tells us it may be proper to advise other penitents to have nothing to do with the society, and to discontinue membership in it, we so advise." Then he quoted some of the Church doctrine in those words of St. Augustine:—"In necessariis, unitas; in non-necessariis, libertas; in omnibus, caritas.—In essentials, unity; in non-essentials, liberty; in all things, charity."

I do not wonder that any Irish priest would turn away from his confessional any Irishman who would kneel at it, confessing to him as one of his sins, that

he had taken a pledge or an oath to fight as a soldier
for the freedom of his country. If I was a priest myself, I would tell the poor slave to give up sinning.
When I came home that day after my visit to Father
O'Brien, I found the whole house laughing at me, and
calling me " fool, fool." It was the 1st of April,
" Fool's Day " in Ireland ; my people made a " fool "
of me in sending me to see Father O'Brien, for he had
never been in, asking to see me. But no matter for
that ; it was a pleasant visit, and the priest laughed
heartily afterward when I was telling him how I had
been " fooled " into it.

One Sunday afternoon, in this month of April, 1863,
I, with some of the boys of the town, made a visit to
Union Hall, a seaside village, some four miles to the
south of Skibbereen. We remained there till eleven
o'clock at night ; met many men of the district, and
enlivened the place with speech, recitation and song.
Next morning Kit-na-Carraiga and a few more of the
wives of the Myross fishermen came in to my shop and
told me as they were passing through Union Hall they
met the magistrate, John Limerick ; that he was raging
mad, and swearing that if he caught Jerrie-na-Phœnix
and his crowd in Union Hall again, they would not
leave it as they left yesterday. Kit spoke in Irish, and
I said to her : " Kit! Innis do a maireach, go riaghmid
sios aris de Domhnaig seo chughain." " Kit! tell him
to-morrow that we will go down again next Sunday."

Next Sunday came, and we were as good as our
word.

After mass, some twenty of us left the town, and

broke into the fields. We started hares and chased them with our screeching. Many of the farmers' sons on the way joined us, and, as we were entering Union Hall, we had a pretty big crowd. But there was a far bigger crowd in the village. It was full of people, because all the morning, police had been coming in on every road from the surrounding police stations, and the people followed the police. The threat of John Limerick, the magistrate, had gone out, and the people came in to see what would be the result. Five or six of the magistrates of the district had come in too. Across the little harbor from Glandore we saw a fleet of boats facing for Union Hall. They conveyed men from Ross, some three miles at the other side of Glandore. As the boats approached our quay John Limerick stood on it, and forbade them to land. "Boys," said I, "never mind what this man says; this is a part of Ireland, your native land, and you have as good right to tread its soil as he has."

With that, Pat Donovan (now in New York). jumped from his boat into the shallow shoal water; others followed him; Limerick left the quay, and they marched through the village, with their band playing, up to the house of Father Kingston.

Limerick gave orders to close all the public houses in the village. I was in at the house of Mrs. Collins, an aunt-in-law of mine, when the police came in, with orders to clear the house. "If you tell me to go out," said I to Mrs. Collins, "I will go out." "I won't turn you out of my house," said she. "If you put your hands on me, and tell me to leave this house," said I to

Sergeant William Curran, or to Dockery (who now keeps a hotel in Queenstown), "I will leave it." "I won't put my hand on you," said the policeman; "my orders are to have Mrs. Collins clear the house, and I can't do more." The police went out; I and my friends went out after them, telling Mrs. Collins it was better for her to close up, for Limerick was lord of the manor, and lord of her license to keep house.

The police in the street arrested Patrick Donovan. Some girls named Dillon, first cousins of his, snatched him away from the police and rushed him into their house. John Limerick read the Riot Act. Potter, the Chief of Police gave the order of "fix bayonets," et cetera. The women in the windows, at each side of the street, were screaming in alarm. Patrick Spillane, the Master-instructor of the Skibbereen band (now in Rochester, N. Y.), stood up in his carriage and addressed the people, denouncing the village tyranny they were witnessing; Dan. O'Donoghue, one of the bandsmen (a Protestant), in a scuffle with a policeman, broke his trombone. I asked Potter, the Chief of Police, what did he mean to do now, with his drawn swords and fixed bayonets? He said he meant to quell this riot. I told him there was no riot but what was made by Mr. Limerick.

Five or six other magistrates were there. I knew Doctor Somerville and John Sidney Townsend. I got talking to them; they told me to go home. I told them I would stay at home that day only that threats from John Limerick had been coming to my house all the week that if I set my foot in Union Hall again it would be worse for me.

Things gradually quieted down; the police were ordered off the ground, and peace was restored. There were lots of summonses next day; McCarthy Downing was employed for our defence, and some fines were adjudged against a few of the people. But that was not the worst of it. Many of them who filled situations lost their places. A few national schoolmasters, who were in the village that day were suspended, and did not teach school in Ireland since. One of them was John O'Driscoll, who died in Boston a few years ago.

A few days after this Union Hall affair I called into the Beecher Arms Hotel in Skibbereen and met John Sydney Townsend. We talked of the affair of the previous Sunday. I said affairs had come to a queer pass when an Irishman, in his own country, would be forbidden to tread its soil. Why, said I, if you yourself were in a foreign land, and if any one insulted you because that you were an Irishman, you would resent the insult. He took off his coat and his vest, took hold of my hand and placed it on his shoulder, to let me feel his shoulder-blade that was out of joint. "I got that," said he, "in Australia, in a fight with fellows that were running down the Irish." He got that middle name, Sidney, from having lived several years in Sydney, Australia. What a pity it is that men like him will not fight for Ireland in Ireland. Most of them are found on the side of Ireland's deadliest enemy—their enemy, too, if they would only rightly understand it.-

The spirit of the men in the south of Ireland was
running ahead of the times—running into fight with
the laws of the English enemy before the Fenian organization in America or Ireland had made any adequate
preparation for a successful fight. Many of the men
had gone to America, and many of them went into the
American army, to learn the soldier's glorious trade—
as much for the benefit of Ireland's freedom as for the
benefit of America's freedom. Patrick Downing,
Denis Downing and William O'Shea were in Cork
Jail with me in 1859. In 1863 I made a visit to
America and saw Patrick Downing, Lieutenant-Colonel
of the Forty-second Tammany Regiment; William
O'Shea, captain in the same regiment; Denis Downing,
captain in a Buffalo regiment, and I saw Michael
O'Brien, the Manchester martyr, enlisted into a Jersey
regiment. O'Shea was killed in the war. Denis Downing lost a leg at the battle of Gettysburg, Patrick Downing was wounded many times. All dead now, and many
more dead, who with their last breath, wished it was in
a fight for Ireland against England they were dying.
I'll go back to Skibbereen for a while.

Things were getting so hot there in the year 1863,
and there was in the line of business and employment,
such an English boycott upon men who were suspected
of belonging to the organization that many of them left
the town and went to America. I left the town myself, and went with a party of them—Dan Hallahan,
Wm. McCarthy, Simon O'Donovan, John O'Gorman,
Jerrie O'Meara, and others, having made arrangements
with my family to be away a few months.

The word "boycott" was not in the English language then, but the practice of the work it represents had been put in active use against me by the landlords of the district. None of them would deal with me or enter my shop. Small loss that, so far as it concerned the landlords personally. But when it came to be known all around that any tenant who would enter my shop would incur the displeasure of the landlord and the landlord's agent, it was a different thing; it was there I felt their power against me. I sold all kinds of farm seeds, and I found some farmers, who lived five miles out of town, coming in and waking me up in the dead hour of night to buy their supply of seeds from me. Then, some of the landlords that were given to the encouragement of the cultivation of crops for the feeding of cattle, would give orders to the farmers for all kinds of clover and grass seeds, and would pay the shopkeeper's bills for those seeds. I got my due share of those orders during some years; but all at once they ceased coming to me, just as if a council meeting of landlords had been held, and it was decided that no orders be given on my house, and no bills for seeds be paid that were contracted in my house.

I have a letter here by me that was written to me, this time by one of the landlords, who was a kind of friend of mine. He was the biggest man in the country; was often high sheriff, and lord lieutenant of the county, as stately and handsome-looking a man as you could see in a day's walk. He had some regard or liking for me, as you may judge by this letter of his:

O'DONOVAN ROSSA—You slipped out of court yesterday before I could hand you my debt. I am sorry I should have been so long on your black books.

I trust you will pardon me for saying I was sorry at what took place in court yesterday. Men of mind and intellect, as you appear to possess, should not display their powers in trifles. Now, suppose there was a revolution to your very heart's content, and that you were placed in the very position of your warmest aspirations, would it tell well that O'Donovan Rossa had been whistling and knocking at doors to annoy the police.

Believe me, though I do not wish you success in the foregoing, that I wish you prosperity in your worldly welfare. I am truly

T. SOMERVILLE.

The "bill" in question was for seed supplied to the farm steward in his employment.

The "whistling and knocking at doors" in question, I had nothing to do with, and know nothing about. The boys had been out in the woods one night drilling, I suppose. When they had done, they scattered, and came home by different roads. One party of them coming into town, knew that the police were out of town, watching after moonlighters. They knew there was only one policeman left in the police barrack, and that he should stay in it; so when they were passing the house of the head inspector, one of them gave a runaway knock on the rapper. I suppose he thought it was a good joke on the police, who were out looking for Fenians.

Some one saw me passing through the street that night, and I was summoned with others. Tom Somerville was chairman of the magistrates, and I showed him that I had nothing to do with knocking at any one's door on the occasion.

That you may not go guessing wrongly as to how or why Tom Somerville could or should come to grow any friendship or regard for me, I may as well give you my own guess on the subject. He had an only son, who was a captain or major in the English army in the Crimean war in the year 1854. During the days of the fighting, news came that the son was killed in one of battles, and there was much public sympathy with the father. Then news came that the son was living. After that came the news that the war was over, and that the son was coming home. There was preparation in the town for giving him a "welcome home."

John Powers Hayes, the local poet asked me to help him out with some lines of welcome he was writing in acrostic form on "Major Thomas Somerville." I helped him, and then I came in for getting the credit of doing the whole thing. So much so, that after that Tom Somerville was disposed to be fairly friendly with me whenever I came his way. I remember that the last five lines of that acrostic, based on the five last letters of the word "Somerville," ran this way:

Valor's representative! Skibbereen will gladly greet him,
Imbued with feelings of respect she joyfully will meet him;
Loudly to home she'll welcome him—old friends, old scenes, say
    rather,
Like to one risen from the dead, around him she will gather,
Enjoying to see that he again has met his honored father.

And now I have to leave Skibbereen—leave it for good—leave it forever, I may say. Coming on June, 1863, I came to America, having an intention to go back in a few months' time to live in Skibbereen. I never went back to make my home there. Farther on you will learn, how and why this came to pass.

But I often visit there when far away, just as many another Irish exile visits through dreamland, the old hearth of the old home, and sees again the old landmarks of the days of his youth in the old land.

"Many another Irish exile," did I say?—did I call myself an "exile"?—an Irishman in New York, an "exile"! Yes; and the word, and all the meanings of the word, come naturally to me, and run freely from my mind into this paper. My mother buried in America, all my brothers and sisters buried in America; twelve of my children born in America—and yet I cannot feel that America is my country; I am made to feel that I am a stranger here, and I am made to see that the English power, and the English influence and the English hate, and the English boycott against the Irish-Irishmen is to-day as active in America as it is in Ireland. I am also made to see England engaged in her old game of employing dirty Irishmen to do some of the dirty work that she finds it necessary to have done, to hold Ireland in thrall.

At the opening of this chapter I said something about Father John O'Brien in connection with secret societies, and his telling me that bad men generally got to the head of them, who did not use them for good, but for bad. Whatever more I am to say in this book on that subject, I preface it here by saying I am strongly of the opinion that much of the preparatory work that is necessary to be done to make Ireland free must be done in secret; and I am also strongly of the opinion that that work can be done successfully in spite of all the false and infamous Irishmen that England can buy into her service. My eyes are not at all shut to the fact that the spy service is one branch of the English service into which England recruits Irishmen for the purpose of maintaining her hold on Ireland. That branch has to be taken into consideration by revolutionary Irishmen, just as much as the police branch, or the soldier branch of the English service in Ireland has to be taken into consideration. No, I am not at all blind in that light. I have seen too many of those spies during the past fifty years, and have too many times been marked by their employers for one of their victims, to doubt their ubiquity or make light of their labors. Some of them intrigued themselves into very close companionship with me in Irish societies. I caught them trying to kill the work I was trying to do, and trying to kill myself. That doesn't frighten me, though there is something disheartening in the situation of things during the past twenty years. The paralyzation of the Irish revolutionary movement, has been developed to such an extent, the work connected with its resolves has been shunted so far aside, that I cannot help asking myself is it the hand of England that is doing all this; is it the will of England that is working to have nothing done that will hurt or harm England.

I see the hand of England at work during those

twenty years to kill myself out of Irish life, and I see very efficient aid to that end given by some men in Irish societies in America. I see the Dudley woman sent out to assassinate me. I see Labouchere employed to ask questions in the English House of Commons that proclaim me through the world an English spy in the pay of England. That is the English side of the work. The Irish side of the work is this: I have been three times expelled from the membership in the Irish revolutionary societies of America by the controlling powers of those societies. No charges preferred against me, no trial, or no summons to appear for trial. A simple announcement made that O'Donovan Rossa is "expelled" or suspended. That announcement, virtually declaring me a traitor, is sent to every club of the organization throughout the nation, and to every affiliation it has in foreign lands. I met it in many places in England and Ireland. I met it in many places in America. The assassin bullet in my body bespeaks an agency less infamous than the agency that would so assassinate my character—a character that has come to me through some unselfish labor—and much suffering therefor—for Ireland's freedom. I do not see that the moral assassins have done anything for the last twenty years that would enable me to give them the benefit of thinking they are not in the same employment as the Dudley assassins. I print the following two letters as samples of the product of their work:

SAN JUAN, January 1, 1887.
O'DONOVAN ROSSA—Enclosed find $2 in payment

for your paper. Don't send it after the receipt of this letter, for I think you are a traitor, and a British spy.

M. SULLIVAN.

ROCHESTER, N. Y., Aug. 13, 1888.

O'DONOVAN ROSSA :

SIR—For some time past you have been sending your papers to my brother. He says he has notified you to cut them off. He says, and I say with him, that your sheet has never done any good for Ireland, and you are a delusion and a fraud. You don't go much on Parnell, do you? Why don't you do up bloody Balfour, and bring him to his knees? Why? Because a coward always hoots, he don't fight for a cent.

MARTIN J. RYAN.

It is very likely that Mr. Sullivan and Mr. Ryan are good men. I will further say, could I dispossess myself of certain fears that have grown into my mind that if I were to-morrow to go looking for good trustworthy men to do daring and dangerous work for Ireland's freedom, I would first speak to men belonging to the society to which they belong. It is not without my share of sorrow I am obliged to think that such men are in the hands of an organization bound to the peace, and bound to do nothing that will hurt or harm England—without giving due dotice to England first. And I may add, that if any wealthy Irishman in the land offered me a hundred thousand dollars to day for the cause of Ireland's freedom, on the conditions that it should be utilized with the advice and coöperation of the present leaders of the Irish Revolutionary Society of America, I would refuse the offer, so satisfied am I that there is treachery and crookedness somewhere in that leadership.

Le Caron, the English spy, eighteen years ago had the acquaintance of every chief man in the organization; Gibney, the English spy in Doctor Gallagher's case fourteen years ago, had the confidence of the New York chiefs; Jones, the English spy, in the Ivory case in 1896, had their confidence. I look at all this, and I see myself denounced as a traitor and a spy by the men who took Le Caron and Gibney and Jones to their hearts. There is something rotten somewhere, something to be cast out.

In this chapter I have brought myself as far as leaving Skibbereen and coming to America in the summer of 1863. I have in my head many recollections of the trials and struggles of the men at the start of the organization and I have in my possession many letters of James Stephens and John O'Mahony and of all the Fenian missioners, and Fenian centres and Fenian organizers of those times in Ireland and America. I intend in next chapter to take those letters, commencing about the year 1860, print them in the order of date, and edit them with any information I am able to give. That will take attention away from myself for a while, and let you see what Scanlon and Finerty and Fitzgerald and Kelly and other living celebrities were saying and doing those times.

And as I am leaving Skibbereen for good, it is only just and proper I should say a good word for all the good people. who knew me there. I must go to my grave indebted to many of them for much kindness, indebted to many of them living and dead in New York for more than kindness; because in my struggle to fight the battle of life here, and to stand up against the enemies that were raised up against me, to trample me down, I had often need of a helping hand, and I never made that need known to a man who knew me at home, that the helping hand was not extended to me. Photographed on my memory in that light are Tom Browne, and James Scanlan the merchant butchers of Gansevoort Market, and West 40th street, John Howard, of the Kenwood House Hotel; Tim Coughlan, of Kilcrohane, 28th street and Third avenue; James P. Farrell, of Lispenard street; Rocky Mountain O'Brien, Father Denis McCartie, and Jerrie O'Donovan, of Dromore, all of whom knew me when they were boys at home, and whose fathers before them knew me. Jerrie O'Donovan is in Calvary Cemetery a few years, but his children, Leo J. and Alfred J. O'Donovan, of Fordham College—the children of Madame O'Donovan, of No. 37 West 36th street, New York, may live, as I hope they will, to be proud to say that their father was a trusted, true and tried friend of O'Donovan Rossa's.

I have spoken of Father John O'Brien in this chapter. He is in Ireland still, and is a Catholic curate still. When I was in Ireland four years ago, I got this letter from him:

ARDFIELD, CLONAKILTY, March 31, 1894.
MY DEAR JER—Somebody sent me a copy of your

paper, in which you recalled to mind a funny incident of "All fool's day," 1860.

Should you include this out-of-the-way locality in your programme of travel now, I promise you as hearty a "welcome home" as you will get from any of your friends in old Erin.

Our meeting in the "Common mountain" will not be a case of "Fool, fool," like that of 1860, in Skibbereen long ago.

Do you remember the Prince of Wales' marriage, and the illuminations at the newsroom?

Accept my sincere congratulations on your surviving through so many trials, to see once more your native land. You spoke of knowing your old friend Flor McCarthy forty years. It is forty-three years since Morty Downing and Jer. O'Donovan Rossa were introduced to your old and sincere friend.

JOHN O'BRIEN, C. C.

CHAPTER XXI.

JAMES STEPHENS AND JOHN O'MAHONY.

AFTER the arrest of the Phœnix men in December, 1858, James Stephens went to France. In April, 1859, when I and my companions were in Cork Jail, he wrote this letter to John O'Mahony:

No. 30 RUE DE MONTAIGNE, PARIS, April 6, 1859.

MY DEAR O'MAHONY—The contemplated modification of our body, as well as the still more important step spoken of to you and friends the night before I left New York, you are henceforth to look upon as facts. I need scarcely say, however, that it will be wise to limit the knowledge of such a fact as the latter to such men as Doheny, Roche, Cantwell, etc., and to command all parties to whom such information is given to observe secrecy—not whispering it to the very air, without special permission from you.

I have reason to believe myself fully justified in the course decided on. Indeed, on meeting our friends here, I at once saw the necessity of remodeling, and in many instances, utterly doing away with the test. Not that the men at home had given any sign of blenching; on this head I have every reason to be satisfied. One Centre only had given way, owing, probably, to our inability to communicate with him often enough—to the utter darkness, rather, in which he had been left almost from the very first. This man has declared off; so that

however repentant and anxious to resume his work, he
shall never more hold higher position than that of rank
and file, till he shall have won his grades on the battle-
field.   Such be the guerdon of all waverers; the fate
of the coward, much more the traitor, shall his be such
as to make him curse the day he was born.   Two other
Centres, though staunch and true, and longing for the
death-grapple, have been able to give nothing to our
force but their own earnestness.   Of two more again,
our friend could say nothing, having found it impossible to meet them.   We know, however, that one of
these last had accomplished the work at first entrusted
to him; and the other, though in a bad view, had done
something.   These are the shadows; now for the lights.
As many of the Centres, known to our friend, had ex-
ceeded their numbers as the Centres who (though
formidable, and working earnestly), had not been able
to complete theirs.   Thus, every Centre (balancing one
with another) represents a full regiment.   To com-
pensate for the lost Centre and the two ineffective ones
(the other two are merely doubtful—rather to be counted
on than otherwise), three new Centres had been added.

So much for the members, which, everything considered, are up to what we could have reasonably expected, and fully up to the figure I gave you.   Add to
this, that the spirit and bearing of the men were excellent; the only drawback on this head being, that, where
the hand of British Law had fallen, there the craving
"to be at them" was most impatient of the curb.   Who
will be base enough to say now that these men—our
brothers—are not to be relied on.   Cowardly slaves,

and knaves, alone believe it.   Let God be thanked for
the day on which you and I, and a few other intelligent
men, decided on taking our stand, come weal or woe,
by the people of Ireland!   The woe, I firmly believe,
has passed away forever: the weal is coming fast, with
laurels and the songs of triumph!

Oh! we have reason to be proud of our toiling countrymen, and cheerful for the future.   Nor does the
necessary modification of the test lessen this a whit.
It merely proves that our brothers are conscientious.
Away with the shallow prate of their being servile to
priestly or other influence, where freedom of their country is at issue.   This sort of calumny was useful to the
bungling chiefs we wot of, chiefs who would fain pass
for martyrs, though the honor of their country were
smirched by it.

The people of Ireland are not servile to the priests,
even now, when they are being put to so hard a proof.
A proof how different from that of '48!   For what man
could have given a reason worth a flea-bite against
taking up arms against slaughter—against slaughter,
however great, in a fair fight—aye, or even foul?   The
arguments of such man might be met by the unques-
tionable—unquestioned—example of the highest eccle-
siastics of our Church, not excepting popes and even
saints.   Whereas now, there is an appearance (an appearance only, I maintain, for I defy all men to give
me a single rescript bearing directly against us) of
hostility on the part of the Church, which, wielded
skilfully by the men so revered by our brothers, may
well strike terror in the believing soul.   I will, how-

ever, go so far as to assert that, even where the words
of the priest are implicitly believed, numbers of the
people would accept the worst—that is, threatened
damnation—rather than be false to the cause of Ireland! Can as much be said for any other men on earth?

I regret that numbers of the people would do so; and
these, together with those who, happily, do not scruple
to take the test, would give us an organization equal to
the work to be done.

But, convinced of the earnestness of the men so
suffering through their conscience; who so callous as
to persist in subjecting them to a life of ceaseless
agony? I believe, too, that however unswerving in
their truth to us, the arms of these men would neces-
sarily be feebler in the day of strife. Besides, the conditions of a test would keep vast numbers, not a jot
less eager for the fray, out of our ranks forever. I say
nothing of the risk involved in the test. That risk,
however, is, while a serious consideration for the chief
who would not needlessly sacrifice a single man, but a
slight check on the people who would be—nay are —
deterred from joining us by the voice of the priest.

It was, in order effectively to countercheck that voice
that I decided on the course you are aware of. And
now I feel bound to say, that spite of my faith in the
result of the struggle, the necessity of prompt and ef
fective succor on the part of our brothers in America,
seems great as ever.

I am convinced, that with a little assistance—even
without any—from America, we can bring the men at
home to a fight; but to produce anything better than

disastrous massacre, a good deal must be done on your side.

On the other hand, I am equally convinced that a great deal may be done by you, if the work began by me be fairly carried out. And here, I speak in the name of God and their native land, to the men who encouraged, or got others to go into this movement, that they do the work of earnest men, laboring night and day for their country and their honor, so that their last hour may be free from remorse or shame, and those who come after them may proudly say:

"Is truadh gan oighre 'n ar bh-farradh."

For the bearer of this, John O'Leary, I expect the highest possible courtesy, respect, and even deference, as my representative; and, through me, the representative of the Irish cause; you will soon perceive that he is an able man of high intellectual culture; his bearing, too, will prove—what I assure you of—his high principles of honor, and convince you how devotedly he loves Ireland. To you, however, I might say that, spite of all these high qualities, our differences on many serious things are so very great that, had I a choice of men of such intellectual calibre and honor, I would not urge on him a mission so little to his taste. For, in the abstract—as a matter of taste as well as judgment—he is not a republican.

This alone would seem to disqualify him for the work to be done by him in America.

But while averse to the republican form of government in the abstract, he is ready to accept it when it represents the national will.

We know that a republican must represent the will of revolutionized Ireland; and, consequently, that he is virtually the loyal citizen of our young republic. Still, it was better that principles of government, etc., were not discussed with him before some of our extreme friends. His faith in the success of the movement, too, is not at all equal to mine; but he believes the probability of success sufficient to, not only justify, but imperatively call on every Irishman to coöperate with us. Lastly, he does not know that I am equal to the task I have undertaken; but, if not the most effi cient of organizers, in his opinion I am second to no Irishman of his acquaintance, and superior to anybody he knows able and willing to do the work. For all these reasons I deem it unwise to send him through the States; he has neither the opinions nor the faith in the cause, that could ensure the requisite results. But he can do the work you are at in New York. He can live without that essential nutriment of so many of our friends:—talk; and, without any compromise of either himself or the cause, give quite as much information to the curious as I am at all desirous they should have. You may have it made known to all but a few of your friends, that the actual state of things at home imperatively necessitates a certain reserve—that any serious departure from such reserve would be a breach of Mr. O'L.'s instructions; that I myself had become convinced of the necessity of limiting my confidence on essential matters as much as possible, being guarded even with you, and speaking of certain things under the command of secrecy.

By observing these directions, and keeping all merely curious—or others, except for the transaction of business—away from him, he will fulfil his mission as effectively as anybody, however in accordance with our opinions.

He is making such serious sacrifices, too, in order that my plans should not be thwarted, and I am so grateful for this, that, independent of his services to the cause, I am desirous he should be much as possible at his ease. To effect this, it may be necessary to convey to our friends that, in his private residence, he should not be subjected to what somebody terms "promiscuous visitings."

Having decided, then, that O'L. should remain to do your work in New York, on you devolves the working tour through the States.

You are better known now than before taking the position you were placed in some months ago ; indeed, I heard nobody spoken so highly of, once I got out of "the great patriotic influence."

With such a reputation in your favor, and the intelligence contained in this letter, I believe, judging from what I experienced myself, that your success is beyond a doubt. Your mission will be justified, I have no doubt, by the late trials and their result. It will be seen that the government is in earnest—resolved, if needful and possible to crush out what the London *Times* calls our "accursed race." It will be seen that to procure conviction, they were found to pack a jury ! Best of all, that O'Sullivan, of Bonane, seeing that justice was not to be had in British courts of law in Ire-

land, withdrew from the wretched mockery of trial by
such a jury, and met his sentence of ten years' penal
servitude like a man.   Honor, to the first martyr of our
cause!   Should the present administration remain in
office—(my friend O'Leary has just informed me that
Lord Derby has dissolved parliament).   So, we shall
have a general election!   Why, next to a European
war, a general election is about thè best thing that
could have happened for us!   And the enemy—God
increase their difficulties!—shall have the European war
to boot!   Oh! if all your transatlantic talk should turn
out other than the vilest driveling, this very year shall
see the Sunburst in the old sacred Isle!

As the present administration does retain office, then,
at least for some months, and all ambitious of leaving
their mark in Ireland, we shall have more perjuries,
more packing of juries, more convictions and punish-
ments, and (thank God!) the manifestation of more
manhood in the land.   For, as I was certain, even before my return, the men at home shall be found firm;
circumstances have proved, as already mentioned, that
they are firmest—most eager for the strife—where the
hand of British law has fallen.

Think of this, and go cheerfully on your way; think
of it, and go with the firm resolution to let nothing—I
will not say make you yield, or even falter, but—let
nothing ruffle your temper for an hour.   Think also,
that from no living man—not excepting myself—do
our brothers, the men in the gap, at home, expect more
than from you; that so much confidence and love deserve more than the small sacrifices (small in your eyes

and mine, though so justly large in the eyes of many of our countrymen) you have hitherto made, and that nothing short of effective work can keep you from going into the grave most deeply their debtor. For theirs is the coin—love, esteem and confidence—that has its equivalent in heroic devotion alone. It will not do to say you are ready to give them life—the common soldier will give that—for a few cents a day. Give them your heart, brain and soul—best given by the toil that shall give them the freedom yearned for by them as earnestly as by their sires, through so many ages of blood and woe. Work, brother, as you love me. Your labors may save me. For, my resolution remains unshaken—to free Ireland or perish. Set to work soon as you have read this. Get every one of your friends (no matter how humble, the humble man may be able to recommend you to some generous heart or willing arm in one or other of the States) to give you letters of introduction. Procure these letters by the hundred—by the thousand, if possible. Let the letters be brief, and to the point, so as not to take up too much room. For the same reason, you might have them written on a single leaf, and dispense with envelopes.

In connection with these details I deem it necessary on account of notions of yours to tell—nay, command —you to procure clothes suited to the climates through which you have to pass, as well as to the ideas of the people you may come in contact with. Trifling as these matters may seem, the neglect of them might occasion deplorable consequences to the cause as well as to yourself. A very essential counsel comes now. Write at once to each of the centres, and (where there is no centre) sub-centres of the American organization.   In your letters quote any portion of this letter you think it judicious to communicate.   Call on them to forward all the men and money possible to New York, giving instructions to the men to see O'Leary, who knows what to do about sending them to Ireland.   Of course the money orders must be sent in O'L.'s name; the receipts, however, are to be signed for you, as your name is to stand before the public as central receiver.   Of course, there will be no need of keeping it on the public papers after you return to New York.   You will do well to get a couple of hundred of the organization rolls struck off, so as to be able to establish systematic work in the various places in which it is as yet unknown.   Take a copy of the accompanying diagram with you.   The headings of the columns explain its object—to enable me to communicate with every man who goes to Ireland.   Take down the name, birthplace, &c., &c., of each man on one of those forms—a separate one for every place from which you send men; be particular about every point, especially the pass words; enclose the form in an envelope, and forward it sealed, to O'L.   These various envelopes will be brought by the persons he sends to me, together with similarly enclosed forms for the parties he sends to Ireland from New York, as you send them from the various places on your route.

The forms you send to New York to be forwarded to me must be seen by no eye but your own, on account of the passwords, which would be useless to me if known to any other; for the same reason, the forms sent by O'L. must be seen by him only. As most of the men sent home will be able to undertake the organization of a company—nine sergeants, each with nine rank and file—and that none of them will have any scruple about a test, give them one to administer to any parties at home, equally free from such scruples. For, in every instance in which we find them so, the test will be kept up. The form of the test, I leave to yourself, merely telling you that the oath of secrecy must be omitted. The clause, however, which binds them to " yield implicit obedience to the commands of superior officers " provides against their babbling propensities, for, when the test in its modified form is administered, you, as the superior official, in the case of the men you enroll, command them to be silent with regard to the affairs of the brotherhood, and to give the same command to the men of the grade below them, and so on. But the test, in its modified form, is not to be administered to any one who considers it a cause of confession.

I expect you to be ready for the road a week after O'L.'s arrival. When writing to the Centres and sub-Centres, as already directed, you might request them to send your letters of introduction to their friends; some of these you would receive before leaving New York, and the others would be forwarded to you by O'L. at one or other of your resting-places. Your tour will be very different from mine with regard to time. I give you three months to accomplish your work. This will enable you to spend a week, at need, in every large city where celts do congregate, and to make short excursions, out of the main route, to small places highly recommended to you. The route I leave to the judgment of yourself and friends; only recommending you to make first for the South, so as to lessen the chance of being clutched by yellow fever, or other blessings of that delicious clime. I recommend you to leave no town without sufficient money to take you, at least, two journeys onward; one town might be a failure.

I have done. Good cheer, firmness, perseverance and God speed you on the way.

A few words more. When you find yourself in a large city, likely to detain you long enough to be able to hear from O'L. don't omit writing to him; you might even telegraph from such city, if not, that you were going there. All O'L.'s messengers will come to me by the Fulton or Arago; that is, once a month.. Procure a list of the sailing dates of those boats, so as to be able to forward all the money possible, to be brought to me by said messengers.

It is past one o'clock in the morning (meaning an hour past the witching time); and so, I must close with brotherhood to all, and a prayer, that none of you be found wanting. It is not easy for me to close, without special remembrance to my friends. But I must do it, else, another hour would not suffice to write down even the names of all entitled to it. But, none are forgotten. Omitted to say that, when writing to Centres and sub-Centres—well, on reflection, it seems to me that my words involve what I was about saying. Still, as they may not be over clear, better you should inform them of O'L.'s arrival, not forgetting the importance I attach to him; and, at the same time, announce your own tour. You must have observed the omission of the friend's name who has worked so untiringly and well with me from the beginning. Of course, also, you have guessed the cause of the omission. The fact is, he is a little known, not to say a specially marked man, and so, I must not make him too sure a hit for them— in case of miscarriage in the present instance; that is, of this letter, which has to pass through hostile ground. I deem it necessary to suggest the greatest reserve with regard to names in general, and specially with regard to prominent names. Adieu. Health and fraternity.

INNISFAIL (James Stephens).

P. S. The only two of my acquaintances, in France, from whom, for the present, I could expect, not to say ask, money, are not in Paris. Both reside in the country, coming occasionally to Paris. One of them will be here in a fortnight or so; though aware of this I wrote to him last week. The address of the second I did not get till yesterday, and shall write to him also, this very day. On this head, I expect to have something cheerful to say in my next dispatch. Tell Roche and Mr. O'Dwyer so. In the meantime do not see Roche short; I will make good what you advance him. Our friends the Militaires, I have kept aloof from, clearly because these gentry must be entertained in a way the present exchequer would not admit of—they must see no want of the sinews of war. But I could lay my hand on a few even now, and answer for what I said on this head with my honor.

CHAPTER XXII.

A LETTER OF MUCH IMPORT, WRITTEN BY JAMES STEPHENS, IN THE YEAR 1861.

THOUGH I spoke of the McManus funeral before, I have now to speak of it again. I find among my papers a letter written by James Stephens to John O'Mahony, the week after the funeral took place in Dublin. It deals trenchantly with the milk-and-water Irish patriots of that time and even of this time who are ever telling us that "England's difficulty is Ireland's opportunity," and ever calling upon us to "bide our time," and do nothing until that time comes.

This is that letter :

BROTHER—Your last letter (30th Nov.) was placed in my hand yesterday by Lieut. O'Connor. On the whole it is the healthiest, and consequently the most pleasant communication I have had from you for years. This is owing to its freedom from what looked like a chronic disease in you—fault-finding in general and a proneness to advice, and even lecturing, men of ripe years who have proved themselves the only practical workmen this country has produced in our time. I say this without the most remote intention to hurt you in any way, and solely that you may henceforth avoid what has been not alone irritating to me, but calculated to

lower you in the estimation of men who would otherwise think highly of you. Now, if ever, there should
be a thorough understanding and union between us,
and to this end it is incumbent on us to cut as little as
possible against the grain. A word to the wise. Even
in this last letter, you complain of not having been
written to; from which it follows that you had not received a letter of mine written immediately after the
funeral. If the post office has not begun to play on us,
your complaint has been proved a vain one long ago.
The letter of mine alluded to was a hurried answer to
this constant complaint of yours anent non-correspond-
ence; but, if necessary, I could say a great deal more
than my letter contained. About the same time, I sent you
twenty copies of the *Irishman*, twenty of the *Freeman's
Journal* and twenty of the *Express*. These three papers,
as you are aware, represent three sets of opinions—the
National (for unfortunately or fortunately, as the case
may be, we have no other *national* journal than that
brassy, mendacious, silly, sordid and malignant *Irishman*), the Whig and the Tory; perhaps the article of
the last organ is the most telling of all. My letter,
should you have received it, gives a far more correct
estimate of the power, feeling and discipline manifested
by us at the funeral; but should my letter have gone
astray, Jeremiah Kavanagh, who will hand you this,
can make up for everything. And here, I may as well
say a few words about the American Deputation. The
Brothers, without exception, have given thorough satisfaction; Jeremiah Kavanagh, especially, has been of
important service to us, owing not only to his zeal and

subordination, but also to his natural talents as a ready
and effective speaker. But I wish it to be distinctly
understood that I am thoroughly satisfied with all the
Brothers. On their return, they can be of much service to us here, not only in the fulfilment of their usual
duties, but in holding up to just scorn and reprobation
the vile press and sham patriots we have to deal with—
the brood who have so long passed as the "Trusted
Leaders" of the people. By Demas, we have scared
and routed them somewhat here; but the *coup de grace*
can be given them yonder by the Deputation. As you
are wise and true—to yourself, to us, and to your
country—do not neglect to favor all willing hearts in
this great duty.

Crisis or no Crisis?—*that* is the question. Another
question, of far more importance to us, is this: If a
real crisis, what will be its consequences to us? I shall
offer a few observations on these two points. If there
be one thing, in connection with the cause of Ireland,
I more cordially detest than any other, it is what scrib-
blers or spouters call "a Crisis." It has been the
chronic bane of Ireland—a more fatal bane than famine
or any other the enemy have had, to perpetuate their
rule. A bane—a scourge—a disease - a devil's scourge
it has been to us. Its best known formula has resolved
itself into this: "England's difficulty is Ireland's opportunity." Blind, base and deplorable motto—rally-
ing-cry—motive of action—what you will. May it be
accursed, it, its aiders and abettors. Owing to it, and
them, the work that should *never* have stood still, has
been taken up in feverish fits and starts, and always

out of time, to fall into collapse when the "opportunity," predestined to escape them, had slipped through their hands. Ireland's trained and marshalled manhood alone can *ever* make—could ever have made—Ireland's opportunity. And this opportunity, the manhood of Ireland alone, without the aid of any foreign power—without the aid of even our exiled brothers, could have been *made* any time these thirty years; and, whether England was at peace or war, with this manhood alone we could have won our own. But our duped and victimized countrymen, giving ear to the imbecile or knavish cry of "English difficulty," stood, with mouth agape, and over and over again, waiting—"biding their time"—till the opportunity came, and left them as before. Accursed, I say, be the barren, lunatic or knavish clods who raised this dog-souled cry—a cry to be heard even *now*, in the mouths of the slanderous brood who, as you say, "first misled and then abandoned a brave and devoted people." They are, I say, raising the cry once more—this cry of—a crisis—"England's difficulty." By the time this reaches you—before it reaches you—you shall have heard of the "Mass Meeting" at the Rotundo. I shall speak of it myself by and by; but for the present, I pass on to the—crisis! *Is* it to be a *real* crisis after all? I am far from convinced of it. Nothing, far as I can see, has taken place to preclude an arrangement—a compromise of some sort. It seems to me that the reasons for this, especially on the side of America, are very cogent. I waive the question of the actual state of Jonathan—a state which, according to your own account, bodes something

like decomposition—a crumbling into utter chaos.
How would a war with England set this to right? Are
the men at Washington so ignorant of human nature
as to hope, even in the face of a foreign foe, for a fusion
with the South? Then look to Europe. There, the
feeling, and what is of far greater weight in human action, the interests of all are decidedly with England.
It is by no means impossible—even improbable—that
France will be thoroughly with England. America
cannot possibly be blind to this; if blind now, her eyes
will be opened, probably, in time to stave off a collision.
Granted, however, that human passions, human blind-
ness—shall hurry the States into this war with England, and that we shall have a bona fide crisis. Granted,
too, that Europe shall rise above mere interest, stand
aloof from the fray, and leave England to fight it out
single-handed. What will then be the consequences to
us? Do you hope for good results? I am not by any
means sanguine; or, to be thoroughly outspoken, it
seems to me—I apprehend—that, in the case in question, far more evil than good shall accrue to us. Once
engaged with England, our communications with
America are at an end; at least, no men can come
home, and even money, only in an indirect and roundabout way. Then, the cry will be on your side, "let
us settle our own difficulties first—let us drive the
enemy from our shores, and then we shall do your business for you." How long will this state of things last?
How many of the best of our race shall be sacrificed in
this way? And they, poor dupes and victims, shall be
all the while dreaming that they are serving their na-

tive land! Then, again, some popular soldier, gifted with more heart than brain, or without much of either, may get it into his head to prepare an expedition, "homeward bound." Let us suppose he has forced the double blockade—yonder and here—and that he has actually set foot on Irish soil. He landed where he could; but, for the sake of argument, I suppose he landed on some point where we are strong. To suppose the contrary would be to talk of utter ruin to us and the cause of Ireland forevermore. For we have but this one chance. Any man who holds the contrary, is incapable of making up the sum—two and two are four. There he is, then, on some favorable point. How many men could he bring to us under the circumstances? Granted —again for the sake of argument—that the number is considerable. As we have had no understanding with him—as he takes us as much by surprise as the enemy —we have only to make the most of the—shall I call it Godsend? Then again—but I will not go on in this stain of conjecture. I shall merely say that I augur no good for us from this war, so much desired by certain Irish patriots. The consummation most devoutly to be wished for by us is this: An arrangement or compromise of some kind between North and South, and the consequent disbandment of the army. Then, as well as meantime, our communications would be open with you; money and men might be coming over to us, and we would choose our own time for the first blow. Indeed, the advantages to us appear to me so manifest, in this latter case—that of England keeping out of the struggle—that it would be boresome to you to point them out. Were we in the field, it would be clearly an advantage to us to have England in a death-struggle with America; but I am more than doubtful of the advantages to be gained by us should this struggle begin before we rise. But of course—or is it so?—we can do nothing to bring about or prevent this war. You say that, should it take place, "your purpose is to offer your own services and those of your friends to the United States government to serve against England, in Ireland if possible, but if not, anywhere." I look upon this as wise, and fully approve of it. You will recollect that, in my letter of the 8th of June last, I counselled you to make yourself thoroughly aware of the spirit and action of those amongst whom you were living, and then take action yourself, always aiming at the greatest service to Ireland. Now, in case of a war with England, all the Irish race on the American continent will be into it; so that you could not stand aloof without the utter loss of your influence. Clearly you must to the field, and the more prominent your position, the better for Ireland. Granted, then, that you are in the field, and in a foremost position, I would not allow myself, even then, to be too hasty in urging on an expedition. I should keep up my correspondence with home, and be sure that everything was right there, convinced that, without a vast power of trained men at home, armed already, or to be provided with arms by me, the expedition—if not far beyond anything that has ever in that way steered for the Irish shore—could only compromise the last chance like every preceding one. I would not, like so many ignorant or silly men, fancy that 10,000 or 20,000, or even 30,000 Irish-Americans, could if landed on our shores, give freedom to my country, unless, as already said, a vast power of trained men, armed already, or to be armed by me, were ready to fly to my standard. I would not allow myself to be deluded by the lunatic dream, that a mob, however numerous or numberless, could make victory a certain or even a probable thing. I would believe, on the other hand, that a trained power at home—say of 100,000 men—already armed, or for whom I bought arms, could—nay would—be sure to do more with the aid of so small a number as 1,000, than an auxiliary force of even 30,000 could ever effect, if backed by a mere mob, whatever its number. I would therefore and as already said, be sure that there was at home a strong power of trained men to coöperate with the force brought by me, and till I was sure of this, nothing could force me to undertake a descent on the Irish shores, convinced that such descent, so far from serving my country, would only deprive her of the last chance of freedom. These are amongst the many things sure to be suggested to me, should I ever find myself in the position I supposed you in *toute a l'heure*. Let us be provided against all contingencies.

In haste, yours faithfully
J. KELLY, (JAMES STEPHENS).

That is a letter entitled to serious consideration from the Irish newspaper men of Ireland and America who occasionally write of "England's difficulty being Ireland's opportunity." And much more is it a letter

worthy of serious consideration from the patriotic Irishmen enrolled in military regiments, and military companies, connected with Irish societies in America.
Those men have the proper Irish spirit—the spirit to
become proficient as soldiers—with the hope that some
day an opportunity may come to them to fight for the
freedom of their native land. But this thing of waiting for that opportunity, instead of making it, (which
Irishmen could do, and should do) has taken many an
Irish soldier to his grave without doing any fighting for
Ireland.

If the Irish men and Irish societies and Irish soldiers
of the world do nothing to make "difficulties" for
England but what they are doing at the present day, I,
too, have little hope but that I will be in my "long
home" before I see Ireland free. For I, too, from my
earliest days, and all the days of my life, desired to be
a soldier for Ireland—desired to be among the men who
would be at the front in the face of danger, daring and
doing all that brave men could dare and do for their
country's freedom.

When John O'Leary was writing his "Recollections
of Fenianism" in the Dublin papers, in the year 1896,
he said that when the Phœnix prisoners were in the
Cork Jail, word was sent to them by James Stephens
not to accept their release from jail on the terms of
pleading "guilty."

I know that the prisoners got no such word—for I
was one of them. The men of the organization who
were in Cork City were somewhat disaffected; they
spoke to us as if the whole work was abandoned after

the arrests. There was general disorganization and demoralization.

After our release from prison Mr. Thomas Clarke Luby visited the south of Ireland a few times. He was in communication with James Stephens in Paris, and with John O'Mahony. A letter he wrote to John O'Mahony in August, 1860, will give the reader an idea of the difficulties that beset the organization that time. This is it:

DUBLIN, 25th August, 1860.

MY DEAR MR. O'MAHONY—I shall commence this letter by informing you that when your agent James Butler arrived in P——, our friend there decided on associating me with him in his Irish mission. Accordingly, copies of your correspondence with Chicago and St. Louis were placed in my hands; also, copies of all the passages of your letter to James, embodying charges, and, lastly, a long and able statement written by our friend. I was instructed to accompany your agent through the country; to make use of those papers; to place the charges contained in them before the principal shareholders of our firm; to explain the greater or less amount of truth existing in those charges; to lay before our friends fairly and squarely the question—whether our friend should withdraw from the management of the firm, or remain at his post; to try to produce a pressure from the members of the firm here on those across the sea, and to cause such steps to be taken as would give you satisfactory means of demonstrating, in the teeth of all reports to the contrary effect, that the transactions of the firm here were bona fide transactions. With this view, to cause letters to be written by friends of ours, in various localities through the country, to their friends in America, calling on them to repose unlimited confidence in you, and to sustain you in all your efforts; and, finally, I was to write and sign a document expressing the most unbounded confidence in you (as you will see, I have written one, expressing unlimited confidence in both you and our friend;) and to procure as many signatures to the document, of principal shareholders, as I could.

I have carried out those instructions to the best of my ability, and in fact, my success in the business has gone beyond my warmest anticipations. I would have written to you sooner, in order to relieve the anxiety which I know you must feel, were it not that I still was hoping to send my communication by Mr C. Besides, as you will gather from the ensuing portion of this letter, the work to be done was not completed; and indeed, owing to unavoidable circumstances, it is even yet incomplete. However, I can no longer withhold from you the cheering intelligence I have to give you. Therefore, I have at last decided on sending you a letter by post.

But, let me here, in the first place, assert emphatically that never have more impudent and calumnious falsehoods been uttered than the statements regarding our business madly hazarded by that unfortunate rash man over there.

To dare deny that our firm was bona fide and sol-

vent! Placing out of view for a moment the result of
my movements, Mr. C.——, and Mr. B——, of St. Louis
will, on their return, furnish you with a triumphant ref-
utation of the monstrous and barefaced calumny. Nay,
their letters must already, I should think, have satisfied
you about our solvency. Why, even your friend Mr.
K——, who saw comparatively little, learned enough, I
fancy, to enable him to convince you that our transactions here are bona fide. I would almost venture to
maintain that our County Cork branch alone, even
now, comes up to the full height of what James orgi-
nally engaged to do. What, then, shall we say when
we take Kilkenny and the other districts into our calcu-
lation?

But, to give you a summary of the results of my
mission: Since I received our friend's instructions I
have seen twenty principal shareholders, not to speak
of numerous lesser ones who called on me in various
places. Of these twenty, no less than nineteen signed
the paper of confidence, and signed it in a manner which
quadrupled my delight at getting their signatures.
They listened to the tale of the calumnies of that un-
happy man, but also with unspeakable scorn and in-
dignation.

I cannot give you any adequate idea of the warmth
with which I was received by some of the shareholders
and their friends. My only complaint was, that their
ardor occasionally outran discretion. Seeing those
things with my bodily vision, and, at the same time calling to mind the outrageously impudent statements
which had been made in certain quarters, I often

fancied myself in a sort of dream. I do not deny that
in two or three places I found apathy. But in spite of
such drawbacks, I derived more pleasure from this last
trip than from all my former ones put together. Almost
everything satisfied me. In some spots, where, up to
this, was comparative coldness; for the future expect
enthusiasm. I got but one refusal, and even that did
not by any means amount to a withdrawal of confidence. Indeed, the refusal was based on grounds
simply childish. This occurred in Waterford City;
but I have discovered another friend there who, without interfering with the former agent, will act with
youthful energy. Lest I should forget it, let me add
that shortly some new travelers will be added to the
firm.

But, to return. I got three signatures by letter since
I came back to Dublin. The letters shall be sent as
vouchers. As my tour was unavoidably shortened,
Mr. C—— procured me another signature; while Dan,
who recently received a remittance will, in two or
three days, send me not less than six more. Altogether,
I should have from 27 to 30. This is surely wonderful, considering all things. Bear in mind, that two
places in North Tipperary (where things are more or
less in confusion) and three in Waterford County,
(which I have reason to believe more or less good), with
three indifferently managed places in other directions,
must all remain unvisited. This, for many reasons,
which can be explained hereafter.

I had almost forgotten to add here, that I expect that
numbers of letters will be written by friends of ours in

various parts of Ireland, calling on their friends at the other side to sustain you. In a word, the confidence of our shareholders cannot be overturned. I may as well state now, that the prospect of a visit from you delighted all. This visit will produce the greatest results. Nothing should prevent it from taking place.

I might for a moment speak my own mind. When our concern began, I was not over-sanguine. But now, supposing I were not already a shareholder and yet could know everything I do know, I would at once become a shareholder, aye, without a moment's hesitation or loss of time. I say it emphatically; we have to-day a better starting point than any we have had up to this.

This belief of mine is shared by most of our friends. Even J. P. Leonard of Paris, (coldly as he is wont to look on our prospects, and little prone as he is to indulge in sanguine anticipations)—agreed with me so far, two or three days ago. But, when I speak thus confidently, recollect that my confidence is based on the hope that we shall now act on the minds of our friends across the sea in such wise as to make them react on us in a regular go-ahead style. We bear, recollect, a certain brunt, which as yet they have not to bear. It is little enough, then for them to attend chiefly and efficiently to the financial department. Besides, have not our friends here sunk large sums, too?

But, if the two battledores, so to speak, cannot keep the shuttlecock flying, backward and forward, without stop or fall, things must go wrong. In short, there must be incessant activity, alike with you, and with us ; and intercommunication and enterprise, too.

In fact, some few of our shareholders in the South are beginning to lose faith in your branch, and to think more and more every day of self-reliance. They are in sooth, a little disgusted with the great promises and little performance of some men at the other side who, let me add, seem so ready to censure shortcomings, for which in reality, they have only themselves to blame, and to believe the vilest slanders, backed by testimony insufficient to convict, the basest of mankind.

I remain, dear Mr. O'Mahony,
Very truly yours,
THOMAS CLARK.

Then, on the American side of the water, there were rumors going around to the prejudice of John O'Mahony, and of his efforts to spread the movement. Parties were saying that everything in Ireland was dead; that there was no organization there; that what was there, died out with the arrest and imprisonment of the men there.

To contradict those reports it was deemed necessary by James Stephens to get to a document the signatures of the centres who were again working actively in different counties of Ireland, and to send that document to John O'Mahony. Mr. Luby exerted himself to get those signatures. Here is what he says to Mr. O'Mahony, sending him the paper:

DUBLIN, Sept. 9, 1860.

MY DEAR MR. O'MAHONY—I send you the

document of confidence with the signature of twenty-five officers of the " A " class or, as our American friends I believe, call them, head-centres. Considering that circumstances compelled us to leave many good men unvisited, this is far from being a bad result. We are all in good spirits at home here. Many circumstances combine to enliven us now; among other exhilarating causes, the prospect of a speedy visit from you is an exhilarating one.

And here is a copy of the paper:

We, the undersigned local representatives, in Ireland, of the Irish Firm—over the American branch of which John O'Mahony has been appointed Supreme Director—hereby express our unlimited confidence in the ability and integrity with which that gentleman has conducted our affairs in America; and, also, our admiration of the noble constancy which has enabled him to sustain our interests unflinchingly amidst the severest trials, and in the face of the most shameful and unmerited calumny.

We also testify, in the strongest manner, our approval of the conduct and devotion of James Stephens, in the general arrangement of the firm, under similar trying circumstances, and, finally, we confirm both these gentlemen in the authority originally conferred upon them; and express our unalterable determination to stand by them while they represent us, against all their enemies, whether open or disguised—their enemies being ours, also!

1. Peter Langan, Dublin.
2. Thomas Clarke Luby, Dublin.

3. Joseph Dennieffe, Dublin.
4. Charles Beggs, Dublin.
5. James W. Dillon, Wicklow.
6. Thomas Purcell, Bray.
7. William Butler, Waterford City.
8. John Haltigan, Kilkenny.
9. John O'Cavanagh, Carrickon Suir.
10. Edward Coyne, Callan.
11. Thos. Hickey, Coolnamuck Co., Waterford.
12. Dennis D. Mulcahy, Jr., Redmondstone Co., Tipperary.
13. Brian Dillon, Cork City.
14. William O'Carroll, Cork City.
15. Jer. O'Donovan-Rossa, Skibbereen, Cork.
16. Daniel McCartie, Skibbereen, Cork.
17. James O'Mahony, Bandon Co., Cork.
18. Thomas P. O'Connor, Laffana, Tipperary Co.
19. James O'Connell, Clonmel.
20. William O'Connor, Grange, Clonmel.
21. Michael Commerford, Newtown, Carrickon Suir.
22. Mortimer Moynahan, Skibbereen Co., Cork.
23. Eugene McSwiney, Toames, Macroom.
24. Denis O'Shea, Kenmare.
25. Martin Hawe, Kilkenny.

The following two letters from Michael Commerford, of Carrick-on-Suir, and Martin Hawe, of Kilkenny (still living, 1898) bear testimony as to the truth and time of my story.

HIGH STREET, KILKENNY, Sept. 7th, 1860.
In compliance with yours it is with much pleasure I

state that I place the greatest confidence in the honor and integrity of the two gentlemen who have labored so hard to reëstablish the true Irish manufactory, which goods are just now in very great demand. Should either of those two gentlemen withdraw, I will never deal with the firm after.

Yours fraternally,

MARTIN HAWE.

NEWTOWN, CARRICK-ON-SUIR, 8 August, 60.

DEAR MR. LUBY—I authorize you to sign my name to the papers expressing confidence in the devotion and wisdom of our leaders, James and John.

MICHAEL COMMERFORD.

Keep up your spirits. We are all well and determined. Your friend T. O'C. waited on me.

M. C.

Mr. Thomas Clark.

CHAPTER XXIII.

JOHN O'MAHONY, WM. SULLIVAN, FLORRY ROGER
O'SULLIVAN, BRIAN DILLON, JACK DILLON, MICHAEL
O'BRIEN, C. U. O'CONNELL, JAMES MOUNTAINE, AND
OTHERS.

THE two letters published in the last chapter, written
by James Stephens and Thomas Clark Luby to John
O'Mahony, at the start of the Fenian movement, speak
for the Irish side of the house. The following letter,
written by John O'Mahony to William Sullivan, of
Tiffin, Ohio, at the start of the movement, speaks for
the American side. I may add that there is not a line
or a word added, omitted or altered in this original
manuscript letter of John O'Mahony's:

No. 6 CENTRE St., N. Y., 4th April, 1859.
TO WM. SULLIVAN, ESQ:

MY DEAR SIR—I rest satisfied that our organization
cannot now go down in Ohio while under the earnest
and influential auspices of yourself and your brothers.
It is but natural that our progress should be slow at
first, particularly as our finances do not yet warrant us
in sending round agents to the different centres of the
Irish-American population. Neither have we at our
disposal in this country the right kind of man to send
forth as our representative. I could not myself be

300

absent from this for many days without injury to the movement. We must then wait until the arrival of Mr. O'Leary, who must be now on his way out. As you are most probably already aware, he was to have met Mr. Stephens on his landing, and, having given his report of the progress made by the so-called Phœnixes for the last five months, to have come directly to this, with instructions for our further guidance. After seeing me and staying a few days to rest himself in this city, he will set out on his tour of organization. You will be likely to meet him here when you come in the middle of the month.

We must calculate upon a certain amount of opposition from some of the priests. I do not, however, consider it judicious to come into collision with them openly. Those who denounce us go beyond their duty as clergymen. They are either bad Irishmen, who would not wish to see Ireland a nation, or very stupid and ignorant zealots, who do not understand what they are about. Our association is neither anti-Catholic nor irreligious. We are an Irish army, not a secret society. We make no secret of our objects and designs. We simply bind ourselves to conceal such matters as are needful to be kept from the enemy's knowledge, both for the success of our strategy and for the safety of our friends. I hold that I do not exceed the bounds prescribed by my religion when I swear this, nor shall I ever tax my conscience with it in the confessional. It is ridiculous for men to denounce us for enrolling ourselves under the Irish banner, when they say nothing against those who enroll themselves under the Ameri-

can banner, or even under the banner of such private
adventurers as General Walker and others, whose sole
apparent aim is most unjustifiable plunder.   However,
there is no use in arguing with members of the priest-
hood on such points.   It is better to avoid their de-
nunciatory attacks by modifying the form of our pledge
so as not to be obnoxious to spiritual censure, even by
the most exacting ecclesiastic in America.   They cannot deny the goodness, justice and even piety of the
object we propose, and, if there be a shade of sin in the
words by which we pledge ourselves to effect it, let
those words be so altered as to be perfectly innocuous
to the soul.   This can be done wherever a clergyman
insists upon it: but where there are liberal and enlightened priests, there need be no change.

In every case, it will be well to give but as few se-
crets as possible to individual members.   They can do
good work without knowing all that is doing, and who
are doing it.   They should be taught that it is enough
for them to know that those in immediate communication with themselves are trustworthy, and that they
will truly and faithfully discharge the duties of their
position.   Men need not be sworn previous to helping
us along.   They see enough by the newspapers to show
them that the time for exertion is come now—that Ireland is thoroughly aroused and that a crisis in England's
fate is fast approaching from her external enemies.

A member of the Belfast Arms Club has arrived
here within a few days.   He was the secretary of the
men lately arrested there.   The news he brings is
highly encouraging.   The Ribbonmen, throughout the

North, are fully determined to join the Phœnixes, as they call them. In Belfast they have 20,000 stand of arms. Their organization extends through all Ulster and much of Connaught and Meath; it is also widely spread through England and Scotland. This party was not included in my friend's estimate. It is most important that we get into direct communication with it, for by it we could cripple England, by attacking her at home in her large towns. The fear of such a contingency would force her to grant us peace after a short struggle. All these matters must be looked to.

The news from these states has been rather more promising during the past week. The organization is extending rapidly, though as yet but little money has come in since I left. Boston is the best city I have on my roll. In it a full centre is now almost completed. What I like best about its members is that they do their work systematically, each sub-centre sending weekly the regular dues. A list has been also opened there for the contributions of men who will not be initiated. Branches of our society have been also started in Vermont, Maine and Connecticut. From Pennsylvania I have received a most satisfactory communication from the Railroad men. If the plan proposed by them is well carried out, it will bring overwhelming numbers into our ranks. I will speak more about it when I meet you.

In Milwaukee and Chicago, I expect that great things will be done under the auspices of Mr. Lumsden, whom you may know. The result of the late trials will, I hope, excite our countrymen to work everywhere. It is our first triumph, and, though but a partial one, it has proved that our home organization is almost spy-proof.

Present my compliments to your brother, Mr. Edmund Sullivan. I felt greatly disappointed at not having seen him again at my office previous to his late departure from this city. Tell him that the brothers in New York are beginning to exert themselves more earnestly than of late. On yesterday, I had a very enthusiastic meeting of men who will work, if I mistake not. It is hard to get the mass of the Irish in New York to believe that any one can be serious who speaks of freeing Ireland. They have had their hopes disappointed, when raised to the highest pitch, twice or three times within the five years I have been here. Then, the majority of them are mere dupes of designing politicians who scoff at the notion that any one could be so green as to hope for Ireland. But this must soon cease. True men are beginning to see that we are really in earnest, and they will not much longer heed the sneers which the venal and corrupt have always at hand for every noble and disinterested action.

I remain, dear sir,
Yours very faithfully,
JOHN O'MAHONY.

That letter was written in the year 1859. This is the year 1897. Nigh forty years ago. For any hope of Ireland's freedom in my day, I would, before my God, rather see Ireland as it was that day, than as it is to-day. That day, there were no weeds in the field.

To-day the field is nothing but weeds—with the patriots of the day grazing on them—to free Ireland; growing fat and contented on them, too; satisfied they'll be able to arrive at freedom in the *next* generation. Go b'hfoire Dia oruinn!

I bring into my book that letter of John O'Mahony's that it may live in the history of Fenianism, to stand against what may be said about the movement being opposed to the Church.

The demonstrations about the McManus funeral in Cork and Dublin, demonstrated to the English in Ireland that the spirit of rebellion was strong in the land; and all the English agencies of business were set to work to destroy it. Clerks were discharged from business; licenses to carry on business were refused; the man who was in business found that his credit was stopped, if he didn't stop his politics—in a word many had to stop, and had to prepare to leave the country. All through the years 1862 and 1863, this fight was going on, and continued on, from the start of the Irish People newspaper in November, '63, up to the suppression of that paper, and the suspension of the habeas corpus act in September, '65. During those three years, John O'Mahony kept saying that it had a bad effect on the spirit of the organization in America, that so many men belonging to the organization in Ireland were leaving Ireland. James Stephens kept telling him, he could not help it, that they had to leave; that they were among the best of his men—making themselves so active, zealous and independent, that they became marked men. While it broke his heart to have them be obliged to go, he could not refuse giving them the few words of introduction to some friend in New York that they asked for when they were leaving Ireland. I have some of the letters of those times. When I show you five or six of them, you will be able to judge of the spirit of the times, and of the condition of things that was to be met with in those days.

Here—the first letter that comes to my hand, is a letter of Florry Roger's. Shall I put it aside? No, no; Florry Roger has a place in my memory, and must have a place in my book. I met him a few times, and met a noble man. He was arrested as one of the Phœnix men when he was a medical student in Killarney. After release from prison, he went to Dublin and got employed in a drug store in Queen street. He died the following year. This is the relic of his I hold:

No. 46 QUEEN ST., DUBLIN, 8th Nov., 1861.

MY DEAR O'DONOVAN—I casually learned by some paper that you were in town. I slindged over to the Shelbourne Hotel to-day thinking to get a glimpse at you, but I was informed by Mr. Generally-useful, that you did not put up there. I therefore address this to Colonel Doheny for you—being in my opinion the surest means of arriving at the knowledge of your whereabouts. As I am anxious to see you, will you do me the favor of calling over here to-morrow, that we may have a chat together on the state of the weather, and crops in the South.

Oblige your very faithful,

F. R. O'SULLIVAN, JR.

The O'Donovan Rossa, care of
Col. Doheny, Shelbourne Hotel,
Kildare Street.

Next is a letter from William O'Carroll, who was one of the centres in Cork city:

CORK, Oct. 10, '61.

MY DEAR O'DONOVAN—Something has come to my ears lately. It may be no harm to give you a wrinkle on the matter. Sir John Arnott is negotiating with John McAuliffe about his house and stock in Skibbereen. It seems that the latter is your next-door neighbor, and your landlord, and that the former has your mansion taken, too. My friend in the house was telling me that Sir John, and Grant and McAuliffe and a few others had a kick-up about many things—not the least of which was your castle. . . . You now see the position of things. You will certainly come up to the funeral. I will be glad to have a chat with you then. We are making every preparation we can. I am, your friend,

WILLIAM O'CARROLL.

That William O'Carroll had to leave Cork next year, 1862. He went to Australia. With him, went another centre, James O'Mahony, who kept a draper's store in Bandon. The two wanted me to go with them. I didn't go. This is one of O'Mahony's letters:

CORK, March 15, 1862.

MY DEAR O'DONOVAN—I suppose you expected to hear from me ere this. I have spent the greater portion of the past fortnight in Cork City, but will be returning to Bandon on next Monday. I had hoped that either myself or my wife, or both, would have paid you

a visit to Skibbereen ere this, but the weather was so
unfavorable that we could not attempt moving.   They
are making great preparations for the annual ball
here   'Tis likely I'll not make my appearance there at
all, though at first, I was determined on going.   Still,
all things considered, I think it better not to go.

Your friend,
JAMES O'MAHONY.

Twenty-two years afterward, 1884, I had a letter
from Melbourne, from James O'Mahony.   Here are
some passages of it:

> "I do not think where'er thou art,
>   Thou hast forgotten me."

MY DEAR ROSSA—I wrote to you three times since
we last met last at the Rock mills.   I have often
thought of your farewell words after I took your photograph from you that early morning in Patrick street:
" No ship that was ever built should take us away from
Ireland."

Yours as ever, go dilis,
JAMES O'MAHONY,
Seamas laidir Ua Maghthamhna.

Go bhfeiceadsa an la go mbeidh raas air an Sagsanach.
A luingeas dha mbath, air lar na fairge.

John Lynch who, five years after, died in the next
ward to me in a London prison, was an officer of that

banquet committee in Cork City, Patrick's day, 1862.
He sent me this letter of invitation:

NATIONAL READING ROOMS,
TUCKEY ST., CORK, Feb. 26, 1862.
MY DEAR SIR—I am directed by the committee to
ask your attendance as a guest at our Soiree and Ball
in the Atheneum on St. Patrick's night, to celebrate
our National festival.

Trusting that you will make it your convenience to
attend, and awaiting the favor of a reply, I am, dear
sir, yours very truly,   JOHN LYNCH.

Mr. O'Donovan Rossa, Skibbereen.

I went to the banquet. Jerrie Hodnett, of Youghal,
presided. Father Ned Mulcahy, Timoleague, delivered
an address in the Irish language, and Brian Dillon
raised the roof off the house singing "O'Donnell Aboo"
and "Is truadh gan oighre 'nar bhfarradh." Father
Ned is dead. Riding by his side at a funeral one day,
he told me, he had had his parishioners ready to start
into the field with him in '48, if there was any fighting
going on anywhere. He was one good Irish priest.
Oh, yes; I believe there are lots of good Irish priests
who aren't known to be good, but who would show
themselves good if the people were any good. When
people show themselves slaves, it is not the duty of
priests to make soldiers of them. It is not for such
work as that, that men are ordained priests.

Brain Dillon died in prison. I have here a letter of

introduction that he gave Michael O'Brien, the Manchester Martyr, to John O'Mahony, when Mike was
leaving Cork in 1862. I may as well let you see it;
blessed are the words of the brave dead:

CORK, 23d April, 1862.

DEAR SIR—I had the pleasure of introducing the
bearer, Mr. Michael O'Brien to you, the evening you
visited the National Reading-room in Cork. He was
the Secretary of that room, and was since '58 an active,
zealous brother and " B " of mine. He will himself
tell you the reason of his visit to America, where he is
so well known as to make this introduction of mine
quite superfluous.

The news of the Colonel Doheny's death has caused
a wide-spread feeling of sorrow here. I trust in God,
should his remains be ever brought over to Ireland,
their landing will be the signal for that resurrection of
the old land for which he labored so earnestly and
well. All friends here deeply sympathize with Mrs.
Doheny in the loss she has sustained, and it ought assuredly be a consolation to her to know that in the
hour of her affliction, thousands of the truest in the old
land have offered up their prayers for the repose of the
soul of the eloquent, noble-hearted man and patriot
who was her husband.

Mr. O'Brien will tell you all about the departure of
Messrs. O'Carroll and O'Mahony to Queensland.

Fraternally yours, BRIAN DILLON.

29th April, 1862.

DEAR SIR—As you will perceive by date at the

head of this, Mr. O'Brien has remained here a week longer than he at first intended. This delay has enabled me to communicate with Skibbereen. Donal Oge (Dan McCartie,) sends by him a letter to you. You will have read in the *Irishman* before this Rossa's letter. Its terseness and pointedness has settled the whole thing. * * * * * * *

Another "B" of mine, William Walsh, of Cloyne, accompanies Mr. O'Brien. He is a shipwright and is compelled to emigrate, there being no work for his trade in Cork. He is an honest, earnest young man; he intends joining the Phoenix Brigade, in the hope of learning something that he could turn to good account, should opportunity ever offer here.

Fraternally and faithfully yours,

B. DILLON.

I have not printed the whole of that letter. Where I make star-marks: * * *, reference is made to some newspaper fighting I was engaged in at the time. Nearly every one belonging to the fight is dead—except myself—and I don't want to keep it up in these "Recollections" of mine.

Michael O'Brien comes before me again, in a letter of introduction he has to John O'Mahony from Mr. O'Connell. These are the words of it:

CORK, May 1st, 1862.

BELOVED BROTHER—This will be handed to you by brother Michael O'Brien, who has held on here as long as he possibly could. He has been out of employment for the last five months; and you can conceive what he mentally endured all the time. Seeing he could get nothing to do here, he at last resolved to turn his face to New York, in the hope of better fortune. Above all things, he desires to acquire military knowledge in the Phœnix Brigade. He will tell you, himself, why he was first thrown out of employment; and you can rely upon what he says, as he is genuine unsophisticated honesty itself, and as firm as a rock.

Yours fraternally and affectionately,

CHAS. U. O'CONNELL.

This is a letter of introduction brought from Mr. Stephens to Mr. O'Mahony by a Drogheda man. I knew him; but as I do not know whether he is living or dead—in Ireland or America—desiring the honor of publication or not, I do not print his name. I print the letter to show that Drogheda was not behind-hand in the organization at the time:

Tuesday, May 26.

BROTHER—The bearer, Mr. — —, of Drogheda, is compelled, through the oppression of his employer to seek a temporary home in the States. I regret his going, as he has proved himself a good workman, having as B., enrolled certainly fifty men in his native place. He, of course, is anxious to see you. He does not, however, expect a commission, or anything else that I am aware of, save only to know you and be placed under you, as our head in the States. Nothing of consequence has occurred since Chas. O'Connell left.

Yours fraternally,
J. KELLY.

The following is part of a letter of introduction brought from James Stephens to John O'Mahony by John, the brother of Brian Dillon:

CORK, June 11, 1862.

BROTHER—The bearer, Mr. John Dillon, has done the work of a B. This alone should be a strong recommendation. He is, moreover, a brother of Mr. Brian Dillon, one of our staunchest and most effective A's. He leaves in search of work (he is a ship carpenter), which cannot possibly be had here. The pagan knows him well; anybody can see that he is the stuff of a soldier.

A word about the men who have already gone out, or who may go out in time to come, I deem it necessary to say something about them as, owing to your complaints on the subject (to me and others in Dublin, but especially to parties here), a bad feeling has been created —a feeling calculated to do serious injury, if not properly explained. Neither I nor the parties going out expect any assistance from you or our friends— they have all gone, and mean to go on what you call "their own hook." To insinuate, much more to state unequivocally, that you fear their becoming a burden upon you, is keenly hurtful to these men. It is painful, too, to these men, to find themselves criticized for doing what they cannot help. Your having written here to this effect would have prevented several of these men from calling on you; and finding no proper party to communicate with, they would probably write home to say that we are nowhere in New York. You must see at a glance, the consequence of this. Of course, if I send a special message to New York, it will be only fair to see to his personal wants. But I have sent no such man since my return to Ireland.

No sooner did I find myself in possession of even limited means than I took the old track once more. I left Dublin on the 31st of May, and have since visited the counties of Kildare, Carlow, Kilkenny, Tipperary, Waterford, on to Cork. I could not now do justice to the firmness of all our friends; but such is my faith in them that I can surely defy, not only the clique but all influences whatever. Our position here is all that heart of man could wish. I speak for what I have already seen, and doubt not that my whole course shall give the same results. Much new ground has been broken, and the old soil is being tilled to its best. Here in Cork I cannot help saying a few words about O'Carroll. I can find no extenuating circumstances in his case; at least, I have been unable to find any, up to this.   Yours fraternally,

                                    J. MASON.

Well, I don't know; I only know that William O'Carroll, of Cork City, and James O'Mahony of Bandon were two of the first men in the south of Ireland that Mr. Stephens got into the organization; that it was through them he got introduced to Dan McCartie and O'Donovan Rossa in Skibbereen, and that they worked hard in the organization for some time. They might have cooled down a little after the arrests; I know they felt as if they had been deserted, or left to themselves, the time that I and my companions were in Cork Jail. In the Australian letter of James O'Mahony from which I quoted before, there is another passage I may quote. He says "You know my funds were always at the command of 'Seabhac'—(Shouk—the Hawk,) and that as long as I had a red cent, it was forthcoming. The amount was large as you may know." I know, that in the first years of the organization, many men in many counties of Ireland, spent their own money organizing. I don't like to see a bad word said of any one of them, who might have broken down under the work.

James Mountaine is dead. In honor to the memory of one of the Protestant National Irishmen of Cork City, I will publish this letter of introduction that he brought from James Stephens to John O'Mahony:

DUBLIN, Oct. 27, 1863.

BROTHER—The bearer, Mr. James Mountaine, is a friend, though paying but a flying visit to America (he is going to see his son, a surgeon in New York, and will stay but six weeks or so in the States), it would grieve him to leave, without taking your hand in his. When in yours, you should grasp that hand firmly, for it is that of as brave and true an Irishman as you know. He is one of the few who, with a good deal to lose, as the saying is, still clings to the cause as of old

—nay, as years and prospects increase, they but add to his zeal and devotion. He is one of the few, too, who are sure to rally round me in times of trial— whose friendship is shown at need, in better coin than words. It is now some time since I asked you for a favor. In the present instance I do so, and request that you will show Mr. Mountaine all the consideration in your power. All that he expects and would accept, is that you should receive him as a brother, and speak of him as a man who is at all times ready to fight or die for Ireland. For my part, I would gladly go out of my way, to meet and welcome, and be a brother to such a man. Mr. Mountaine would, I am sure, be delighted to see some of our military friends in their element; and, should an opportunity offer, I bespeak for Mr. Mountaine every attention you can pay him. Yours as ever, fraternally,   J. POWER.

This extract of a letter from Stephens to O'Mahony, April, 1862, is interesting:

The Dublin organization has nearly trebled within the last three months. And as it is in Dublin, so it is elsewhere. Our doctrine alone has life in it. The very class we found it so hard to reach till this year— the farming class, are now craving for our approach. But with all this, there is so strong a desire for in-telligence—for frequent communication with *me*—that whatever the risk and inconvenience, I must go amongst them. In England and Scotland as well as at home, I am called for clamorously. In the name of God and

of Liberty, will our friends yonder ever rise to a sense
of duty, and the want of the hour.   I should forget
everything did they give me but three months uninter-
rupted work now.   What might I not do!   Then, as
already said, I could go to America with such creden-
tials as no Irishman ever brought there before me.
The results produced here, together with my knowledge
—or belief—of what is in me, lead me to the conviction that my toil yonder shall produce necessary
fruits.   I have never heard, nor can I ever conceive,
anything to shake this faith in myself, and in my
countrymen in America.   J. S.

One morning in Skibbereen, I got a letter from
James Stephens, asking me to send Patrick Downing
to him to Paris.   I went to Pat Downing's house, he
was in bed, I ordered him to get out of bed and go on
to Paris.   I asked him where was the parcel of letters
I gave him to put in hiding for me.   His father was
building a house next door.   He showed me a stone in
an angle of the wall.   " The letters are inside that
stone," he said.   Very likely they are there this day I
am writing.   Patrick J. Downing had been in America
in 1853, and came back home about 1855.   When the
Stephens organization started in 1858, he became the
most expert at learning drill from the drill-master that
James Stephens sent down to instruct us.   When that
drill-master, Owens, left us, Patrick became our instructor.   He was arrested as one of the Phœnix men
in December, 1858.   He was in the dock with me, in
presence of Judge Keogh, in the Cork Court house,

Patrick's Day, 1859. I find him bringing a letter from James Stephens to John O'Mahony, bearing the date of "Paris, 5th of March." The year must be the year 1860. This is the first paragraph of it:

PARIS, 5th March.

BROTHER—This will be given you by Patrick Downing, one of the "State prisoners." He is a townsman and particular friend—a blood relation too —of Donal Oge (McCartie,) who, should I forget to bespeak bearer a cordially honorable reception, would not fail to secure it from him.

Indeed bearer is of the stuff that recommends itself, and should give you a high opinion of the manhood of his district; for, what but a high opinion can you form of a district, the sub-centres of which are all like my friend, Mr. Downing. He has been by my side for the last fortnight; and every day has raised him more and more in my estimation. I answer for it: Circumstances shall not swerve *him* from what he believes a high and holy duty. Receive him then, in all earnest brotherhood—be a real brother and a friend to him.

JAMES STEPHENS.

Patrick J. Downing learned the drill of a soldier, by moonlight, on the hillsides of Ireland. So did three of his brothers. The four of them gave their services as soldiers in the American war; Denis, as captain of a company in a Buffalo regiment, losing a leg at the battle of Gettysburg. Patrick rose to the command of

Colonel in the Forty-second New York (Tammany) Regiment.

He died in Washington a dozen years ago. I went to Washington to his funeral. After the requiem mass, the priest who celebrated the mass, spoke some words to his memory. I could not help thinking—sadly thinking, how the Irish race are scattered, and how strangely they sometimes meet; far, far away from home!

Colonel Downing and Father Nunan were no blood relations; but here was I between them; the dead soldier—the grandson of my father's sister; and the priest—the grandson of my grandfather's sister.

CHAPTER XXIV.

ADMINISTERING RELIEF TO POOR PEOPLE—A FIGHT
WITH THE LANDLORDS.

IN the summer time of the year 1862 something occurred that brought me face to face with the English
landlord garrison of the South of Ireland; something
snowed me the spirit of exterminating the old Irish
race, that possesses some of these landlords. Rumors
reached Skibbereen in the month of May that much
distress prevailed in the islands of Sherkin and Cape
Clear—Innis Cleire—" the island of the clergy"; that
the people were dying of starvation. Special messengers from the island waited on the Skibbereen Board of
Guardians, and pressed for immediate relief. A committee of the Board, consisting of McCarthy Downing,
Martin Jennings and James Murray, were appointed to
take the matter in hand. They resolved to send a ton
of meal into the islands immediately. The regular relieving officer, James Barry—Shemus Leathan, as he
was called—was old and infirm; it was necessary to
get an active man who would act temporarily as relieving officer, and act immediately; Mr. Downing sent for
me, and asked me to undertake the work; that a boat
with four men was at the quay that would take us in
to the islands with a ton of meal. I told him I certainly
tainly would go on such a mission. I called on a neigh-

320

bor of mine, Michael O'Driscoll, to go with me, and he readily assented. We got the meal on board the boat that night and next morning we set sail for the islands.

The first island I met was the island of Sherkin—that island of which Thomas Davis sings:

" Old Inis—Sherkin's crumbled fane looks like a moulting bird ;
  And in a calm and sleepy swell the ocean tide is heard."

The boatman told us that the distress was greater in Innis Cleire than in Innis Sherkin ; that the people in the farther off island were dying of starvation, and that it would be better for us to go on to Cape Clear first. We accordingly decided to do so ; and we decided to land three sacks of the meal in Sherkin, for distribution there next day on our return from the Cape.

It was a beautiful summer evening ; the boat was steered into a little shingly cove ; a man was stretched on a grassy bank, as if asleep ; we called him to help us to take the sacks ashore ; he turned his head high enough to look, and lay back upon the grass again—taking no further notice of us. I leaped ashore, and found that the man was unable to stand on his legs ; he was dying of hunger—a man named O'Driscoll, over six feet, and about twenty-six years of age.

My wife had thought I would be out on the islands for a few days, and she had sandwiched up as much food for me as would feed me for a week ; Michael O'Driscoll's wife had done the same for him ; we took our lunch baskets from the boat, laid them before the hungry man, and left him to help himself while we were landing the meal into the house of a Mrs. Hughes near by. We made a fatal mistake; we were accessory to the death of the starving man; he had eaten more than was good for him; he was dead when we returned to the island next day.

We got into Cape Clear about nine o'clock in the evening. News had reached there that we were coming. Father Collins was on the strand, with conveyance to take the meal to his house, near by. We distributed some of it that night; the priest sent word through the island to have the poor people be at his house next morning to take their share of the relief. We had supper and sleep at Father Collins's, and next morning before breakfast we distributed the meal.

We brought with us a gallon measure, and a half-gallon measure. A gallon holds about seven pounds of meal, and we were to distribute our relief as nearly as we could within the bounds of the Poor Law Outdoor-relief regulations—giving no single individual more than three and a half pounds of meal.

When we had supplied the relief to all that called, we had about a hundred pounds of meal left. We decided to leave it at Father Collins's until we would call again, which we expected to be the following week.

After breakfast, Father Collins took us to see a bedridden woman who was living in a cleft of a rock on a hill back of his house. He went on his hands and knees getting into her house; I went in after him in the same fashion; and there was the poor woman stretched upon flag-stones covered with heath. She could not sit up to cook the measure of meal that we gave to a neighboring poor woman for her. Father

Collins suggested that as we had some of the meal left, it would be no harm to give this neighboring poor woman an extra measure of it in consideration of her attendance upon the sick woman. We acted upon the suggestion, and gave the extra measure. I lost my job by doing so. Further on, I will come to the story of it.

Father Collins accompanied us to the other end of the island to take the boat for Sherkin. The walk was about three miles. We entered many houses on the way. Some of them had flags for doors—the wooden doors having been burned for firing. In one house were five or six children; one of them was dead— evidently dead from starvation. I reported that case of death to the first coroner I could communicate with when I reached the mainland; an inquest was held and the coroner's jury brought in a verdict of: "Death from starvation."

On Thursday, Board day, the following week, I gave in my report to the Skibbereen Board of Guardians. The landlords of the islands—the Beechers—were there. They are what is called "ex-officio guardians" —that is, guardians of the poor by virtue of their pos- sessing the lands of the poor—for the O'Driscolls owned the lands of Sherkin and Cape Clear till the Beechers came and swindled them out of these lands, as I will show you by Irish history, by and by.

The John Wrixon Beecher who was in the Skibbereen Board room that day that I gave in the report of my visit to the island is the Beecher that was married to Lady Emily Hare, the daughter of Lord Ennismore. He scrutinized every item of my report; and he asked for a postponement of its full consideration until another Board day. That Board day, he was on hand with all his friends; he laid hold of that item of my having given the extra measure of meal to the bed-ridden woman; he declared it to be a violation of the Poor Law Rules and Regulations; he proposed that I be dismissed from the situation of temporary relieving officer; that I get no salary for the time I served, and that I be made to pay out of my own pocket for the extra measure of meal I illegally gave away.

The fight on that subject continued for four or five weeks, during which time I visited the islands four or five times.

McCarthy Downing was in a fix. He was the land-agent of much of the Beecher estate; but his heart was with the people. I wrote to the Guardians and the Poor Law Commissioners some letters at the time, and in the copies of the letters before me now, I see Mc-Carthy Downing's pencil-writing, toning down some expression of mine, and substituting words of his for words of mine. I told him I would take the case into court, and sue the Guardians for three months' salary. He said he could not act as my attorney, but advised me to employ Chris. Wallace or Tom Wright. I did so, and I got a decree against the Guardians for the quarter's salary.

This story in my recollections will be better understood by my giving you to read the following letters which I wrote at the time:

SKIBBEREEN, May 28, 1862.

TO THE SKIBBEREEN BOARD OF GUARDIANS :

GENTLEMEN—On Friday, the 23d inst., I left at 12 o'clock noon, with one ton of meal, for distribution among the poor of Cape Clear and Sherkin Islands.   I arrived in Sherkin about 3 o'clock, and left seven and a half cwt. of the meal at the house of Dan Minihane. I made arrangements to have word sent to all the poor whose names were taken down by Mr. Barry, that they may attend next day.   I then proceeded toward Cape Clear with twelve and a half cwt. of the meal, but did not land before half-past seven o'clock, as the weather was most unfavorable.

That evening and next morning I gave eleven cwt., two quarters and eleven lbs. of meal to 81 families numbering 225 individuals.   Among those are five or six farmers with families, apparently in the greatest destitution—who would not go into the poorhouse.   In the house of one—Thomas Regan of Lisamona—a child was dead, and from her wretched appearance I considered she died from want and starvation.   I left undistributed in Cape Clear about one cwt. of meal.   I came to Sherkin Island on Saturday, and distributed the three sacks of meal I left there the previous day, among 53 heads of families, and single old infirm persons, numbering 172 individuals.   About 40 were left unsupplied with any, and I requested some of those supplied to assist the others until I could come again.   It is, of course, possible that in discharging so urgent a duty, and so promptly, some mistake might have been made ; but I did my best.

The people appeared more wretched and distressed in Cape Clear than in Sherkin. In both places many of them said they may not want poor-law relief long, as they had hope that Father Leader would return with money to get fishing gear for them, which would be a means of affording them remunerative employment, and permanent relief. The entire number relieved are 397 individuals, comprising 139 heads of families and single persons.

Yours respectfully,
JER. O'DONOVAN-ROSSA.

The following is a copy of a bill I sent in to the Board of Guardians, with accompanying letter:

THE BOARD OF GUARDIANS,
SKIBBEREEN UNION.
To JER. O'DONOVAN ROSSA, Dr.
1882 To salary as relieving officer, per
appointment by a committee of
the Board of Guardians, for three
months £12 00 00
To boat hire for second week . . .   10 00
                                        ————————
                                        £12 10 00

GENTLEMEN—As you have appointed a relieving officer in my place, I believe you are all under the impression that my services are virtually at an end. As this is the day, then, for paying the officers, I put in my bill. I have heard it said I would get only a fortnight's salary, though the situation has yet involved me in five weeks' attendance upon you, and I believe will occupy more of my time.

If you are disposed to give me only a fortnight's salary, I shall claim my right to the entire three months' salary, as per appointment; and then, I think I can show what has so often been talked of at the Board, that my discontinuance in office was owing to a cry of politics gotten up against me, and against the committee who appointed me—a cry unworthy to be raised, where the discharge of a duty to the suffering poor was alone involved.   I remain, gentlemen,

Respectfully yours,
JER. O'DONOVAN ROSSA.

Here is a letter I wrote to the Poor Law Commissioners, Dublin, at the time:

SKIBBEREEN, June 7, 1862.

THE POOR LAW COMMISSIONERS,
DUBLIN:

GENTLEMEN—On the 22d of last month a committee of the Skibbereen Board of Guardians requested me to go into the islands of Cape and Sherkin with one ton of meal to distribute among the destitute poor people there, whose names were previously taken down by Mr. James Barry in his application-book and report-book— which names I copied.   I went with all possible haste, and distributed the meal.   I returned, and, according to the instructions of the clerk of the Union, placed the names of the recipients on the register.   He then gave me a "statistical report book," directing me to enter the cases in the columns of the first section of the act. I found that this section contained no column for many of those I relieved; and, seeing that they were relievable under the second section of the act, I placed them in its columns.

I was not in presence of the Clerk of the Board while doing this; nor was I told that a resolution was passed by the Board to the effect that none should be relieved except those coming under the first section.

Before going into the islands I called on the clerk for a book of instructions; but he had none. I called to the committee; they had none. But they gave me a copy of the Poor Law Commissioners' circulars of the year 1848 or thereabouts. Receiving those, to act by them as part of my instructions, it is not to be wondered at if I relieved parties who did not come under the first section of the act. It is true I gave a little meal to five or six small farmers—but their families were apparently in the most wretched state of destitution. In the house of one, I saw a dead child, who, I believe, died from want of the necessaries of life. *That*, a coroner's jury subsequently affirmed. The father of the child would not go to the poorhouse. I gave the apparently starving family a little meal—as I could do according to my instructions. But the lord of the soil comes forward in the Board room yesterday, and the previous Board day, with a statement on paper to the effect that out-door relief was not wanted in the islands —signed by the tenants, including the father of the deceased child—he the lord of the soil, saying, that the relieving officer, or some other person, must be held accountable for meal given to any person not coming under the first section of the act.

I certainly acted in ignorance of the resolution previously passed at the Board. And, if I knew it, it is as certain that I would not go into the islands, fettered up in such a manner. But I thought, from all that I had seen and heard of the existing distress, and from the statements made by Sir Robert Peel in Parliament, and his replies to various deputations, that the commissioners had unlocked all the sections and clauses of the Poor Law act, and directed the guardians of the different Unions to avail of them, and to put on them the most liberal construction for the relief of the destitute poor.

The clerk of the Union has returned the statistical book to me, telling me it is not properly filled; that he cannot receive it unless all the cases are relieved under the first section of the act. Under all these circumstances, I respectfully refer to you for instructions as to how I am to satisfy the clerk, or otherwise act.

It seems I am no longer the Guardians' Relieving Officer. They appointed another yesterday, though the committee who appointed me led me to understand I would hold the situation for three months.

For the truth of that statement, you may refer to that committee.

I would not seek such a situation; but having been requested to discharge its duties, in a pressing emergency, I do not like to be set aside for having done so, efficiently.

To be candid with you, I believe I incurred the displeasure of most òf the landlord guardians on account of my having reported the child's death to the coroner of the district, and they immediately cried out that my appointment was political, and resolved to cancel it. I remain, gentlemen, your obedient servant,

JER. O'DONOVAN ROSSA.

I have made the remark that the Beechers of a few hundred years ago, swindled themselves into the lands of the O'Driscolls in Cape and Sherkin and other islands of "Carbery's hundred isles." Not only that, but they and their descendants since, have been trying to wipe out the old Irish stock entirely. It. is not agreeable to have around you people you have plundered, and reduced to pauperism and starvation. Doctor Dan O'Donovan, in his sketches of Carbery, says:

"In a copy of an inquisition taken in Ross Carbery in the year 1608, all the various lordships, royalties, rents and dues are detailed, and the boundaries strictly defined of the country or cantred of Collymore, called O'Driscoll's country. It contained 65 ploughlands— 39½ on the mainland and 25½ in the islands. The names of their castles would also indicate the flourishing conditions of the occupants, viz, Dun-na-sead, which means the castle of the Jewels, and Dun-an-oir, the golden fort.

"Walter Coppinger had been an arbitrator in deciding a dispute regarding landed property between Sir Fineen O'Driscoll and a relative of his named Fineen Catharach. Coppinger got an order out of Chancery

against the heirs of O'Driscoll.   Coppinger, after the
justices had issued a commission to Sir William Hull,
Mr. Henry Beecher and Mr. Barham to examine into
the case, made a private contract with Beecher, and
granted him a lease of the whole."

And so, the juggling went on, till the O'Driscolls
came in to be pauper tenants in their own lands, and
the Beechers came in to be millionaire landlords over
them.

CHAPTER XXV.

JOHN O'DONOVAN, LL. D., EDITOR OF THE ANNALS OF THE FOUR MASTERS.

THE life of my early manhood is full of my acquaintance with John O'Donovan, the great Irish scholar; and when now—forty years after that acquaintance—I am writing my "recollections," it would not be right to pass the old times by, and pass the old friends by, without saying a word about them. I will, therefore, devote this chapter to the letters of John O'Donovan that are here before me. When writing to me he used to touch upon all subjects : Genealogy, politics, public men, history, seanachus, sinsearacht, his family, his friends and his children. His son Edmond, whom I knew when he was a child, and who, when grown into manhood, became active and prominent in the Fenian movement, and active and prominent as a war correspondent in Asia and Africa, for the London journals— killed in the Soudan, or some other expedition—will be recognized in these letters of his father that I am going to show you. I will also show you, at the end of the chapter, three letters of Edmond's own.

The old Dublin *Penny Journal* of my boyhood days was a very interesting journal to read. In it were papers on Irish genealogy, written by John O'Donovan. I was interested in the genealogy of my own name, and in the nickname of "Rossa" attached to it; because it it was only in whispers, my father and the families of his five uncles who lived in the town, would speak that nickname—though all the neighbors around called them "Muintir-a-Rossa." The secret of the privacy was this: The nickname came to the family from their having owned the lands around Rossmore some generations before that, and from their having been deprived of those lands because they would not change their religion and go to church. The Hungerfords and the Townsends and the Bernards and the other "people of Quality" around, were in possession of those lands now; my people were defeated in the battle for their rights; they were allowed, here and there, by the Cromwellians, to live as tenants on their own lands, but if they stuck to the name "Rossa," which the people gave them, it would imply that they held fast to the desire "to have their own again,"—and that was a desire they did not want to make manifest.

Reading John O'Donovan's papers in the *Penny Journal*, I took it in my head to write to him. I have not a copy of the letter I wrote, but the nature of it may be judged by this letter of reply that I received from him:

DUBLIN, No. 36 UPPER BUCKINGHAM ST.
December 24th, 1854.
DEAR SIR—It amused me very much to learn that you have taken me for a Protestant! I have not the honor of having had one Protestant ancestor, from 1817 to 493, when St. Patrick cursed our ancestor Lonan, in

the plain of Hy-Figenti. We have all remained unworthy members of the Church of Rome ever since!
(The Protestant wives all turned to mass.) But I am
sorry to think, and to be obliged to confess that we
have not been a pious, wise or prudent race, and I am
convinced that we are doomed to extinction.

Many curses hang over us! (if curses have aught of
force in modern times). Saint Patrick cursed Lonan
in 493; the holy Columb MacKerrigan, Bishop of
Cork, cursed our progenitor Donovan (from whom we
all descend), and our names Donovanides, in the year
976, in the most solemn manner that any human being
ever was cursed or denounced; and, so late as 1654, a
good and pious Protestant woman's family (the children
of Dorothy Ford), cursed Daniel O'Donovan of Castle
Donovan, and caused a "braon sinshir," or corroding
drop, to trickle from a stone arch in Castle Donovan,
which will never cease to flow till the last of the race
of the said Daniel O'Donovan is extinct. It appears,
from the depositions in Trinity College, Dublin, that
the said Daniel O'Donovan and Teige-a-Duna Mc-
Carthy hanged the said Dorothy Ford at Castle Donovan, to deprive her and her family of debts lawfully
due unto them.

You and I escape this last curse, but we reel under
that pronounced by the Holy Columb (if indeed, its
rage is not spent). God's curse extends to the fifth
generation, but I believe man's goes further. But in
addition to these ancient maledictions, I, and my unfortunate sept of Ida in Ossory labor under two other
denunciations which hang over us like two incubi!

I return you my warmest and best thanks for your kind invitation to Skibbereen, and hope to make a tour thither next autumn, but I will not be very troublesome to you, as my stay will not be long.

Wishing you many happy returns of this holy season, I remain yours truly

JOHN O'DONOVAN.

To Mr. Jeremiah O'Donovan-Rossa.

I have about thirty or forty of those letters of John O'Donovan, written from the year 1854 to the year of his death, 1862. They are very interesting to me and to men like me. They may never see the light of day if I pass them by now. But, I cannot publish. the whole of them ; I will run 'through them and show you the ones that I consider interesting, as throwing some light on the character, the thoughts, the opinions, and the genial family surroundings of the greatest Irish scholar of this century. His next letter is this :

DUBLIN, Dec. 31st., 1854.

DEAR SIR—The old name of Castle Salem was Kilbritton. This castle was the chief residence of McCarthy-Reagh, by whom it was erected. The O'Donovans had nothing to do with this castle, notwithstanding the authority of the ignorant historian Dr. Smith !

The Professor Donovan, who wrote the article on coffee in 1834, is my friend Michael Donovan, of No. 11 Clare street, Dublin, who is a very distinguished chemist and member of our Royal Irish Academy, where he frequently reads papers on the most scientific

subjects. He wrote several works which were published in Lardner's Cyclopedia, on galvanism, chemistry, domestic economy, etc. He has made a discovery
in chemical science which he has as yet failed to establish ; that is, the process of turning water into gas.
He was given up the Gas-house at Dover to test this
discovery; the house got burned, for which he had to
stand his trial ; but he succeeded in proving that the
house was burned by the workmen, who were preju-
diced against him. His father was born at Kilmacow,
near the River Suir, in the county of Kilkenny, within
sight of where I was born. I was born in 1809 in the
parish of Atateemore, in the barony of Ida, and
county of Kilkenny. But we are not in any way related. His grandfather turned Protestant about the
year 1750, since which period his family have been the
wealthiest Donovans in Ireland, except perhaps, those
of Ballymore, County Wexford.

You may rely on it that "Felicitas Columba" knows
nothing of the O'Donovans-Rossa except what I have
published in the appendix to "The Annals of the Four
Masters." I have no sympathy with falsehood in any
shape or form, and a lie (white, black or red,) coming
from a minister of any religion, (which I am told
"Felicitas" is), is doubly hideous. We have truths in
vast abundance, and the discovery of them in history
and science is a praiseworthy result of patient investi-
gation ; but no false assertion should be ventured
upon. Truth will ultimately triumph over falsehood,
and those who have attempted to sustain false asser-
tions, are contemptible in the estimation of the honor-

able, and the lovers of true truth. Believe me to be
yours sincerely,

JOHN O'DONOVAN.

I here pass by some letters on genealogy, which may
be considered interesting only to myself and to my
family name and connections, and come on to this one:

DUBLIN, 29th May, 1856.
JEREMIAH O'DONOVAN-ROSSA,

DEAR SIR—Please read the enclosed American letter
and return to me. It is rather to show the spirit of
the Irish mind in America. I would do anything in
my power to encourage nationality, because we are becoming extinct very rapidly.

I have it in contemplation to try and notice the
three branches of our sept in the "Danish wars" to be
published by Dr. Todd. I have furnished him with
very many notes on other subjects and families, and I
feel satisfied that he will insert what I intend to furnish
him on the three septs of our family, namely, Clan-Cahill, MacEnesles and Clan-Loughlin. Of the first,
Morgan O'Donovan, of Montpelier, Douglas, Cork, is
decidedly the head and chief representative; of the
second, either you or some one of your relatives; and
of the third, my old friend Alexander O'Donovan, of
Kilrush (if he be alive), or his next of kin.

I am of a senior branch of the Clan-Cahill, and, as
we always believed, descended from the eldest son,
Donell O'Donovan, who died in 1638; but we lost our
birthright by the crime of our ancestors, by the just

decree of the laws of God and man, and we ought to be thankful for not having become extinct; for we are widely spread throughout Leinster and America, and we are likely to last to the end of time. Behold us all in the following table:

1. Donal O'Donovan, married to Joanna McCarthy, of Castle Donovan, who died A. D., 1638.

2. Edmond, married to Catharine de Burgo, killed 1643.

3. Conor, married to Rose Kavanagh.

4. William, married to Mary Oberlin, a Puritan, died 1749.

5. Edmond, married to Mary Archdeacon, died 1798.

6. Edmond, married to Ellen Oberlin, died 1817.

7. John O'D. L.L. D., married to Mary Anne Broughton of Cromwellian descent.

8. Edmond, born 1840, died 1842; John, living, born 1842; Edmond, living, born 1844; William, living, born 1846; Richard, living, born 1848; Henry, dead, 1850; Henry, born 1852, living; Daniel, living, 1856.

Eight sons, without any daughter intervening, is a sort of effort of nature to preserve the name.

I can hardly believe that Mr. John D'Alton will live long enough to bring out another edition of his book, because he is very old and feeble. I shall, however, write him a note on the subject of your branch of our sept Hy-Donovane, which I hope he will be tempted to print (if he prints at all), because one of them—Captain Donell Boy MacEnesles O'Donovan was very distinguished, and was restored to property under the Act of

Settlement and Explanation. If he does not print it, I shall be on the lookout for some other national work in which to insert it. In the meantime, I hope you will now and again, write to me, and believe me to be your affectionate clansman,

JOHN O'DONOVAN.

Next comes this letter:

DUBLIN, June 12, 1856.

DEAR SIR—I have just received your letter dated 9th inst., enclosing note from my neighbor John D'Alton, which I can hardly read, the handwriting is so unearthly. I did not pass through Skibbereen at the time you mention. So that you might have looked for me, but I fear you would have learned that I was in the North, among the Presbyterians. I am very glad that you have satisfied yourself that you are of the MacEnesles O'Donovans, (MacAneeis is the local name), because I had written in my published pedigree of the O'Donovans, before I ever had the honor of receiving any communication from you on the subject, the following sentence:

" The editor has not been able to identify any living member of this sept," (of MacEnesles).

Aneslis, who was the second son of Crom O'Donovan, 1254, had four sons, Donogh More, Rickard, Walter and Randal, who became the founders of four distinct septs, who all bore the generic tribe-name of Clann Enesles, or MacAneeis, and whose territories are mentioned in various inquisitions, etc. The townland of

Gortnascreena, containing three plough-lands (in the parish of Drimoleague), belonged in the year 1607 to the Sliocht Randal O'Donovan. In the same year the sept of MacEnesles possessed the townlands of Barna-hulla, (now Butler's gift), and also the lands of Meeny and Derryclough Lower, in the parish of Drinagh.

On the 20th of August, 1632, Dermot MacTeige MacEnesles O'Donovan was possessed of the lands of Lisnabreeny, west of the parish of Glenawilling, or Kilmeen, and I take this Dermot to be your ancestor.

If you descend from Dermot MacTeige MacEnesles, who lived at Lisnabreeny in 1632, and may have lived down to 1688, you do not want many generations in your line, with your present knowledge.

I will do all I can to fill up this chasm. You come of an older sept than Rickard O'Donovan, the clerk of the Crown. Yours ever sincerely,

JOHN O'DONOVAN.

In reply to that letter, I wrote the following one to John O'Donovan, a copy of which I find among my old Irish papers :

SKIBBEREEN, June 14, 1856.

DEAR SIR—I have received your welcome letter and am convinced beyond a doubt that I am descended from Dermot MacEnesles, who, as you say lived at Lisna-breeny in the year 1632. I made mention to you in one of my former letters, of a great-grandaunt's daughter of mine, Nance Long, (that time living), who was a bit of a genealogist, and I am sorry that she forfeited my good

opinion of her veracity, by telling me that her grandfather Teige a Rossa was a grandson of Teige Mac-
Aneeis, who lived in Glean-a-Mhuilin; and, as I thought
there was no MacAneeis, but the first named, I believed her as much as I would believe a man of the
present day who would tell me he was a grandson of
Brian Boru. She also said it was her grandfather who
first came from Kilmeen to the neighborhood of Ross
Carbery, where her uncle Denis (my great-grandfather)
married Sheela Ni Islean, or Julia O'Donovan-Island.
She used to speak much on the downfall supposed to
be brought upon the Rossa family on account of such
an alliance. To use her own words, her "grandfather
was deprived of all his land by the Cromwells; and the
Donovan Islands, having come by riches some way, were
glad to catch any of the family."

If you had any truthful correspondent about Ross,
when editing your "Annals of the Four Masters," he
would or should have told you of my Clan-Donovan,
my grandfather and five brothers of his (all with families), were then living at Milleenroe and Carrigagri-
anane. The names of these six brothers, Anglianized
were: Jer, Denis, Conn, Dan, Flor and John. I was
surprised they did not perpetuate the name of Teige,
and on making inquiries to that effect, I learned that
they had an uncle of the name who was a poet, was
considered eccentric, and was known by the cognomen
of Teige-na Veirsee; and they feared the eccentricity
may follow the name. But the present generation
(mostly now in America), have adopted it again.

As you have helped me, down as far as Dermot, **son**

of the above Teige MacEnesles, I will give you the
descent from him, and if it agrees with the intervening time, there can be no reason to doubt its correct-
ness.

My father, Denis, was born about the year 1790,
married in 1818, and died in 1847. He was son of
Jer, son of Denis, son of Teige. The old woman's
grandfather and his grandfather, being Teige Mac-
Enesles, or Teige MacAneeis, he must have been the
son of the Dermot MacTeige MacEnesles mentioned in
your letter. Yours, ever obliged,

JER. O'DONOVAN-ROSSA.

That letter brought this reply:

DUBLIN, June 23, 1856.

DEAR SIR—I have received yours of the 14th inst.,
and was glad to learn that there is a representative of
the second branch of the O'Donovans, namely of Mac-
Enesles, locally shortened to MacEneeis. I will prepare any note you like on this sept, and your descent
therefrom for Mr. Alton's second edition of his thick
book on King James II.'s Army list, but I suppose he
will want you to pay for giving it insertion.

Mr. Windele, of Cork, tells a story about the
O'Connells of Bally Carbery, in Kerry, which affords a
fair specimen of the kind of family history given by
" Felicitas Columba " and other writers like him.

On one occasion, McCarthy More sent to the Castle
of Bally Carbery for tribute, but the lord of the castle
took the messenger and hanged him. Now who was

O'Connell of Bally Carbery? He was McCarthy More's constable, holding three acres of land, and the wardship of the castle.

This description of history is truly disgraceful, in any country whose history is known. The Red Indians, who have no documents, may enjoy any stories of this kind that are consistent with their traditions; but the Irish have records which leave no room for fictions like that given by Windele.

I met a young friend of yours in the college the other day, whose name is O'Mahony. He is a Protestant, but a very intelligent, nice young fellow.

Yours truly,
John O'Donovan.

That O'Mahony was Thaddeus, the brother of James O'Mahony of Bandon, of whom I spoke in a previous chapter. In a subsequent letter my correspondent says:

"Your friend O'Mahony has been recently married, and I am told that he gives out that he was once a priest."

I don't think he was ever a priest, but I think he had an uncle a priest. His mother's name was Kearney; she lived and died a Catholic, and I think she had a brother, a Father Kearney, who was stationed one time, somewhere near Bandon. Yes, Thaddeus O'Mahony of Trinity College, married a Protestant, became a Protestant minister, and died—I don't know what.

Writing July 3, 1856, John O'Donovan says: "What puzzles me most is, why the epithet, or appellative of

Rossa clings to your sept. The O'Donovans of Rossmore are mentioned in an inquisition taken at Cork on the 3d of April, 1639, when Thaddeus MacDonogh O'Donovan was ten years dead, leaving a son, Teige O'Donovan, his son and heir, who was of age when his father died.

"Where is Rossmore situated, and what reason have you for believing that your appellative of Rossa is not derived from that place."

I told John O'Donovan that that was the place from which the appellative of Rossa was derived. That the family lived there; that the family tradition was, that they were driven out of it by fines, inquisitions and confiscations—fines for not attending service in the Protestant churches—inquisitions into titles to property, when they had no titles but what belonged to them as being Irish, and owners of the soil upon which they and their fathers were born; and consequent confiscation of their lands, for not paying the fines, and for not being able to show an English title to their property. That is how nearly all the lands of all the old Irish families were confiscated into the possession of the descendants of the Englishmen who hold them to-day. The more modern and more distinguishing appellative of Rossa—from Rossmore—followed my family when they were driven from Rossmore, and the Clan-name of MacAneeis (MacAeneas) was dropped from the tongues of the people.

Rossmore is the same place as Kilmeen, and Lisnabreeny, and Glean-a-Mhuilin are neighboring townlands in the parish of Rossmore or Kilmeen.

This is the next letter:

August 26th, 1857.

DEAR SIR—When I arrived here yesterday, the servant girl told me that a young Mr. O'Donovan had called early in the morning. I thought it might be Mr. John O'Donovan of Enniscorthy, but I have since seen him and he told me it was not he. I thought it might be Henry Donovan the mathematician, but I find it was not. After making several inquiries among my Donovan friends, I have come to the conclusion that it must be you. The girl describes the gentleman who called, as about twenty-three years old; brown-haired, tall, and thin in the face. He had with him, she says, a countryman from Clare or Kerry.

I waited within in the evening till 8 o'clock yesterday.

I am going to the Arran Islands in the Bay of Galway on the 3d of September, with the British Association, and on my return I am thinking of going to the South to see my O'Donovan friends.

I make my first appearance at 11 o'clock to-morrow, before the Savans of Europe, on " The characteristics of the Old Irish Race " I feel rather nervous, but I hope I won't fail altogether.

Should you come to Dublin soon again, please to let me know where a note could find you, and how long you will remain, for then I will be able to go for you, or send a messenger.

I stay within this evening till 8 o'clock, expecting

you might call; but I must go out then, as a member of
the British Association.

Yours sincerely,.

JOHN O'DONOVAN.

The English war of the Indian Mutiny was going on
in the year 1857. England was blowing the Sepoys
from the cannon's mouth; and whenever England won
a battle there were days of fasting and prayer declared
in England—and Ireland, too—to give thanks to God.
Of course, it was taken for granted that God was at
the side of England—for England had the heavy cannon, and the giant powder, and the mitrelleuse artillery.

I suppose I, in writing to John O'Donovan, told him
that I fasted fiercely, and prayed hard one of those
days, as I find he makes allusion to the matter in this
letter:

DUBLIN, October 9th, 1857.

DEAR SIR — I was much amused by your description
of the braon-sinshir which is likely to extinguish us all.
Deborah Ford was hanged about Shrovetide, 1641, by
O'Donovan (Daniel, son of Donell, son of Donell-na-g
Croicean,) and Teige-a-duna McCarthy of Dunmanway.
If the drops had ceased on the death of the late General O'Donovan of Bawnlahan, in 1829, the tradition
would have been oracular; but the drops are likely to
continue to fall as long as the grouted arch retains its
solidity.   Drops of this kind are shown in various parts
of Ireland.   A drop like these fell on the tomb of

O'Fogarty at Holy Cross Abbey, but ceased when the last of the race was hanged at Clonmel for Whiteboyism! Another braon aillse continued to fall on the tomb of the White knights at Kilmallock, till the last of the direct descendants of these knights died without issue.

What the drops of Castle Donovan may do it is hard to divine. I do not believe that the Clan-Donovan are a long-lived or a prudent race. They are all fond of their drop, and I believe that they are likely to become extinct in Ireland, or to be removed westward to the new world by the steady encroachment of the Saxon race.

The drops will surely outlive the present Montpelier family, but they have nothing to say to the murder of Deborah Ford. They should have ceased at the extinction of the head of the Bawnlahan family in 1829. But this family is not yet extinct, and the deadly drops hang over them like fatal swords.

There were O'Donovans at Crookhaven, whose pedigree is preserved. Is Timothy O'Donovan of Arhahill still living? Is Richard Donovan of Lisheens House at Ballincolla still living?

I was glad to hear that you fasted and prayed on Wednesday last. In the last century, the Milesian Irish showed a great disinclination to pray for the success of the arms of England. Timothy O'Sullivan wrote about 1800, on the proclamation of George III.

Go sintear mo phiob-sa le ramharcorda, choi'che ma ghiodhfiod air maithe leosan—

> " May my windpipe be stretched by a very stout cord,
> If e'er for their welfare, I pray to the Lord."

But we are getting more and more English and loyal every century. Timothy O'Donovan of the Cove, is one of the highest Tories you have in Cork County— though a great Papist; and so is his relative Rickard Donovan, clerk of the Crown.

The O'Donovan writes to me—October 8th, 1857. "We have just now an abatement of an awful storm and deluge of rain, such as rarely occurs. I trust it may not have damaged those two noble ships, Austrian and Great Britain, that left this port on Monday and Tuesday for India, with 2,000 soldiers."

Yours as ever,
J. O'Donovan.

Irish tories are those Irishmen who side with the government of Ireland by England. The O'Donovan of Montpelier was a tory and a Protestant; Timothy O'Donovan of O'Donovan's Cove, was a tory and a Papist. Those two held landlord possession of lands that belonged equally to their clansmen; England protected them in that landlord possession of the robbery from their own people, and that is why and how those Irish landlords all over Ireland back England in maintaining a foreign government in their native land.

And here, I may as well pause to let my readers see some old historical records that will corroborate what I, in a previous chapter, said about my people being deprived of their lands because they would not turn Protestant; not alone my people, but all the people of the old blood of Ireland from Cork and Kerry to Donegal and Antrim.

The Skibbereen *Eagle* of February 19, 1898, reprint-
ing a historical paper about my native diocese, from
the *Lamp*, says :

Though the diocese of Ross was small, it was not
too small to tempt the rapacity and greed of the Reformation leaders. A certain William Lyons, who was
an apostate from the beginning, was appointed Protestant Bishop of Ross in 1582. He met with a characteristic reception from the brave and zealous priests
and people of Ross. All the plate, ornaments, vest-
ments and bells connected with the cathedral and mon-
astery, as well as a chime of bells in solid silver, valued
at £7,000, were secreted in the strand at Ross Bay.
And so well was the secret kept, that though the
priest and friars were tortured and hanged—in the
hope that love of life would tempt them to disclose the
hiding place, the treasure remained undiscovered to
this date.

The people were not behind hand in their opposition.
Determined that the residence that had been conse-
crated by so many saints and patriots should not be
contaminated by the presence of an apostate, they set
fire to the old Episcopal mansion, so that the intruder to
the See of Ross had to report to the Commissioners, in
1615, that on his arrival he found no residence, "but
only a place to build one on." Lyons, however, was
not to be denied a place whereon to lay his head. He
built himself a house at the cost of £300, a large sum
for those days, "but in three years it was burned by
the rebel, O'Donovan." The Protestant Bishop, for
want of something better to do, turned planter ; for we

have a record that he was commissioned "to find out
ways and means to people Munster with English inhabitants."

Elizabeth at this time was Queen of England, and in
the first year of her reign were passed these laws:

First year of Elizabeth, Chapter 2, Section 8. And
all and every person or persons inhabitating within this
realm shall diligently and faithfully resort to their
Parish church or chapel, or to some usual place where
Common Prayer and other Service of God is used or min-
istered, upon pain that every person so offending shall
forfeit for every such offence twelve pence, to be levied
by the church wardens of the parish, by way of distress on the goods, lands and tenements of such offender.

Statute 23 of Elizabeth, Chapter 2, says:

"And be it likewise enacted, that every person who
shall say or sing mass, being thereof lawfully convicted,
shall forfeit the sum of two hundred marks, and be
committed to prison in the next jail, there to remain
by the space of one year, and from thenceforth till he
have paid the said sum of two hundred marks. And
that every person who shall willingly hear mass, shall
forfeit the sum of one thousand marks, and suffer imprisonment for a year.

"Be it also further enacted that every person above
the age of fourteen years who shall not repair to some
church, chapel or usual place of Common prayer, but
forbear the same, contrary to the tenor of a statute
made in the first year of Her Majesty's reign, for uni-
formity of Common prayer, and being thereof lawfully

convicted, shall forfeit to the Queen's majesty for
every month which he or she shall so forbear, twenty
pounds of lawful English money."

The 29th statute of Elizabeth, Chapter 6, Section 4,
says :

" And be it also enacted that every such offender in
not repairing to Divine Service, who shall fortune to
be thereof once convicted, shall pay into the said receipt of the exchequer, after the rate of twenty pounds
for every month. And if default shall be made in any
part of any payment aforesaid, that then, and so often,
the Queen's Majesty shall and may by process out of the
said exchequer, take, seize and enjoy all the goods, and
two parts as well of all the lands, tenements and hereditaments, leases and farms of such offender, as of all
other lands, tenements and hereditaments liable to such
seizure, leaving the third part only of the same lands,
tenements and hereditaments, leases and farms to and
for the maintenance and relief of the same offender, his
wife, children and family."

Elizabeth dies in the year 1603 and James I.,
comes to the throne. He makes all haste to confirm
all that Elizabeth had done to plunder and persecute
Irish Catholics, and gets his Parliament to pass these
acts :

Statute 1., James, Chapter 4. "And be it further
enacted by authority of this present parliament, that
where any seizure shall be had of the two parts of any
lands, tenements, hereditaments, leases or farms, for
the non-payment of the twenty pounds due, and payable for each month, according to the statute in that

case made and provided; that in every such case, every such two parts shall, according to the extent thereof, go toward the satisfaction and payment of the twenty pounds due and payable for each month, and unpaid by any such recusant."

Statute 3 of James, Chapter 4, says:

"Inasmuch as it is found by daily experience, that many of His Majesty's subjects that adhere in their hearts to the Popish religion, by the infection drawn from thence, and by the wicked and devilish counsel of Jesuits, Seminaries, and other like persons dangerous to the Church and State, and so far perverted in the point of their loyalties, and due allegiance unto the King's Majesty, and the Crown of England, and do the better to cover and hide their false hearts, repair sometimes to church, to escape the penalty of the laws in behalf provided.

"Be it enacted by the King's Most Excellent Majesty, the lords spiritual and temporal, and the commoners in this present parliament assembled: That every Popish recusant, convicted, or hereafter to be convicted, which heretofore hath conformed him or herself, and who shall not repair to church and receive the sacrament of the Lord's supper, he or she shall, for such not receiving, lose and forfeit for the first year, twenty pounds a month; for the second year for such not receiving, forty pounds a month, until he or she shall have received the said sacrament as is aforesaid.

" And if after he or she shall have received the said sacrament as is aforesaid, and after that, shall eftsoons at any time offend in not receiving the said sacrament as is aforesaid by the space of one whole year ; that in every such case the person so offending shall for every such offence lose and forfeit three-score pounds of lawful English money."

Then, to meet the cases of estated and wealthy Catholics who would rather pay the fines and forfeits of twenty, forty and sixty pounds, than attend the Protestant churches, an act was passed to deprive them of two-thirds of their lands, tenements, leases and farms. Here are the words of that act:

"Now, forasmuch as the said penalty of twenty pounds monthly is a greater burden unto men of small living, than unto such as are of better ability, and do refuse to come unto Divine Service as aforesaid, who, rather than they will have two parts of their lands to be seized, will be ready always to pay the said twenty pounds, and yet retain in their own hands the residue of their livings and inheritance—being of great yearly value, which they do for the most part employ to the maintenance and superstition of the Popish religion. Therefore, to the intent that hereafter the penalty for not repairing to Divine service might be inflicted in better proportion upon men of great ability : Be it enacted that the King's Majesty, his heirs and successors, shall have full power and liberty to refuse the penalty of twenty pounds a month, and thereupon to seize and take to his own use two parts in three of all the lands, tenements, hereditaments, leases and farms, and the same to remain to his own and other uses, interest and purposes hereafter in this act provided, **in** lieu and in full recompense of the twenty pounds monthly."

I heard at my father's fireside, before I was able to read a book, about those laws which I am now copying from an old law book of the seventeenth century. All my readers are victims of these laws. Father Campbell and Father Brown, the priests of my parish to-day, are victims of them. They, and the many other good priests who are tenants on the estate of the *United Irishmen* newspaper, ought not to blame me much, if I was ever during my life, ready and willing to join any society of Irishmen that were aiming at destroying English rule, and English government in Ireland.

I am not done with John O'Donovan's letters. I regard them as historical—historical, after we are all dead; so I let you see some more of them.

DUBLIN, October 24, 1858.

MY DEAR FRIEND—My second son, Edward, desires me to send to you his first attempt at painting the armorial bearings of the O'Donovans. He drew them very well in pencil, but he spoiled his drawing in laying on the colors, at which he is not yet sufficiently expert. He has been about a year at drawing under the tuition of Mr. Bradford of the Jesuits' Seminary, No. 6 Great Denmark street, but I have determined upon *with*drawing him from this amusement, as he was spending all his time at drawing cats and dogs, and neglecting his more important duties. He has been put into Homer and Euclid this quarter, which will occupy all his time.

A young friend of mine, William John O'Donovan of the Middle Temple, London, has been making re-searches in London about O'Donovans, and has found some particulars about the sept of Kilmeen, or Mac Enesles, which escaped me. I will write to him on the subject when I hear of his arriving in London. He is a very young man of some fortune, and a most enthusi-astic herald and genealogist.

Since I wrote to you last, I lost my only brother, and am now the last of my generation. He left one grandson of the ominous name of Kerrigan (which was the name of the old bishop of Cork who left a curse on our race for their having murdered Mahon King of Munster, the brother of Brian Boru). My brother's daughter, Adelia ni Donovan was married to Thomas Frederick Kerrigan, the only son of an old merchant of New York. She had no money, of course, and the old man turned his son out of doors for this imprudent marriage. Then the son went to California, where he went through a variety of adventures. At length the father died, and the hero of California has returned to his wife and child, and taken his father's place in New York.

I enclose you his note to me, from which I infer that he believed I had known all about my brother's death; but I had not known a word about it except in a dream, from which I would venture to calculate the minute at which he died.

The enclosed extract from a note from the Reverend Mr. Hayman, Protestant minister of Youghal, reminded me of you, and I send it, hoping that you will be able

to tell me something about the Nagles mentioned by
him. I remain, dear sir, yours ever sincerely,

JOHN O'DONOVAN.

DUBLIN, 36 UPPER BUCKINGHAM STREET,
October 25, 1858.

DIARMUID O'DONNOBHAIN
(MAC ENESLES, ROSA-MHOIR.)

MY DEAR FRIEND—The O'Donovan and I are good
friends? He seems to me to be a kind and good man,
and really an Irishman of some spirit. I gave the
young gentleman of the Inner Temple, London, a letter of introduction to him last August, and he spent
about ten days with him at Montpelier, while he was
examining the registry of Cork, for O'Donovan Wills.
He told me that The O'Donovan treated him with
great urbanity, hospitality and kindness. This young
gentleman is of the Wexford Sept of the Hy-Figenti;
is about twenty-six years old, six feet two inches tall;
a Protestant, (but he is likely to be fished up by the
Pope some day or another, like the Ramm of Gorey!)
Next year, during the vacation, he promises to examine
the Herbert documents for me. Herbert had given me
permission to examine his papers several years since,
but I have not been able to take time to go to Killarney. This young gentleman has been in receipt of
£350 per annum in right of his mother, who died
when he was eighteen months old. His father, who is
about sixty-seven years old, married a young wife a
year or two since, but he will leave this young Mr.
John O'Donovan £400 a year in addition to what he

has already. He is the cousin-german of the Captain
E. O'Donovan, who took the Russian battery at Alma,
and of Henry O'Donovan who was shot through the
head at the taking of the Little Redan at Sebasto-
pol.

As I feel convinced that you take a great interest in
all true branches of our name, I enclose you a letter
from a Daniel Donovan of Queenstown (Cove of
Cork) who appears to me to be a very respectable and
worthy man, though little known in his neighborhood,
except as a baker. Who is he? I firmly-believe that
the name will become important again, though now
sunk low enough as regards landed property.

I forgot to ask you in my last letter what happened
our American friend, your cousin Florence, who expected to be appointed Consul at Cork. Has he written to you since? Has he any desire to return home?

I do not believe that my ancestor Edward comes
under the curse of the Braon-Sinshir of Dorothy Ford,
for he was killed by a cannon ball, which I think I
have, about six years before she was hanged by Daniel
O'Donovan and Teige-a-doona McCarthy; but I labor
under the curse of the holy Bishop Kerrigan, and so do
you, and the whole race; but I believe—hope—it lost
its withering force, or that its fulminatory influence
was nearly spent after the fifth generation. Curses
among the Jews exhausted themselves in the fifth generation. The Irish belief is that the curse returns on
the pronouncer if it was not deserved. Our ancestor
really deserved the curse pronounced on him.

Let me congratulate you on the subject of your

many sons. I am particularly fortunate in that respect, for I have no daughter to run away with any Kerrigan ; but, as the Emperor of China said : " Where there are many sons, there are many dangers." Excuse hurry, late toward midnight, and after a hard day's work. My sight is failing.

Yours sincerely,
JOHN O'DONOVAN.

DUBLIN, Nov. 10, 1858.

MY DEAR FRIEND—You will oblige me by returning to me the descent of the Rev. Mr. Hayman of Youghal (with any remarks you have to make on the Nagles), at your earliest convenience. I want to try what my grenadier namesake in London can make of it. He is pedigree-mad, if any man ever was so, and would read a whole library for one fact relating to any branch of the O'Donovans.

Write me such a note as I can send him (without making any allusion to Protestants) and I will get him to make any searches you like about the Kilmeen or Glean-a-Mhuilin Sept.

My eldest boy John entered Trinity College, Dublin, on the 5th instant, and was admitted to contend for mathematical honors. He feels himself like a fish out of water among the Tory Protestants, after leaving the Jesuit fathers of Great Denmark street.

It is reported here that a young Ireland war is beginning to be organized in Cork and Kerry, but I do not believe it. You need not make any allusion to this in your notes, because my young friend is an aristocrat, though he hates the Saxons more than I do.

Yours in great haste,
                    JOHN O'DONOVAN.

The "Young Ireland War" as he calls it, got me into prison a few weeks after he wrote that letter. He wrote it on the 10th of November, 1858. I was arrested on the 5th of December, and kept in Cork Jail until August, 1859; but that did not make John O'Donovan afraid of writing to me. I wrote to him on some subjects from Cork Jail. He was in England at the time, and I got this letter from his son Edmond, who was then fifteen years old.

DUBLIN, June 20, 1859.
MR. O'DONOVAN ROSSA, COUNTY JAIL, CORK.

SIR—My father and my brother John are at present in Oxford, else you would have long since received an answer to your letter. As you would probably wish to write to him again, I send you his address, which is in care of Dr. Bandenel, Bodleian Library, Oxford. We expect them home about the 24th of July.

I remain your, etc.,
                    E. O'DONOVAN.

That is the Edmond O'Donovan who became so celebrated as a war correspondent in Asia and Africa, for the London papers, and who was killed in the Soudan in the year 1882. About June the 14th, 1859, his father wrote me this letter:

DEAR SIR—I have received your letter of the 5th instant, and was glad to hear that your enthusiasm had not cooled down. I was, since I wrote to you last, away in the beautiful land of the Saxon, where they seem to know as much about us as they do about the Pawnee Loups of North America. I worked in the British Museum, the Tower of London, the State paper office, the Lambeth Library, all in London, and in the Lambeth Library at Oxford. The State papers are full of most curious information relating to Ireland, which will be published some time between this and the day of judgment, for the enlightenment of posterity, but not in our times.

John Collins of Myross, the last Irish poet and antiquary of Carbery was an Irish Senachy without any critical knowledge whatsoever.

The tribe of the O'Donovans which he calls Mac-Aeneus or MacAongus, had never any existence under that appellation, but the O'Donovans of Glenawilling, are frequently mentioned in old Irish pedigrees, under the name of MacEnesles, and in the public records under that of MacEnesles-Mac-I-Crime. This MacEnesles family was the third (second by descent) most important sept of the O'Donovans of Carbery, and the descent of their ancestor Aneslis, or Stanislaus, is given thus by MacFirbis:

1. Donovan, ancestor of the O'Donovans, slain, 977, by Brian Boru.

2. Cathal, fought at Clontarf, 1014.

3. Amhlaff or Auliffe, flourished 1041.

4. Murrough. 5. Aneslis. 6. Raghnall or Reginald.

7. Mulrony. 8. Crom, slain, 1254, by O'Mahony in Glanachryme near Dunmanway.

9. Cathal, a quo Clancahill, anciently of Castle Donovan in Drimoleague.

Aneslis, a quo MacEnesles of Glenawilling.

Loughlin, a quo the Clan Loughlin of Cloghatradbally.

10. Donogh More, son of Aneslis.

The pedigrees of the Clancahill of Castle-Donovan, and of the Clan Loughlin of Kilmaccabee and Reenogriana are preserved, but that of the sept of Mac Enesles (now locally Mac MacIninish) has been entirely neglected. The last distinguished man of the sept was Captain Daniel Boy O'Donovan of Kilcoleman, who had served his Majesty faithfully beyond the seas, 1641. In 1632, Dermod MacTeige MacEnesles O'Donovan possessed the lands of Lisnabreeny West, in the parish of Kilmeen; but here I loose sight of them altogether! They had no local historian. Aneslis their ancestor had four sons, Donogh More, Rickard, Walter and Randal, who became the founder of four distinct septs generally called in the public records, Slught Eneslis MacIcroyme. Denis na Meeny, so much talked of by John Collins, was one of this sept.　　Yours ever sincerely,

JOHN O'DONOVAN.

After I came out of jail, our correspondence continued; I will continue it here by showing you this letter:

DUBLIN, March 1, 1860.

MY DEAR FRIEND—I have just received your note, and was glad to see your handwriting. I should be glad to contribute in any way to illustrate the literature of old Ireland, but my hands are more than full just now. I have too many irons in the fire, so that some of them must get burned. My boys are of no help to me, because they have too many studies to attend to, and I do not like to interrupt them. I have the eldest in Trinity College, and three others at the Jesuits' Grammar School, where they are making considerable progress in classic and science. I have buried the youngest, Morgan Kavanaugh O'C. O'D., who died on the 11th of February, 1860, at the age of one year and forty-nine days, so that I calculate he went off the stage of this world without any stain from ancient or modern sin. I have no reason to be sorry for his departure from this wicked world. But his mother is so sorry after him that she refused to take food for two days, which has brought her to the brink of insanity.

I was glad to learn that Henry O'Donovan, Esq., of Lissard, had an heiress. He may have a house full of children now, of both sexes, as he has broken the ice, notwithstanding the curse of the Coarb of St. Barry. Our ancestor Donobhan, son of Cathal, was certainly a singularly wicked and treacherous man, but it is to be hoped that his characteristics have not been transmitted, and therefore that the curse of the good Coarb of St. Barry has spent its rage long since. But still if you view the question fairly, you will incline with me to believe that the curse still hangs over us:

1. Castle-Donovan was forfeited in 1641, and given away, forever.

2. My ancestor Edmond killed the son of O'Sullivan Beare, and was killed himself in 1643, leaving his descendants landless. Right!

3. The race of Colonel Daniel O'Donovan became extinct in 1829, in the person of General O'Donovan, who left the small remnant of his patrimonial inheritance to Powell, a Welshman. Curse!

4. The present O'Donovan is childless. His brother Henry has one daughter, who, if she be the only heir, will leave the name landless.

These four reasons, adding to them your imprisonment in 1859, convinces me that the curse of the good Coarb still hangs over us all. But I hope we may escape it in the next world!

John O'Mahony (the descendant of the real murderer of Mahon, King of Munster), who was proclaimed here in 1848, is now in America, a greater rebel than ever. His translation of Keating's history of Ireland is rather well done.

Wishing you every happiness, I remain dear sir, yours ever,   J. O'DONOVAN.

DUBLIN, March 21, 1860.

MY DEAR FRIEND—I have promised to write for Sir Bernard Burk's "Family Vicissitudes" a few articles on fallen Irish families, and I was thinking of giving a note of James O'Donovan of Cooldurragha, whom you told me was in the poorhouse, Skibbereen. You mentioned to me that he had no son. Perhaps you might not think it troublesome to ask himself if he would like this notice of him to appear. If he should like it, you will oblige me by letting me know exactly what he has to say on the "vicissitudes" of his family. I know you have a quick apprehension and a lively imagination, and I will therefore expect from your pen a curious story from the dictation of James O'D. himself, on the vicissitudes of his family. I believe that his descent is pure, and that he is now the senior representative of Donogh, the fourth son of O'Donovan by the daughter of Sir Owen McCarthy-Reagh. This is a high descent for one who is a porter in the poorhouse, and I think his story might be worked up into a narrative that might do justice to the genius of Plutarch.

Your friend Edmond, the painter, has got free access to the records of the Ulster King's Tower. I am almost afraid to let him indulge his tastes for heraldry; but I am willing to let him go there every second day, on condition that he will not neglect his classical studies. Should you be writing to your cousin Florence, of New York, you will oblige me by asking him to call on my nephew-in-law, Thomas Francis Kerrigan, telling him that I wish them to become acquainted.

This has been a very severe March, but as you have youth, health and enthusiasm on your side, you must have come off more scathless from the effects of it than one who is a regular Mananan Mac Lir—a regular thermometer—from the effects of rheumatism.

Yours, ever sincerely,

JOHN O'DONOVAN.

As he asked me to see James O'Donovan, I saw him.
He was a porter at the entrance gate of the Skibbereen
Poorhouse, at a salary of twelve pounds a year.

When he would have a vacation day, he'd come into
my house in town. One day I told him what John
O'Donovan wanted me to get from him. He did not
like to give it; he was afraid it would injure him.
Henry O'Donovan brother to " The O'Donovan " was
an ex-officio poor law guardian; Powell, the Welshman,
who inherited the lands of General O'Donovan was an
ex-officio P. L. G., and if he, James, got anything published about who and what he was, they may think he
had some design upon ownership of the lands of the
O'Donovan clan, which they held because their fathers
and their kin turned Protestant, while James' fathers
remained Catholics, and so lost their patrimony; so
James did not like to give me the information John
O'Donovan wanted, for fear it would—to the loss of
his situation—prejudice the landlord guardians against
him, most of whom were the possessors of the plundered
property of the people.

I told that to John O'Donovan, telling him I did not
like to press James to give me his story.

The next of his letters is this:

DUBLIN, March 24, 1860.

MY DEAR FRIEND—I have received your letter, and
was exceedingly sorry to hear you had lost your wife
—a great loss in case of ardent affection on both sides;
but you are young and vigorous; and time, the dulce
molimen—the soft soother—will finally reduce your

grief to "a softer sadness." Your imprisonment must have weighed heavily upon her spirits.

My nephew-in-law seems to be a sensible man of the world. He seems to be a great Catholic. Of his politics I know nothing, but calculate that they are ultramontane; and I think Finghin Ceannmor and he would agree very well. I have no faith in politics of any kind, nor have I any trust in Whig or Tory. I was glad to learn that poor James was in good health, and not utterly destitute. I hope you will be able to get out of him all the Shanachus that he has in his head about the Clann-Donnabhain. I am sure it would offend him to hear that Donell-na-g Croicean, who died in 1584, was unquestionably a bastard— Teige, his father, was never married. Donell-na-g Croicean "kept" Eileen ni Laoghaire — Ellen O'Leary, but afterward married her. Domhnall, their son, married Juana, daughter of Sir Owen Mc-Carthy.

Daniel, their first son, is the ancestor of General O'Donovan, of Bawnlahan, who died in 1829. Teige, their second son, is the ancestor of Morgan, now O'Donovan. Donogh, the fourth son is the ancestor of James of Cooldurragha.

It is useless to tell him this, because he would not believe it, though it was sworn to by "Sir Finghin O'Driscoll, and divers other good and trustworthy witnesses"; but he heard from the Clan-Loughlin and other septs of the O'Donovans, that such was the tradition.

This illegitimacy of the senior branch is, in my opinion, another result of the curse of the good Coarb of St. Barry.

I have given in the Appendix to the Annals, all that I could find about James' pedigree; but what I want from him now is his story of how the property gradually passed from him and his ancestors, giving dates as often as possible, and also the cause of the loss of the lands. It is very curious how the descendants of the youngest son, Kedagh, succeeded better than any of the rest, except the Protestants.

How many acres did James farm when he was married?

My western correspondents always speak of him as a poor, struggling farmer, but a man of strict probity and high principles. Does any other male descendant of his ancestor Donogh or Denis survive? If there is none, does it not strike you that the curse is at work in removing the name out of Clancahill? I am actually superstitious on this point. I believe that most members of the family are high-minded, and remarkably honest, but I believe, also, that they are reckless, addicted to drink, and irritable to a degree that counterbalances all their amiable characteristics. I am anxious to preserve a memorial of James, as by all accounts, he has been a virtuous, honest and honorable man; and only unfortunate, as being overwhelmed by adverse circumstances, or perhaps, as not having sufficient craft or cunning to grapple with the world. I enclose you the Jesuits' letter about my boys. These Jesuits are very clever. I also enclose a note from W. J. O'Donovan of the Protestant sept of Wexford, who

beats us all hollow in enthusiasm for the name and its
pedigree.

Hoping that you keep up your spirits, I remain,
dear sir, yours ever sincerely,   JOHN O'DONOVAN.

DUBLIN, March 27, 1860.

MY DEAR FRIEND—You told me when last in Dublin, that the family of Deasy were Irish, and were
called in Irish, O'Daosaigh. Are you quite certain
that the O' is prefixed to the name by the Irish-speaking people of the County of Cork?

We have in the County Kilkenny a family of the
name of O'Daedi, anglicized Deady, and I have been
long of the opinion that your Deasys of County Cork
are the same. You have a Dundeady in the parish of
Rathbarry, in your county, a well-known promontory.

You will oblige me exceedingly by asking James of
Cooldurragha, whether the Deasys are a Cork family,
and what the name is called by the Irish-speaking people. Please to ask James the following questions:

First.—Are there O'Deadys and O'Deasys in the
County Cork?

Second.—If not; how long have the O'Deasys been
in the County Cork; and where did they come from?
What is the tradition?

We have O'Deadys in Ossory, but believe that they
came from Munster; and John MacWalter Walsh, in
his dirge, lamenting the downfall of the Irish, sets
down O'Deady as one of the Irish chieftains next after
O'Coileain, now Collins. This looks odd; for I cannot
find any Irish chieftain of the name of O'Deady in the

Irish annals, or Irish genealogies. I have several relatives of this name.

Third.—How long have the Deasys of your county
(of whom is the Attorney-General Rickard Deasy)
been in the County Cork? Are they aborigines or late
comers? If aborigines, where were they seated? If
late comers, how is it known that they are of Irish descent? How long are they among the rank of the
gentry? Are there many of the name in the county?
Are they a clan anywhere? I suppose they are
O'Deadys.

Fourth.—Did James ever hear of a sept of the
O'Donovans in the County of Cork, who were not descended from Crom, or the Donovan who captured
Mahon, King of Munster at Bruree? It appears there
was a sept of the O'Donovans of the same race as
O'Driscoll of Colthuighe, before the race of the treacherous Donovan of Bruree had settled in the O'Driscoll
territory; but I fear they cannot now be distinguished.
They were seated in Tuath-Feehily, near Inchydoney,
on the Bay of Clonakilty.   Yours ever,
                                    JOHN O'DONOVAN.

                        DUBLIN, March 29, 1860.
MY DEAR FRIEND—I return you the letters of Donal
Oge and Edward O'Sullivan (Edward, the Cork but-
ter merchant, now dead—1898), and thank you most
heartily for the read of them. Donald Oge (Dan
McCartie, now in New York—1898), seems very
clever, but the other seems wild. Your cousin,
Finghin Ceannmor and my nephew-in-law in New

York may be of mutual advantage to each other, as they seem bent on business and industry. I fear your political friends are too sublime in their notions to herd with either of them.

You will oblige me by getting hold of Shemus of Cooldurragha soon as you can, or his brother. Have they any share of education? I suppose John Collins was their chief tutor.

I was often invited by the O'Donovan and his brother Henry to visit them, but I have never been able to spare time. I thought to send Edmond last year, but his mother would not let him go. Next summer or autumn I may take a stroll to the Southwest with one of two of the boys, to show them gentes cunnabula nostrae.

Meantime, believe me, yours ever,
S. O'DONOBHAN.

DUBLIN, April 20, 1860.

MY DEAR FRIEND—Many thanks for your letter about the Deasys. I fear that their pedigree is not on the rolls of time, and that we can never discover any more about them.

Your observations about the Pope have amused me very much. My faction of boys are divided into two deadly political enemies to each other on the subject, and I can hardly keep them from fighting on the subject. One party is for our Holy Father the Pope and his temporal power, and another for ceding him his spiritual power only. They are all for Napoleon;

which, in my opinion, is not fair, and they hope that
the Bourbons will never be restored.

My eldest son John, got the prize for chemistry in
the Museum of Industry here, which was a great effort
for him, being just turned off seventeen and having to
contend with the practical young chemists of Dublin.

My second son, Edmond, is actually mad at his her-
aldic studies, though I have been constantly telling
him that it is an obsolete science, and that mankind
will soon do very well without it. But my admoni-
tion is slighted, and he continues to cultivate the old
knightly science. You will soon see some of his doings
in my article on Wilhelm Count Gall Von Bourkh of
the Austrian service, from whose brother Walter we
descend collaterally.

My third son, William, is the cleverest of all, and is
likely to become a Jesuit or a Passionist. He is en-.
tirely for the Pope and his temporal power; and in-
clines to sneer at the *Nation* and *Irishman* equally.
We get both these eccentric Irish newspapers. My
fourth son Richard is all for statistics and geography.
He knows more of European statistics than any boy of
his age in the world (except, perhaps, some of the
mnemonistic students) but he is wicked and selfish and
will be very lucky if he is not yet killed fighting
against the niggers.

Hoping to hear of your second marriage (which is a
right, natural and proper thing), I remain, dear sir,
your well wisher, JOHN O'DONOVAN.

While I was in prison, from 1865 to 1871, Edmond

O'Donovan was taking an active part in Fenian politics. In that enterprise he had traveled through Ireland, England, Scotland, and had made a few visits to America. After I left prison and came to America, I got this letter from him;

COUNTY DURHAM, ENGLAND,
May 9, 1872.

MY DEAR ROSSA—Twenty times within the past four months, I have sat down with the intention of writing you a long letter; but as often those circumstances over which one has no control interposed their ill-favored presence. Even as it is, I cannot catch time for an interchange of thoughts, and only scribble a few lines to ask you to get our friend whom it concerns to look after two gentlemen of my acquaintance, now on your side of the Atlantic, and who complain they can't get credit among you. Their names and addresses are as follows: Thomas Smith and Owen Murray, late of the North of England. Address, under cover, to John Kelly, Spuyten Duyvil, Westchester County, N. Y. If you would kindly see after this I would be obliged.

I duly received your card, per favor of Mr. Scanlan, to whose letter, by the way, I have never since replied, and about which you must apologize for me, should you see him, as he is an old and valued friend.

I address this to the private address on your card—under cover, to Mrs. Kelly.

I have been reading your letters to the Dublin *Irishman* with great interest, and having the misfortune to know something about the United States, through two visits made during your imprisonment, I can thoroughly appreciate and feel for your unenviable position of nineteenth century knight-errant and Paladin in the cause of distressed virtue.

Be assured that if ever I take up such a rôle—and you must pardon my saying so—I will display greater discrimination in the choice of a sphere of action. I know well the retort that will spring to your lips—that those "who live in glass houses should not throw stones"—and, that those who constitute themselves champions of a lot of "coundfounded, hairy, greasy foreigners" should not talk of wisdom. But, after all, you know what the United States Germans say—"the longer a man lives, the more he finds out," and I can only say in the words of the immemorial schoolboy, "I'll never do it again, sir."

I was a prisoner of war in Bavaria when I read of your release, and, would you believe it, it was a Roman Catholic clergyman who brought me the news, and was actually—he said—glad to hear of it.

Truth, they say, is stranger than fiction—and as the Turcos used to exclaim, "Be chesm, on my head and my eyes be it," if what I tell you isn't correct.

Time, paper and nonsensical ideas being all run out —with best respects to Mrs. O'D. and all old friends, I remain ever yours,

E. O'DONOVAN.

P. S. Excuse rubbish; the fact being that I am writing a book on metaphysics, and under the circumstances, you cannot expect common sense. E. O'D.

P. A. Collins, of Boston, was active in Fenian politics those days. So was Colonel Tom Kelly, one of the men rescued in Manchester. This is a letter written by Edward O'Donovan to P. A. Collins:

MY DEAR MR. COLLINS—Should any question arise as to the part which Colonel Kelly intends playing in the present arrangement for unifying the I. R. B., of Great Britain—and should any doubt arise as to his abiding by the decision of the committee—a member of which you are, I beg to state that I am authorized by Colonel Kelly to speak for him in the matter, and hold myself in readiness to appear before the convention, or any committee appointed by them to investigate the true state of the case.

Furthermore, I am authorized by Colonel Kelly, should such be necessary for the harmonious working of the parties, to lay before you his complete and entire resignation of all claims to authority over any branch of the organization, either here or in Great Britain and Ireland. Your obedient servant.   E. O'DONOVAN.

P. A. Collins, Esq.

When Edmond was in Asia and Africa, some of the native tribes made him their king. I take from Appleton's Encyclopedia this account of how he came by his death:

" The battle ground had been selected by the Mahdi with his usual sagacity. It was a narrow rocky passage between wooded hills, in which he had placed the guns and rifles captured in former engagements, in positions where they could be used with effect, but where it was impossible for General Hicks to deploy his artillery. Into this ambuscade the Egyptian advance was led by a treacherous guide. The army of Hicks Pasha was totally annihilated. The troops are reported to have fought three days without water, until all their cartridges were expended. General Hicks then ordered a bayonet charge, but the army was immediately overwhelmed, and not a man escaped. The commander-in-chief, with Alla-ed-Din, Governor General of the Soudan, Abbas Bey, Colonel Farquahar, Major Von Seckendorf, Massy, Warner and Evans, Captain Horlth and Anatyaga, Surgen-general Georges Bey, Surgeon Rosenberg, O'Donovan the well-known war correspondent, a number of Egyptian pashas and beys, and all the officers, who numbered 1,200, and soldiers of the army, were slain."

In a book bearing the title of " Mr. Parnell, M. P., and the I. R. B." I read this passage:

" The most distinguished literary man ever known to be in the ranks of Fenianism was undoubtedly Edmond O'Donovan, who was a ' V,' or organizer for the North of England, and afterward the well-known Asiatic traveler and writer."

Looking at the death of the three eldest sons of John O'Donovan—John, Edmond and William—I cannot help thinking on what their father says about his being almost superstitious on the head of that holy curse pronounced against the name. John was drowned while bathing in the river at St. Louis; Edmond was slain in Africa; and William died here in New York a dozen years ago; I saw him buried in Calvary Cemetery. The three were actively connected with the Fenian movement in Ireland. I don't know I may blame myself for having anything to do with that connection.

The father, John O'Donovan, died in the year 1862, at the age of fifty-three, and his co-laborer in Celtic literature, Eugene Curry, died a few months after. God be merciful to them, and to all the souls we are bound to pray for!

Another word; a few words; these few verses from a poem written by Thomas D'Arcy McGee on the death of John O'Donovan will end this chapter:

And thus it is, that even I,
Though weakly and unworthily,
    Am moved by grief
To join the melancholy throng
And chant the sad entombing song
    Above the chief:

Too few, too few, among our great,
In camp or cloister, church or state,
    Wrought as he wrought;
Too few, of all the brave we trace
Among the champions of our race
    Gave us his thought.

Truth was his solitary test,
His star, his chart, his east, his west;
    Nor is there aught
In text, in ocean, or in mine,
Of greater worth, or more divine
    Than this he sought.

With gentle hand he rectified
The errors of old bardic pride,
   And set aright
The story of our devious past,
And left it, as it now must last
   Full in the light.

CHAPTER XXVI.

MY FIRST VISIT TO AMERICA.—MY MOTHER, JOHN
O'MAHONY, THOMAS FRANCIS MEAGHER, ROBERT E.
KELLY, AND HIS SON HORACE R. KELLY, MICHAEL
CORCORAN, P. J. DOWNING, P. J. CONDON, WILLIAM
O'SHEA, AND MICHAEL O'BRIEN THE MANCHESTER
MARTYR.

ON a fine sunny morning in the month of May I
found myself on board the City of Edinburgh steamer,
steaming into the harbor of New York.

She stopped while the quarantine doctor came on
board to make examinations as to the state of her
health.

Gazing around from the deck of the ship, the scenery
was grand—the hills of Staten Island looking as gay
and green as the hills of Ireland.   John Locke's words,
in address to the Cove of Cork, may be addressed to
Clifton :

> And Clifton isn't it grand you look
> Watching the wild waves' motion.
> Resting your back up against the hill,
> With the tips of your toes in the ocean—

And the two forts—Hamilton and Wadsworth—sit-
uate so like to the two forts, Camden and Carlisle, got
me to think that if the ocean was baled out and the
two countries, Ireland and America, were moved over

to each other, Fort Camden touching Fort Hamilton and Fort Carlisle touching Fort Wadsworth, there would be no incongruity or break observable in the grandeur of the scenery, sailing down the River Lee through the Cove of Cork and up the Hudson River through the harbor of New York.

They were war times in America the time I arrived in the country (May 13, 1863). Walking up Broadway, I saw a policeman speaking angrily to another man on the sidewalk near Fulton street; giving him a pretty hard stroke of his stick on the side of the leg, the civilian screeched with pain and limped away crying. An impulse came on me to tell the policeman he had no right to strike the man that way. I did not act on that impulse; I suppose it was well for me I didn't. It showed me there was more liberty in America than I thought there was.

In a few minutes after, I was in the City Hall Park among the soldiers. The ground on which now stands the post office was a part of the park, and was planted with little trees and soldiers' tents. Here I met several people who knew me, and I was very soon in the office of John O'Mahony, No. 6 Centre street.

That night I went with O'Mahony to the armory and drill rooms and other rooms of the Fenian Brotherhood societies. All the Fenians seemed to be soldiers or learning to be soldiers; many of them volunteering to go into the battlefields of America that they might be the better able to fight the battles of Ireland against England. I saw this spirit in most of the speeches I heard delivered that night, and there was speech-making, as well as recruiting and drilling everywhere we went.

I made my home, during the few weeks I was looking around, with one of the Rossa family who came to America in the year 1836—Timothy Donovan, No. 276 Schermerhorn street, Brooklyn.

I brought with me from Ireland, some letters of introduction to people in New York. I had a letter from John Edward Pigott to Richard O'Gorman, a letter from John B. Dillon to Mr. Robert E. Kelly, a tobacco and cigar importer in Beaver street, and several letters from Edward O'Sullivan, a Cork butter merchant, to others. The letter from Mr. Dillon to Mr. Kelly is the letter about which there is a story that I must not forget telling. I delivered it. After reading it, he talked with me in his office for a couple of hours. He asked me about Ireland and the Irish cause—would I give up the cause now, turn over a new leaf, have sense, and turn my attention to business and money making? Also asked me what other letters of introduction I had to friends and how the friends received me. Then he told me what those friends were likely to do, and likely not to do. All that he told me turned out true. "And I suppose Mr. Kelly," said I, "you cannot see the way of doing anything yourself?" "Not much," said he, "not much that will be any permanent good to you. You told me that if you remained for any time in New York you may go into the cigar business in partnership with a cousin of yours. Now, if you do that, I will give you goods to the amount of $2,000; but you'll lose the money and I'll lose the money."

" Then," said I, " why would you give me your goods if you're sure you'll lose the money ? "

" Well," said he, " from the talk I have had with you, I see you are disposed to follow up your past life, and I like to give you some encouragement. There are so few who stick to the cause, once they get a fall in it, or meet a stumbling-block of any kind."

" I thought," said I, "that if I said I would give up the cause, and sensibly turn my attention to commercial business, that then you might offer me the credit of your house." " No," said he, " I wouldn't give you credit to the worth of a dollar in that case."

I did go into business this time, during the few months I spent in New York with my cousin Denis Donovan, in Madison street, but we did not deal in such high class goods as Mr. Kelly imported, and I did not avail myself of his offer of credit. I went back to Ireland in August '63. I was put in prison in 1865; came out of prison in 1871, came to New York and was called upon by Mr. Kelly. At his invitation I called a few times to his house and he called to where I lived, and met my family. In 1874 I rented the Northern Hotel. I called to Mr. Kelly's office, in Beaver street, to talk to him about the offer he made me eleven years ago. He was out of town—down in Cuba; but, said his son, Horace: " There is an order made on the books here, by my father, that you are to get $2,000 worth of goods at any time you desire to have them."

I took about $200 worth of cigars that time—I paid for them before I gave up the hotel business. I have not met any of the family since.

The old gentleman must be gone to the other world. He was what may be called a real old Irish gentleman, with a touch of the Irish aristocrat in him in trim and tone. He must have had his boyhood education in one of the colleges of the continent of Europe in the early years of the century. He was of the O'Kellys of Connaught; tall and straight and handsome; the form of him my mind retains now, may be fairly represented in the form of John D. Crimmins, as I see him passing along the street.

And, the words he spoke to me, did put some life and strength into me, and make me strong to-day, even though the fight I'm fighting be a losing one, and a deserted one—deserted by many who swore to be strong and true to it.

I returned to Ireland in the month of August, 1863. I was in New York during the months of June and July, except one week that I spent in Philadelphia, where lived my mother. I went to see her. She was living with a brother of mine. It was ten o'clock in the evening when I got to the house. She did not know me. She was told it was Jerrie. "No, no, 'tis not Jerrie," and saying this, she passed the tips of her fingers searchingly across my forehead. She found the scar that is on it—from the girl having hoisted me over her head and thrown me on the pavements when I was a year or two old, and then came the kissing and the crying with the memories of the ruined home and the graves we left in Ireland.

In July, 1863, was fought the battle of Gettysburg. The day after the battle a carriage stopped at the door of the house in which I lived at New Chambers and Madison streets. I was told a man in the carriage wanted to see me. The man was William O'Shea of Bantry, who had spent eight or nine months with me in Cork Jail, a few years before then. He asked me to sit with him in the carriage; we drove to some hospital at the west side of Broadway; he registered his name on the books, gave up his money to the clerk, was taken to a ward, and a doctor called. He was dressed in the uniform of a captain; he was a captain in the Forty-second Tammany Regiment; his uniform was all begrimed with earth; he had fallen in the fight; he had four wounds on his body—one bullet having entered in front just below the ribs and come out at the back, and another having struck him in the wrist, traveling up his hand, come out near the elbow. He remained two weeks in that hospital; walked about among the friends in New York two weeks more, then rejoined his regiment, and got shot dead in the next battle. While he was in New York, a brother of his was killed in a battle; he had the brother's body brought on to New York, and buried in Calvary. As he and I were coming from Calvary, we met the funeral of the wife of Colonel Michael Corcoran going to Calvary, and with it we went into the graveyard again.

I have an old relic of his—a letter he wrote me after he rejoined his regiment. In Ireland I familiarly called him "Billy O'."

> With fearless Captain Billy O'
> I joined the Fenian band,
> And swore, one day to strike a blow
> To free my native land.

Here are some words of that memento letter of
Billy O's;

U. S. GENERAL HOSPITAL, No. 1, ANNAPOLIS, MD.,
August 17, 1863.

JER—You see I lose no time in jerking you a line as
soon as I can.

Do, Jer., give me credit for being so prompt and
thoughtful, as it is but seldom I claim praise. Now,
for the history of my route to here.

I got in to Baltimore very peaceably indeed. I had a
little trouble of mind on the cars, but I soon got over
that. My uneasiness was caused by a beautiful New
York girl that was going to Washington to a boarding
school, to complete her studies.

I got into Baltimore about seven o'clock the next
morning after leaving you. I wanted to be here in
time, so as to save my distance, as the horse jockeys
say, which I did in right good order. The next day, I
was admitted into this hospital where I now rest. I'd
have saved three or four hundred dollars by coming
here first, instead of going to New York. Kiss Cousin
Denis and Tim in remembrance of me. Remembrance
to Mr. O'Mahony. Send a line as soon as you get any
news to

BILLY O'.

Accompanying that letter was the following letter:

ANNAPOLIS, MD. Aug. 1 1863.
CAPTAIN WILLIAM O'SHEA, 42d N. Y. VOLUNTEERS,
SIR—Having reported to the Board of Officers for

examination, you are informed that orders from the War Department require that you remain in hospital.

You are hereby directed to report in person to the surgeon, B. A. Vanderkieft, U. S. A., in charge U. S. A. general hospital, Division No.1, Annapolis, Md., for admission and treatment therein. You will comply with all rules and regulations, governing inmates of the hospital, and the instructions given you.

J. S. M'PARLIN.
Surgeon, U. S. A.

On the envelope in which I find those two preceding communications I find indorsed the words: "Capt. Billy O' was killed a month after he wrote this.— ROSSA."

A few nights after the burial of Mrs. Corcoran I was at an entertainment that was at Colonel Corcoran's house; many priests were at it, and many officers were in town on leave and on duty. John O'Mahony told me that Gen. Thomas Francis Meagher was in town the day before, and fixed upon a day that he and I would go out to his home in the Orange Mountains of New York to have a talk about how affairs were in Ireland. We fixed upon a day; Meagher was to meet us with a coach at the railroad station in the Orange Mountains. The appointed day came. On the ferry boat to Jersey City we met Captain Jack Gosson going out to see Meagher too. He was one of Meagher's aides in the war. When we got to the Orange Mountains, Meagher and Mrs. Meagher were at the railroad station before us. We got into the carriage; the general took the whip and drove us to the mansion of his father in-law, Mr. Townsend. After partaking of some refreshments we walked out into the orchard ; birds of all kinds seemed to have their homes there and in the surrounding wood. A little humming bird, little bigger than a big bee, seemed to have its home in every tree. Meagher would go around the blackberry trees and whenever he'd see a large gubolach of a blackberry, he'd pluck it and bring it to me ; he and Captain Gosson all the time laughingly reminding each other of the many strange incidents of battles, and of camp life, and of the many queer things officers and men would do.

O'Mahony whispered to me to entertain Captain Gosson for awhile, as he and Meagher were going to walk up the wood-path to have a private talk. Coming to New York that evening, O'Mahony told me it was for the purpose of initiating General Meagher into the Fenian Brotherhood that he did this, and that he did initiate him.

Meagher was a handsome make of a man that day. Somewhere, I should say, about five feet nine, or five feet ten inches in height, firmly straight and stoutly strong in proportion. When I saw General George B. McClellan some years after, it appeared to me as if he was physically proportioned somewhat like Thomas Francis Meagher.

At the dinner table that evening Meagher and O'Mahony got talking of the draft riots that were in New York the week before. I said I saw some of the riots ; that I saw the crowd that hanged Colonel O'Brien, and saw a man put the muzzle of a pistol to my face, threatening to blow my brains out for lifting from the ground a man who was thrown down by the rioters. "You had a pretty narrow escape," said Meagher.

"Had you been in New York those days and shown yourself to the people," said O'Mahony to Meagher, "you could have stopped all the rioting."

"Not at all," said Meagher, "the people those days were in a mood of mind to tear me limb from limb if they caught hold of me."

I was in at John O'Mahony's office one day. A soldier came in; tall and straight, light but athletic; unloosed his coat, unpocketed his papers and gave them to John O'Mahony. He was introduced to me as Captain Patrick J. Condon, of the Sixty-third Regiment; he brought from the seat of war $600, the monthly contributions of the Army Circles of the Fenian Brotherhood. This was history repeating itself. The history of Irish brigades in the service of France and Spain and Austria records that on every pay day the soldiers would contribute a part of their pay to a fund that was to equip them to fight against England for the freedom of Ireland.

That Captain Condon I speak of went to Ireland to fight for its freedom after the war in America was over. I meet him in New York these days I am writing these "Recollections"; he is as tall and straight and soldierly-looking as he was that day in John O'Mahony's office, in July, 1863, but the hair of his head is as white as the driven snow.

Michael O'Brien, who was hanged in Manchester in

1867, was in New York those days of July, 1863. He
told me that Major Patrick J. Downing of the Forty-
second Regiment was on from the seat of war, and was up
at Riker's Island with a detachment to take the men who
were drafted. We went over to Chambers street and
got from Colonel Nugent, the provost marshal, a " pass "
to visit Riker's Island. Mike O'Brien and I went up
to Riker's Island that evening, and slept in Colonel
Downing's tent that night. Some days after that Mike
came to me and told me he had made up his mind to
join the army. I endeavored to persuade him not to do
so; I told him he had pledged his life to a fight for Ireland, and what now, if he were to be killed fighting in
America? He told me he did not know how to fight
well; that it was to learn how to fight well he was going to enlist; that he had been out to the front to see
Denis (Denis Downing was a brother of Patrick's was
a comrade clerk of Michael's at Sir John Arnott's in
Cork; was now a captain in a Buffalo regiment), and
that he went into a battle that Denis was going into.

What he saw that day showed him that he knew
nothing about war, and he wanted, for Ireland's sake to
learn all he could about it; he had made up his mind to
enlist, and I should go with him to the recruiting office
in Jersey City. I went with him; I saw him measured
and sworn in; the recruiting officer pressing me hard to
go with him. I saw him on the street car that was to
take him to the camp in the suburbs of the city. That
street car came out on the street from under the arch-
way there, near the ferry. Mike stood on the back of
the car; I stood on the street; we kept waving our hats

to one another till the car turned the corner and rolled
out of sight. That is the last sight I had on earth of
one of the truest Irish patriot comrades of my life—
Michael O'Brien the Manchester martyr.

On my way through Chambers street to Provost-
marshal Nugent's office near the Emigrant Savings
Bank, the day I got the "pass" to visit Riker's Island,
some policemen, having prisoners, were going to the
marshal's office, too. Each of them had hold of his
man by the collar of the coat. Those prisoners were
men who had been drafted for the war, and who had
not promptly or voluntarily answered the call the Nation had made upon them for their services as soldiers.
They had gone into hiding, but were arrested and
forced into the fight; and, as likely as anything else,
now that they were obliged to do their duty, some of
them did it bravely, and when the war was over, came
home with all the honors of war.

How often have I thought how well it would be for
the Irish National cause of my day if it had a draft law
that would make its votaries toe the mark at the call
of duty. Those votaries swear it is by the sword alone
they are to free Ireland, but when danger threatens it
how many of them are found to think the country can
be freed without using any sword at all?

That's what made Parnell and parliamentary agitation so strong in Ireland, England and America a
dozen years ago; the leaders of the "sword alone," men
"ratted," and turned in to free Ireland by fighting her
battles in the London parliament. That's what paralyzed the spirit of the Irish National cause and makes

it to-day so dead as it is.   England has the whip hand in Ireland, and is whipping the Irish people out of the country.   In one ship that came into New York harbor this week (April, 1898), 247 young Irish girls came in to New York!

When commencing to write this chapter, I looked into a New York City directory to see if I would find the Mr. Kelly whom I speak of, and who lived in Beaver street in 1863.   I saw the name of Horace R. Kelly.   I wrote to Horace R.   I asked what was the Christian name of his father.   In reply to my inquiry I get this note :

COLORADO SPRINGS, May 8, 1898.

DEAR MR. ROSSA—Your card was forwarded to me here, and in reply, I inform you that my father's name was Robert E. Kelly ; and I am delighted to see how kindly you remember him.

I am no longer in Beaver street ; but have moved to our Factory building at the corner of Avenue A. and 71st street, where I expect to be in about two weeks. I hope you will let me know where I can get a copy of your book, when you will have published it.

I remain, sincerely yours,

HORACE R. KELLY.

It has often surprised me the number of Americans who are in New York, whose blood is Irish, and who would show themselves Irish in heart and soul and pocket, if enslaved Ireland was trying to do anything that would be worth assistance or sacrifice.

CHAPTER XXVII.

GREAT-GRANDFATHER THOMAS CRIMMINS—HIS RECOL-
LECTIONS OF THE MEN OF '98, AND OTHER MEN.

In the spirit of the concluding words of the last chapter, I take *this* last chapter of the first volume of my " Recollections," from the recollections of Mr. Crimmins who has lived in New York for the past sixty-three years. In his early life, he was acquainted with many of the *United Irishmen* of '98, who had made their homes in America, after the years of the trouble. It is among my " recollections," to have met Mr. Crimmins; to have talked with him; and to have received from him information regarding the men of '98 that was not in my possession before I met him. So that it is not at all out of place for me to put it in my book.

I wrote it the day after I met Mr. Crimmins; and this is how I wrote it:

I promised, in a late issue of the *United Irishmen*, to tell something about my entertainment, a night I spent shanachiechting with Father Tom Crimmins at his home. Some nights before that, I met him at a " wake " at Mr. Donegan's house ; he told me so many things about old times in Ireland, and old times in America—historical things I may say, which I did not know, and which you do not now know—that

391

I got very much interested in the information I was getting from him. For instance : there are those monuments in St. Paul's churchyard, near the Post Office, erected to the memory of Emmet and McNevin, of the *United Irishmen* of 1798—it was a surprise to me to hear him tell me that those men are not buried in that churchyard at all; that Dr. McNevin is buried in Newtown, Long Island ; and Thomas Addis Emmet is buried in that graveyard in Second Street, Second Avenue, New York.

I often in the pages of this paper, in writing about Decoration day, spoke of "the graves of Emmet and McNevin in St. Paul's churchyard "; and, as a matter of course, must have often misled my readers. So, it becomes a matter of duty now with mé to lead them right, by giving them Father Crimmins' story. I met his son, John D. Crimmins ; I asked him did he know what his father was telling me—that Emmet and McNevin were not buried in St. Paul's churchyard ? "Why, of course, yes," said he ; " in my young days my father often took me with him to Newtown to decorate the graves of McNevin and Sampson ; and to Second street, to decorate the grave of Thomas Addis Emmet. You see monuments of respect and commemoration erected in the city to General Grant, Horace Greeley, Charles O'Connor and other famous men ; perhaps it was with a feeling of more solemn respect for the memory of the dead, that the men of the preceding generations erected their monuments in the graveyards of the city, instead of in the public thoroughfares."

I went to Thomas Crimmins' house for the special
purpose of taking from him, an elegy in the Irish
language, that he had by heart, on the death of an
uncle of his, Daniel Barry, who was killed by a fall
from his horse at a fair in Dromcolloher in the beginning of this century.   I think it is best for me to let
you see these Irish lines, before I say any more; and,
as I want you to understand them thoroughly, and want
to help you to read Irish, I will make an English translation of them, and place them side by side with the
original.

The name of the poet was James O'Connell; he was
a weaver by trade, and—after the name of his trade—
was called Shemus Fighdeora.   He was learned in the
Irish language, but was unlearned in any other.   His
poem looks to me more like a "caoin" that would be
made over the dead man's body at the wake-house,
than anything else; because, here and there, one verse
is spoken as if addressing the corpse, and the next
verse as if addressing the mourners around.   These
are the verses:

BAAS DONAL A BARRA.

Is dubhach an sgeul ata le 'n innsint,
Idir gall a's gael, air gach taobh da m-bid siad,
An fear muinte, beasach, leigheanta, bhi 'guin,
Air maidin 'na slainte; air clar a's' t-oidhche.

Is dubhach an la, 's is casmhar, bronach,
Gur leag do lair thu, lamh leis an b-pona,
Do b'e sin an tra, d'fag tu air feochaint,
Ce, gur mhairis le sealad, 'na dheoig sin.

Is dubhach an Odhlaig i, go h-oban, da ceile ;
A bhfad o bhaile, o na cairid a's na gaolta ;
A riar na leinbh, gau a n-athair a d-taobh leo,
Ce, gur f hag le sgaipeadh, go fairsing da shaothar.

'S an Tir do baistig tu, a's chaithis do shaoghal ann,
Nior f haigis leanbh bocht dealbh, a beicig,
Gur fuar do chistin, a's do theine bhi eugtha,
A's d'reir mar mheasas, 'ta an tirmisg deunta !

A Dhonail Mac Tomais ! m' ochone ! tu claoidhte,
A mhic an athair, na'r bh'aingis le h-insint ;
Gur a m-barr do theangan, do bhidh dainid do chroidhe-si,
Acht nior ruigis leat fearg, air do leabaig, a's' t-oidhche.

Ni dhearfad dada air a chairid, na ghaolta,
Acht labharfad feasda, air a bpearsan an aonar :—
Do bhi fiall, fairsing, la-marga, agus aonaig,
A's na'r dhun a dhoras, le dothoill roim aoine.

A n-diagh do lamh, ba' bhreagh liom li-ne,
Agus ni do bfearr, na air clar a rinnce ;
A d-taobh an bhearla,—ni dhearfad nidh leis,
Mar ba' Brehon ard thu, air lan da sgrioba.

Da mba' duine mise, do sgrio'ch no leighfeach,
Do raighin chum seanachas fada air a ghaolta,
Do scrutain gasra d'f hearaibh gan aon locht,
A's a gnio'rtha geala, na'r bh-aingis do leigheadh duit.

Anois, o labharas,—ainm dibh, 'nneosad,
Gui'guidhe, " Amen ! "—agus paidir, no dho leis :
Siol de sliocht Bharra—an fear Carthanach, Donal ;
Go d-teig a n-anam go Caithir na Gloire !

THE DEATH OF DANIEL BARRY.

THERE'S a mournful story to-day to tell
Among friends and strangers, where'er they dwell ;
That man so learned, so gentle, bright ;
In good health this morning, now dead to-night.

'Tis a day of mourning; there's grief all 'round—
That your steed unhorsed you, going by the Pound,
That the fall you got made you faint away,
And die soon after, this woful day.

A mournful Christmas is it for his wife,
Far from home and friends of her early life,
Her children 'round her, with their father dead,
'Though he left her plenty, to get them bread.

In this your birth-land, where dead you're lying,
You'd leave no child, with the hunger crying,
Till your kitchen froze, and your fire got out,
And this fatal accident came about.

Daniel MacThomas !   'Tis my grief, you're dead,
Son—of whose sire, nothing small is said ;
Quick, from your tongue, flashed your thought of head,
But you never yet took your wrath to bed.

On friends and relatives, I will not dwell,
But of himself, in person, I can tell :
At home, at market, fair, or any place,
He never shut his door against man's face.

How grand to me—to write as you were able ;
And grand to see you dance upon a table ;
About the language—little need I say
For you, as Brehon high—in that, held sway.

Were I a person who could read or write,
I'd record much about his friends to-night ;
I'd bring before you hosts of faultless men,
Whose brilliant deeds would make you young again.

Now, as I spoke, his name I'll tell to you,
Pray ye, " Amen "—and then a prayer or two
For gen'rous Daniel Barry, dead before ye ;
Pray : May his soul ascend to God in Glory !

That Daniel Barry was called " Lord Barry " by the people around. His father was known as Big Tom Barry—Thomas More. They were of the Barrys of Buttevant. They lost the old castles and the old lands of Buttevant, because their people stuck to the old faith in the days of English penal law, and persecution. They were naturally " disaffected " against the government of the plunderers in Ireland, and it was no doubt, on account of the people knowing that Dan Barry was a rebel at heart, that they honored him with a title, that would be his by right of descent, if he and his house had what properly belonged to them. From old manuscript papers that Father Tom Crimmins showed me, it seems that he and all belonging to him at father and mother's side were not very fond of English rule in Ireland a hundred years ago. Many of them were what are called " Irish rebels," and had to leave Ireland. There is on several of those papers the official stamp of American Courts of Law, carrying the dates of the years 1820, 1812, and 1805. One set of papers show that David Reidy had titles to several lots of land in Cincinnatus, in the county of Cortland, New York.— 5,000 acres—3,000 acres—2,000. That David Reidy was the brother of the wife of Big Tom Barry; and the uncle of the mother of Big Tom Crimmins. David Reidy had to leave Ireland, after the " rising " of '98. Arriving in America, he is found in the United States army, and engaged in the war of 1812. He died without leaving wife or children, in New York City, a few years after the termination of that war, possessed of considerable property in New York county, and Cortland county, Thomas Addis Emmet becoming his executor.

In the year 1835 Father Tom Crimmins came to America—landing from a sailing ship in Perth Amboy, with eighty-six gold sovereigns in his pockets. There were no steamships that time; steamships were not known here till he came here. He came to see about this Reidy property that was so much talked of in the family at home in Ireland, and brought with him as much money as would take him back again. He brought with him letters of introduction to the young Thomas Addis Emmet from some of the old '98 exiles who had been in America after '98 and had gone back to Ireland—letters from an uncle of his, Maurice Barry, a civil engineer who had been engaged on the Down Survey of Ireland, and another civil engineer named Landers who was married to one of the Barry sisters.

When Mr. Crimmins went to Cortland county, he found that the land had been sold for taxes—all, except eighty acres, on which was a cemetery. This eighty acres, except the cemetery part of it, he sold out. A few Irish families were buried in the cemetery, and he did not want to have them disturbed. He then returned to New York.

When he delivered his letters of introduction to Thomas Addis Emmet, he was received with the warmest of welcomes; he was introduced to some of the '98 men who were in New York, and to all who knew his Uncles David Reidy and Dan Barry.

"If any soundings were taken around me as to whether or not I was in need of any help," said Father

Crimmins as he was telling his story, "I knew I had as much money as would take me back home whenever I desired to go back, and I suppose I had pride enough to show that. During my stay so far, I was a guest of Thomas Addis Emmet's at his house.

"It was more worrying and more wearisome to me to be idle than to be at work, so I occasionally made myself occupation in straightening up things about the grounds.

"Then, when I thought it ought to be time for the very best of welcomes to be getting worn out, and when I was talking of leaving, Mr. Emmet and Mrs. Emmet begged me to stay, and take charge of the business of the whole place—farm, cattle, arbory, shrubbery, plants, hothouses, everything. The Emmets used to receive a lot of company; they kept a well-stocked wine cellar; I held the keys of that wine cellar for nine years, and a drop of anything in it, I never tasted.

"By the bye, Mr. O'Donovan, excuse me—won't you have a drink of some kind?"

"No, thank you, Mr. Crimmins."

"Wine, champagne, anything?"

"Champagne, did you say?"

"Yes, yes; I keep a little of everything in the house, though I don't make use of much of it"—

Here he was moving to touch the button, to call some one into the room; I stopped him, telling him I did not taste champagne or anything like it for the last eighteen years. He expressed himself, as glad, and shook hands with me.

"That hand of yours, Mr. Crimmins," said I,

"doesn't feel as if it had ever done much work in its life, or, as if it had been ever fashioned for any rough work." (For a very large man his hand is very small, and his fingers remarkably long and slender.) Smiling, he said I was not the first person that noticed that; adding—"I had not occasion to do much rough hand work in Ireland. I was born at the Cork side of the boundary line, in Dromina; but I lived in Limerick since I was one year old; my mother was born at the Limerick side, in Drumcolloher. She is buried in Drumcolloher; my father is buried in Tullilease. My people had their three farms on the banks of the River Deel—a river that runs through the boundary line of two counties—between Dromina, Milford, and Tullilease in Cork, and Drumcolloher in Limerick; they were large buyers of cattle, and instead of my doing any work on the farm, I used to attend the fairs and markets and attend to the shipping of the cattle to England. So largely were we in this business, that if we missed attending a fair, a dulness in the market would be felt. Coming home from the fair in the evening, to the question asked: 'What kind of a market had ye at the fair to-day?' the answer may be heard—'Indeed, the market was rather slack to-day; there there were none of the Crimminses at the fair.' I had a great friend here in New York, Mr. Crimmins, who knew your people well at home—

"Who is he? Who was he?"

"Oh, he's dead; all my friends are getting dead; he was John D. O'Brien of Drumcolloher, who did business down in Vandewater street.

"Oh, I knew him well, and knew his grandfather better. His grandfather, Big Daniel O'Brien, was the last man I parted with when I was leaving Ireland. He put his arms around me and embraced me—lamenting that his best comrade was going away from him.

"The last time I was in Ireland—nine or ten years ago—I was in to see John O'Brien's brothers, next door to the Victoria Hotel in Cork"—

"I was in there too, Mr. Crimmins. One of the brothers, Michael, was the treasurer of my lecture committee in Cork City, three years ago."

While speaking to Father Crimmins, I got mixed up in my genealogy about the Emmets. He noticed it, when I said something of Thomas Addis Emmet who is buried in St. Paul's churchyard, on whose monument are graven those Irish lines:

> Do mhiannaig se ard-mhathas chum tir a bhraith;
> Do thug se clu, a's fuair se molah a dtir a bhais—

He contemplated great good for the land of his birth
He shed lustre, and received commendation in the land of his decease.

"Thomas Addis is not buried under that monument at all," said Father Crimmins, "he is buried in that graveyard near the Christian Brothers' School in Second street, between First and Second avenues"—

"How is that Father Crimmins," said I.

"I'll tell you," said he: "Some people are not found out to be great till they are dead; when Thomas Addis Emmet was dead to the people of New York, they found out that they had lost a great man; they resolved to erect a monument to his memory, and they erected it in the most revered spot in the city. St. Paul's churchyard was that spot, that time.

" Nor are McNevin's remains buried either, under that monument erected to him in St. Paul's. McNevin was the second husband of his wife. Her first husband's name was Thomas. He was buried where that monument is. The twice-widowed woman's name was Riker. She was a sister to Recorder Riker. The Rikers belong to Newtown, Long Island, and have their grave in Newtown. Mrs. McNevin meant to be buried in the grave of her own family and she had McNevin's remains laid in that grave. Then, when it became a matter of public importance to raise a monument to the memory of McNevin in New York City, there was no difficulty in the way of getting that site for it in St. Paul's churchyard.

" McNevin's remains are buried in Newtown; and in the next plot are the remains of another *United Irishman*—William Sampson. In years gone by, I used to take my boys with me to that graveyard a couple of times a year; decorating the graves, twining the flowers of the two graves into one connected wreath, representative of the two men who were united in Life, being united in Death."

" You said something awhile ago, Father Crimmins, about your first start into business in New York, and about your having a story to tell me regarding it?"

" Yes, yes; I took a contract to do $15,000 worth of work for Mr. Phelps, a banker in Wall street. I did the work. I got the money. When I came home I counted the money, and I found I had twenty-five hundred dollars over my right. I went down to him the next morning, and handed him the parcel of money, asked him to count it, as I thought there was some mistake. He said I should have counted it, and made sure of it, before I left the bank the day before; that it was no proper way to do business, to come in now, telling him the amount was short. 'Oh,' said I, 'Mr. Phelps perhaps 'tis on the other foot, the boot is; you will see when you count the money.' He counted it, and found the $2,500 mistake. He told Mr. Emmet of it; he told every one of it that had any work to do in my line. After that, I got as many contracts as I could fill—without making any bids at all for them. The cry went on the street, that Crimmins was an honest man; and, left to himself would do work as cheap and well as it could be done by any one.

"It was another illustration of the truth of the common saying, that 'Honesty is the best policy.' From the year 1850, up to the present day, I have been doing all the work of the House of Phelps, Dodge & Company."

The foregoing twenty-seven chapters make a complete book. Anything written in them is not dependent for explanation or understanding, upon anything else that is to be written. But I will continue writing the "Recollections" from the year 1863 to the year 1898. They (if I live) will make a second book.

O'DONOVAN ROSSA,

Mariner's Harbor,

New York.

INDEX

Note: A form of relationship after a name indicates relationship to Jeremiah O'Donovan Rossa.